W9-BUQ-919

# PERCUSSION:

## An Annotated Bibliography

*with special emphasis on
contemporary notation and performance*

by

# DIETER BAJZEK

The Scarecrow Press, Inc.
Metuchen, N.J., & London
1988

Library of Congress Cataloging-in-Publication Data

Bajzek, Dieter.
   Percussion : an annotated bibliography with
special emphasis on contemporary notation and
performance.

   Bibliography: p.
   Includes index.
   1. Percussion instruments--Bibliography.
2. Musical notation--20th century--Bibliography.
3. Percussion instruments--Performance--Bibliography.
I. Title.
ML128.P23B34  1988      016.789'01          87-32389
ISBN 0-8108-2107-9

# TABLE OF CONTENTS

## (A) WESTERN MUSIC

## (B) NON - WESTERN MUSIC

## (C) APPENDICES

# ACKNOWLEDGEMENTS

I wish to express my sincere gratitude to Dr. Jeff Pressing, who provided most valuable assistance, supervision and encouragement in my research work for this bibliography. My appreciation too goes to staff members of the Borchardt Library and of the Music Department at La Trobe University (Melbourne) for their patient assistance, to the proprietors of the Billy Hyde Drum Clinic for the generous use of their resources and to Elfriede Senycia for her help in proof-reading this text.

I am personally indebted to Graeme Gerrard for his time-consuming, unselfish and untiring assistance with the VAX computer system in storing my bibliography, and using his ingenuity to see this project through. Finally I must express my heart-felt gratitude to my dear Julia, who gave me the strength and moral support I needed to complete this undertaking.

# PREFACE

The bibliography centres on materials published in the English language during the last twenty years, with the exception of some earlier works of interest and some major publications in foreign languages. It covers a wide range of musical styles and techniques of the Western and Non-Western world, and is intended to be a useful tool of reference for the beginner and professional percussionist, the instrumental teacher, the academic scholar, and the contemporary composer/arranger.

The entries in this bibliography, numbering over 1400, do not refer to percussion music itself (with some exceptions), but concern themselves with journal articles, monographs and dissertations pertaining to all aspects of percussion music, instruments, instrumental techniques and research. The majority of entries are annotated, and for more detailed criteria for annotation, as well as information on multiple listings, cross references, selective treatment of entries, and subject groupings, the reader should consult the Table of Contents and the Introduction of this book.

# INTRODUCTION

This bibliography covers a wide range of styles of music and techniques, but only aims to be comprehensive in the selected areas of contemporary notation and performance, as the title indicates. The entries cover the period of approximately the last twenty years (1965-1985), but some earlier publications of importance and interest are also included. I have mainly considered published material in the English language, with the exception of some important foreign works. It is intended that the bibliography be widely useful as a tool of reference, with material of relevance to the beginner and professional percussionist, the instrumental teacher, the academic scholar, and the contemporary composer/arranger.

It should be pointed out that this is not a bibliography of percussion music itself, but that it refers to articles, monographs and dissertations pertaining to all aspects of percussion music, instruments, instrumental techniques and research. Reference to particular compositions is only included if they

  (a)  are specially designed for the study of instrumental techniques
       (i.e. not intented for concert performances), or
  (b)  include instructive comments for practice and/or performance.

However, a selected listing of percussion music, transcriptions, percussion literature bibliographies, indexes and analyses is provided in the Appendices.

I have also decided to omit material which contains mainly bibliographical information, such as interviews and other news-type reports, unless they also contain enough worthwhile musical information, or are considered important enough from a historical point of view.

Instruments not included here are bells (as in church bells), and mechanical (percussion) instruments. Also no attempt has been made of compiling a discography, or trying to cover the just emerging instructional material available on video tape. For this the reader should refer to (semi) regular reviews in the journals listed and annotated in the Appendix.

As some entries of importance cover areas of interest which are not always easy to classify (e.g. covering several geographical areas), I have listed these in more than one chapter for easy reference. All multiple entries have a cross-reference, and only the first entry has the full annotation. This is particularly obvious in the categories of popular and jazz music, where there is a great amount of overlapping material relating to both areas. However, for practical purposes most entries pertaining to both of these fields are listed primarily in Chapter 6 (Popular and Rock Music), unless they refer extensively to jazz. One of the most obvious signs of the increased attention percussion has received in the last twenty years is the immense quantity of published instruction books for the drum set (covering popular, rock and jazz music). Unfortunately, a great deal of this material is of very poor quality, and the same subjects are treated in similar and repetitive ways in many different publications. Therefore the choice of entries is more selective in these musical styles, to avoid an unnecessary glut of listed materials.

An explanation must also be given for the treatment of annotations in this paper. The reason for the absence of many annotations is due to one or more of the following factors:

(1)  Title of entry is sufficiently self-explanatory and descriptive;
(2)  Entry is not comprehensive enough to make an annotation worthwhile;
(3)  Entry is not relevant enough to the specified emphasis of this bibliography;
(4)  Published material was not available to the author;
(5)  Content and quality of entry was not considered to be of high enough standard to justify an annotation;
(6)  Entry was too far out of date to be relevant enough today in its subject field.

However, many entries in the areas of contemporary notation and performance which have not been annotated, whether by choice, or by necessity, are still included, in order to make this bibliography as comprehensive as possible in these areas. Whenever it was felt that an annotation should be provided, but was not possible due to one or more of the above reasons, a note to this effect is made and, where possible, the reader is referred to a review of this entry elsewhere. Therefore, the amount of annotation, or lack thereof, does not always reflect the author's opinion of the entry's value and quality.

The reader should also note that, due to the fact that the equipment used to reproduce this thesis cannot print foreign symbols, the spelling of certain words had to be anglicized (e.g the German "umlaut" becomes "ue"). Comments printed in square brackets are the author's and are usually intented to be a brief description or clarification.

The usage of different words, such as "manual", "method", "tutor", etc., to refer to teaching and reference texts derives mainly from the terminology found in the entries under discussion. They are, however, not intended to differentiate or classify in any way.

# CHAPTER 1.

## COMPREHENSIVE HANDBOOKS AND GENERAL REFERENCE TEXTS:

### (a) Texts on Percussion Instruments.

1. ADATO, J. & JUDY, G. **The Percussionist's Dictionary.** Melville, NY, Belwin-Mills, 1984, 95 p.
   A condensed, but still fairly comprehensive dictionary, containing:
   (1) Extensive listing, with brief descriptions, of percussion instruments, with translations into English from 26 other languages (in alphabetical order);
   (2) A section of 119 photographs of many instruments listed in the previous section;
   (3) A list of foreign terms and a bibliography.
   It would have been more useful, however, to have placed the photographs next to the descriptions instead of separately.

2. AVGERINOS, Gerassimos **Handbuch fuer Schlag - und Effektinstrumente.** Frankfurt am Main, Verlag Das Musikinstrument, 1964, 105 p. [German]
   The translation of this major book means: 'Handbook of Percussion and Special Effect Instruments', with the subtitle: 'A Guide for Composers, Conductors, Musicians and Instrument Makers.'
   Instruments and percussive terms are listed (in cross-reference) in five languages in alphabetical order (German, Italian, English, French and Spanish), and the instruments and their basic way of playing and musical usage are described (with over 250 illustrations). The list is extensive, including rare "off-beat" instruments, but information on the historical background of instruments and details of ethnic-orientated techniques have been avoided.

3. BARTLETT, Harry R. **Guide to Teaching Percussion.** Dubuque, IA., C. Brown, 1971, 172 p. (This edition revised by R.A. Holloway; 1st ed. publ. 1964)
   This is a heavily revised edition of the original book and is divided into 10 chapters. It is a good basic, all-round tutor, covering a wide range of techniques and instruments. One original and useful feature is the "Functional Classification of Percussion Instruments", where a large number of instruments is listed and illustrated, and each one is discussed under the headings of "Acoustical Features", "Basic Techniques", and "Characteristic Usages". Apart from the orchestral instruments, there are also chapters on Latin American instruments (very brief), set drumming (some basic rhythms), and the marching band percussion.

4. BLADES, James **Percussion Instruments and their History.** London, Faber & Faber, 1974, 509 p. (1st ed. 1970)
   This major work is the largest book published on percussion and is now also available in paperback edition at greatly reduced cost. Among the tables it has a metric conversion chart, a glossary of principal terms in five languages, a separate bibliography to each of the sixteen chapters,

1

five appendices, a very detailed index system, 193 photographic illustrations, 68 drawings, and many musical examples. The first half of the book discusses mainly the history of instruments in different parts of the world, and this part is very extensive and thorough. The other chapters deal with the more recent evolution and playing techniques of percussion in Western music: The Classical Orchestra, The Romantic Orchestra (pts. I & II), Techniques of Contemporary Percussion (each instrument is dealt with separately), Composers' Use of Modern Percussion. The appendices give a brief account of the Americas, Latin American Orchestra, Changing Styles in Light Music, Percussion in Education, and Inventions and Patents.

The chapter about Contemporary Percussion does not go into any detail about the more "unusual" instruments which are being used today. Even the next chapter, which briefly lists and describes many examples of 20th century music, does not deal in enough detail with the problems of performance or notation in any one piece, and seems hardly up to date in this area.

5. CENTAZZO, Andrea **Guid agli Strumenti a Percussione: Storia e Uso.** Padora, Italy, Franco Muzzio & Co., 1979, 255 p.

An extensive work on the full range of percussion instruments. It includes reasonable historic background, classification of instruments, a guide and discussion on notation (incl. symbols), a glossary of names, bibliography and discography, and many good quality photographs and musical examples.

6. CENTAZZO, Andrea **Percussion - New Techniques.** Milan, Italy, G. Ricordi, 1983(?), 85 p.

This is an important book on this specific subject, and is written bilingually in Italian and English. It includes a glossary of percussion terms in four languages, notational symbols, and a recording of sounds discussed in the text. The author explains his selection of instruments in discussion (based on general availability and usage in Western contemporary music). He divides them into three groups of idiophones, membranophones, and electronics and percussion, and discusses contemporary and unusual techniques within these groups, including amplification and electronic timbral modifications.

7. COLLINS, Myron & GREEN, John **Playing and Teaching Percussion Instruments.** Englewood Cliffs, NJ, Prentice Hall, 1962, 134 p.

The first part (c. 90 pages), dealing with snare drum technique in 33 lessons, is still a reasonably good text, presenting reading exercises, articulation, sticking, and rudiments. The other four parts (mallet instruments; timpani; bass drum, cymbals, etc.; and Latin American) are too brief and sketchy to be of much value in a general percussion method.

8. COMBS, F. Michael **Percussion Manual.** Belmont, CA, Wadsworth Publ. Co., 1977, 160 p.

This well organized and presented text is divided into nine chapters and six appendices:

(1)  Snare drum study (85 pages), most comprehensive, using both grips, with rudiments, techniques and many etudes.

(2)  Marching percussion, including some patterns.

(3)  Timpani studies (12 p).

(4)  Keyboard percussion instruments (8 p), very basic.

(5)   Percussion accessories (11 p); fair, but a basic selection.
(6)   Multiple percussion (5 p); a few studies.
(7)   The drum set; covers some dance rhythms.
(8)   Organisation of the percussion section.
(9)   Teacher's guide to beginning percussion.
The six appendices are very useful, including bibliographies of texts and literature, discography and terminology.

9.  GARDNER, Carl **The Gardner Method for the Instruments of Percussion.** New York, Carl Fisher, 1944, 320 p.
    This large method is in three parts, and, although these parts date back some years now, are still reasonable basic tutors - especially the timpani book.
Bk.1: 'Drums, Cymbals, Accessories', 1938, 120 p.
Bk.2: 'Bells, Xylophone, Vibraphone, Marimba, Chimes, 1919, 105 p.
Bk.3: 'Timpani', 1944, 95 p.


10.  HOLLAND, James **Percussion.** London, Macdonald & Jane's, 1978, 283 p.
    This is one of the latest (major) comprehensive books on percussion. It is divided into three basic parts:
    (1)   The Timpani (history - construction - student timpanist), which is quite adequate and fully up to date;
    (2)   The Percussion Instruments, which has three sections: (a) general percussion instruments, (b) keyboard, (c) stands and accessories. Section (a) lists all the instruments in alphabetical order, which seems to me the worst part of the book, as this makes it more difficult to compare (and see at a glance) the instruments with similar timbral sound characteristics (e.g. cymbals, shakers, hand drums, etc.), which can be especially useful to the composer. Otherwise, the instruments and playing techniques are well described and illustrated. Section (c) could have been incorporated into section (a), and there are not many musical examples.
    But part (3) 'In Performance', is very interesting. The very experienced author deals here in great detail with the percussion parts of the works of W. Walton's "Facade", R. Gerhard's "Concerto for Eight", and K. Stockhausen's "Kontakte". He shows the layout of the instruments, practically the whole part of the first two works and much of the third, and debates many problems for the performer. This should give some insight  for many percussionists and composers alike. Tables in the appendices comprise a list of addresses of the main manufactorers of percussion instruments, a short bibliography, and a more extensive discography.

11.  JAKOB, Friedrich **Schlagzeug.** Bern, Hallwag, 1979, 108 p. [German]
    A reasonable overview of Western percussion instruments, with good illustrations, and a fair representation of 20th century applications.

12.  KOTONSKI, Wlodzimierz **Schlaginstrumente im modernen Orchester.** Mainz, Schott, 1968, 90 p. [German]
    Originally published in Polish, here extented and translated into German. This is a clearly put together, instructive and informative book, grouping the instruments into four sections: membranophones, metal idiophones, wood idiophones, and various others.
    It is illustrated, gives short historical and musical backgrounds, as well as basic playing instructions with some idiomatic musical notation

examples. As the title indicates, it covers all the percussion instruments in the modern orchestra, has some comments on and examples of notation, and a small "dictionary" of percussion terms and instruments in four languages.

13. LEACH, Joel **Percussion Manual for Music Educators.** New York, Henry Adler, 1964, 93 p.
A text aimed at the student who wishes to become a music teacher and wishes to know the basics of all the main percussion instruments. Snare drum techniques (incl. rudiments), timpani and mallet instruments take up most of the pages. Some very basic information is also given on several hand-percussion and Latin American instruments, and it includes many illustrations.

14. McCORMICK, R. **Percussion for Musicians: A Complete Fundamental Literature and Technique Method for Percussion.** Melville, NY, Belwin-Mills, 1983, 123 p.
A basic instruction manual, attempting to cover most aspects of percussion. The text is kept simple and easy to follow, and it deals with snare drum, timpani, bar percussion, and accessory instruments. Apart from these orchestral instruments, it also treats Latin American, marching percussion, American and Swiss rudiments, basic drum set techniques, and maintenance. Further references are given with a bibliography and discography, a list of excerpts from the orchestral literature (incl. some examples) and six good pieces for percussion ensemble.

15. MUELLER, K.A. **Teaching Total Percussion.** West Nyack, NY, Parker, 1972, 220 p.
This is directed at the instrumental teacher at high school level and tries to cover all the main percussion instruments (incl. mallet keyboards, timpani, drum set, marching percussion and Latin American). Musical examples are few in number, but the author also emphasizes theory and ear training.

16. PAYSON, Al & McKENZIE, Jack **Music Educator's Guide to Percussion.** New York, Belwin Inc., 1966, 128 p.
This textbook (now slightly out of date) covers a wide range of basic percussion aspects, and is obviously aimed at the general music teacher. The first half of the book describes the main orchestral instruments and rudimentary playing techniques (with photographs of bad quality). This is followed by Latin American instruments, a short chapter on "Dance Drums" (very old-fashioned), a section called "developing Musicianship in the Percussion Section", which includes ideas for musical contests, and a final chapter on marching percussion.

17. PEINHOFER, Karl & TANNIGEL, Fritz **Handbook of Percussion Instruments.** London, Schott, 1976, 256 p. (Origin. published in German by Schott, Mainz, 1969)
One of the major texts on percussion. The subtitle reads: 'Their Characteristics and Playing Techniques, with Illustrations and Musical Examples from the Literature'. Although this was written before some of the other important books on percussion (1969), it is in some areas the most up to date one, as it covers more of the less common instruments than the others.
Excellent charts are: percussion instruments in four languages (the

largest I have seen); a chart of Latin American instruments and their possible substitutes; a comprehensive fold-out table of the ranges of all pitched percussion instruments; and a unique and useful feature (especially for composers), a large and illustrated table of beaters, describing their construction, their common and less common uses. The very extensive number of instruments is defined in detail, each one illustrated and referred to one of the 137 musical examples at the rear of the book.

18.  PETERS, Gordon **The Drummer: Man, a Treatise on Percussion.** Wilmette, IL, Kemper-Peters, 1975, 368 p.
   This is a major book on the history, development, function and usage of percussion instruments and their related music. It is, however, neither an instruction book nor a dictionary. It has no illustrations at all and comparatively few musical examples. The book is laid out in nine major chapters:
   (1) "Percussion - Its Evolution and Historical Setting". The 30 pages cover early percussion (geographically ordered) and Percussion since the Crusaders (in chronological order).
   (2) "The Membranic Percussion" deals with snare, tenor, and bass drums and timpani of the pre-orchestral and orchestral period.
   (3) "The Metallic Percussion" and (4) "The Wooden Percussion" discuss respective non-pitched instruments, whereas Chapter (5) "The Drum: Some Cultural-Historical Comparisons" compares the music of various geographical areas.
   (6) "The Keyboard Percussions" first deals in detail with marimbas and xylophones in different parts of the world (50 pages), then with the remaining bar percussion instruments.
   Chapter (7) deals briefly with some aspects of "Acoustics of Percussion Instruments", and Chapter (8) relates some background of "Percussion Instruments and Jazz."
   In Chapter (9) "Percussion Ensembles" many ideas, complaints and suggestions are brought forward with regard to percussion teaching programs, percussion ensembles (literature and performance) and especially concerning percussion notation and scoring in general. A 50 page appendix section is also very useful and includes:
   (A) Further Percussion Studies (recommendations);
   (B) Abuse in Percussion (personal experiences):
   (F) Percussion Instrument Makers (international list);
   (G) Supplementary References (extensive bibliography).

19.  REED, H.O. & LEACH, J.T. **Scoring for Percussion.** Englewood Cliffs, NY, Prentice Hall, 1969, 150 p.
   Although this book is out of print now, it is still a very informative and well laid-out book in its own right. It is especially aimed at the composer/arranger, gives no historical background or examples from the literature.
   The two main parts of the book are (1) "The Percussion Instruments", and (2) "Notation and Scoring". The first part describes all the main instruments (grouped into mallet percussion, membranes, metallic, wooden, Latin American, others), and one of the good features is the description of timbral sounds possible with various mallets and sticks, and distinctive sound features of each instrument. Although the notation section deals only with the traditional staff notation, it is clear, logical and adequate, and explains idiomatic percussion notation and scoring techniques with sufficient depth.

20. RICHARDS, Emil **Emil Richards' World of Percussion.** Sherman Oaks, CA, Gwyn Publishing Co., 1972, 94 p.

As the subtitle promises: 'A Catalogue of 300 Standard, Ethnic, and Special Musical Instruments and Effects'. There are two parts to the book (Standard Percussion, and the rest), divided altogether into 13 chapters. The instruments are listed alphabetically and illustrated within each chapter. As the descriptions of the instruments are very brief (with ranges included where appropriate) it is a pity that the photographs (black & grey) and/or the printing is of such poor quality, that many entries become almost useless.

21. SMITH-BRINDLE, Reginald **Contemporary Percussion.** London, O.U.P. 1970, 217 p.

This is a very attractively presented (if costly) major book which includes tables like: a short glossary of instruments (four languages); a reasonable bibliography, 56 photographic illustrations; and 183 musical examples. It also includes a recorded disc of 45 different instruments played in various manners.

The seventeen chapters are clearly laid-out and include some useful sections for composers and performers alike. For example, Chapter (3) "Notation for Percussion Instruments", which explains the for and against of different systems; Chapter (4) "Percussion Layouts and the Placing of Instruments"; (5) "Factors influencing Timbres"; (6) "Writing for Keyboard Percussion". Chapters (7) to (14) are detailed descriptions of different instruments (systematically grouped), followed by the articles (15) "The Orchestral Use of Percussion" (describing some "twelve principal roles of percussion"), and a very short (16) "The Percussion Ensemble". One of the first authors to present a clear overview of the new pictographic notational systems used in contemporary music.

22. SPOHN, C. & TATGENHURST, J.T. **The Percussion.** Boston, Allyn & Bacon, 1971, 169 p. (2nd Ed.; first published without Tatgenhurst in 1967, 141 p)

[Basic manual; includes exercises.]

23. WHITE, C.L. **Drums through the Ages.** Los Angeles, The Sterling Press, 1960, 215 p.

This rather strange book, subtitled 'The Story of our Oldest and most Fascinating Musical Instruments', contains a lot of historical information - especially in part one (Primitive Percussion Instruments and their Development) - but is rather badly put together. It is often incoherent and/or vague, offers little constructive advice, and preaches antiquated ideas. Part two deals with timpani only, here still refered to as "tympani."

# CHAPTER 1.

## COMPREHENSIVE HANDBOOKS AND GENERAL REFERENCE TEXTS:

### (b) General Texts on Musical Instruments.

24. BENNETT, R. **Instruments of the Orchestra.** Cambridge, Cambridge Univ. Press, 1982.
(Optional audio cassette available)

25. BUCHNER, Alexander **Folk Music Instruments of the World.** New York, Crown, 1972, 292 p.
This large-formatted book is mainly a photographic documentation of traditional Instruments and their players from all parts of the world, with many examples of percussion instruments (207 photographs, some drawings and very little text).

26. DONINGTON, R. **Music and its Instruments.** London, Methuen, 1982, 232 p.
A brief chapter on orchestral percussion Instruments gives basic descriptions and some musical considerations.

27. FOX, L.M. **Instruments of Processional Music.** London, Lutterworth, 1967, 127 p.
(For book review see 'Music in Education' 31/328: 642, 1967.)

28. HEADINGTON, C. **The Orchestra and its Instruments.** New York, World, 1967, 95 p. (Also published by Bodley Head, London, 1967)

29. MARCUSE, Sibyl **Musical Instruments (A Comprehensive Dictionary).** New York, Doubleday & Co., 1964, 608 p.
The instruments receive a brief description, some historical background, and are cross-indexed.

30. MARCUSE, Sibyl **A Survey of Musical Instruments.** New York, Harper & Row, 1975, 863 p.
This is major reference work and covers Western and Non-Western cultures. Parts I & II, Idiophones and Membranophones (c.170 pages), deal with all types of percussion instruments, including detailed surveys of their historic development and descriptions of their construction (no illustrations).

31. MIDGLEY, Ruth **Musical Instruments of the World.** New York, Bantam Books, 1976, 320 p.
This pictorial encyclopedia of instruments contains a large number of percussion instruments from all over the world, illustrated in detailed drawings of over 70 pages, with enough information to make it a good, basic reference book.

32. SADIE, Stanley **The New Grove Dictionary of Music and Musicians.**
London, Macmillan, 1980, 20 Vols.
This is the largest musical dictionary (in the English language),
containing a wealth of information relating to percussion. A large
amount of revisions and additions have been carried out since the
previous edition, and this proves to be especially beneficial in the area of
percussion. However, for annotations of contributions relating to
percussion instruments the reader should refer to the entry 'The New
Grove Dictionary of Musical Instruments' by the same editor (see
following entry), as most articles from that smaller and more specialized
work are extracted from this large Grove Dictionary. Other articles of
interest to be found in this reference text are in the area of ethnic and
traditional music, history, composition and notation.

33. SADIE, Stanley (Edi.) **The New Grove Dictionary of Musical Instruments.**
**(3 Vols.)** New York, Grove's Dictionaries of Music, 1984, 2800 p.
This is a major reference source and contains a vast amount of
information about percussion instruments. Countless numbers of
instruments are listed, including a large number of ethnic and Non-
Western instruments, with the most useful benefits being the extensive
and thorough cross-references and bibliographies.
For example, the entry "Drum" (pp 601-611) covers bass drum, tenor
drum and snare drum only, but lists many hundreds (!) of other drums
which have entries in this dictionary. All major instruments have a
coverage of historic background, construction details, playing
techniques, some references to literature, and are amply illustrated with
photographs, diagrams, musical examples, maps and charts. Many of the
feature articles on Western instruments are written by James Blades,
and many of these contributions are practically the same as in 'The New
Grove's Dictionary of Music and Musicians' (1980).

34. STEWART, Madeau **Instruments of the Orchestra.** New York, Van
Nostrand Rheinhold, 1980, 176 p.
The full title of this book is 'The Music Lover's Guide to the
Instruments of the Orchestra', and it is a beautifully printed 'coffee-
table' book with nice, clean drawings and photographs.

35. THE DIAGRAM GROUP **Musical Instruments of the World.** New York,
Bantam Books, 1978, 320 p.
The subtitle reads: 'The first and only comprehensive illustrated
encyclopedia of its kind (More than 4000 drawings)'. It is certainly
original, presents an excellent overview, and is very well designed. It
covers an enormous number of instruments, with brief descriptions and
fine, detailed drawings. There is the usual classification (Hornbostel &
Sachs) of four groupings, plus very informative chapters like
"Instruments around the World", "Musical Ensembles" (traditional), and
"Instruments through the Ages". These are cross-indexed to the main
part of the book, which contains c. 80 pages on traditional percussion
instruments from all parts of the world, as well as orchestral
instruments.

36. WINTERNITZ, E. **Musical Instruments of the Western World.** New
York/Toronto, McGraw-Hill, 1967, 259 p.

# CHAPTER 2.

## CONSTRUCTION, MAINTENANCE AND REPAIR

37. BAKER, Donald R. 'Percussion Maintenance and Repair.' **The Instrumentalist** 35: 62+, Feb. 1981.

38. BENJAMIN, R.E. 'Finding and restoring relic Drums.' **Modern Drummer** 2/1: 12-3, 1978.

39. BRITTON, M.W. 'Fear not the Kettledrum.' **The Instrumentalist** 22: 64-6, June 1968.
    An article on solving technical problems with the timpani, e.g. correct "collar size", setting and maintaining proper pedal tension and repair, and trouble shooting for unclear tone.

40. CLINE, Dallas (Edi.) **How to Play Nearly Everything.** New York, Oak Publications, 1977, 63 p.
    A delightful collection of ten chapters (by ten different authors) on the playing techniques, and sometimes construction, of such 'high-brow' instruments as the bones, kazoo, and more. Of special interest to the percussionist are these rare set of instructions:
    (1) 'How to Make and Play the Bones' (Sue E. Barber, pp 6-17).
    Very detailed instructions; rhythms, articulation, technique, and bibliography.
    (4) 'How to Make Music on a Handsaw' (Charles Blacklock, pp 27-35).
    Clear, illustrated instructions on this rare art, and plenty of advice.
    (6) 'How to Make and Play a Washboard' (Peter Menta, pp 40-4).
    Gives some historical background on this dying skill, playing instructions, and discography.
    (9) 'How to Play the Spoons' (Barbara Mendelsohn, pp 50-57).
    Explains in detail the one- and two-finger methods, beats, roll, and various rhythms, special "hot licks", and discography.
    (10)'How to Make and Play the Bodhran' (Dan Milner, pp 58-63).
    Basic information only in this chapter on the music, instructions on building the drum, and how to play it.

41. COMBS, F. Michael 'Timpani Repair and Maintenance.' **Music Educator's Journal** 66: 56-7, Feb. 1980.
    Basic repair hints for the timpanist-handyman on pedals, dents, unclear tone problems, squeaking, and general maintenance.

42. CREAMER, David 'Refinishing your Drums.' **Modern Drummer** 8/12: 92-100, 1984.
    Detailed instructions on how to repair and finish wood shells.

43. DAVENPORT, David 'The Art of Tempering the Kettledrum.' **Percussive Notes** 19/2: 62-4, 1981.
    This is a helpful and thorough description on how to prepare the drum for mounting a new head, fine-tuning, and achieving an "ideal" timpani tone.

4. EPSTEIN, Michael 'Drumsticks: The full Story.' **Modern Drummer** 7/7: 26-8, 96-101, 1983.

    An overview of the characteristics of materials used, descriptions of the various designs of drumsticks being manufactured, and the advantages, types of sound-production, and durabilities thereof.

45. ERICKSON, Robert 'Tunable Tube Drums.' **Percussionist** 12/3: 90-95, 1975.

    Invention and building of tube drums made of plastic tubes, their usage and improvements (from 1967-1975).

46. FLAHERTY, P. 'Keyboard Mallet Recovery.' **Woodwind World, Brass and Percussion** 17/4: 40-1, 1978.

47. FOLEY, Patrick 'Re-covering your Drums.' **Modern Drummer** 8/5: 102-3, 1984.

    [Practical advice and instructions.]

48. FORD, C. (Edi.) **Making Musical Instruments.** New York, Pantheon, 1979, 192 p.

    (Not available for annotation; for book review see 'Journal of the Lute Society of America' 12:82-4, 1979.)

49. FRANCOIS, Jean-Charles 'Percussion Sound Sculpture.' **Percussionist** 18/3: 40-70, 1981.

    This is an edited version of Chapter VI from the author's forthcoming book 'Aspects of Contemporary Percussion' and discusses the construction and physical and musical usage of such new "sound sculptures". Subheadings of the article are: "Gamelans; The early Percussion Practices of John Cage; The Micro-Intonalists; Set-ups, Frames, Consules; Heterogenerous Timbral Spaces; Performance Electronics and an Example of Sound Sculpture; Two Worlds of Sound (Conclusion)."

50. FROCK, G. 'Maintaining Concert Percussion Equipment.' **The Instrumentalist** 38: 80+, Sep., 1983.

51. GOLDSMITH, David 'Foot-operated Muffler-Dampers for Timpani.' **N.A.C.W.P.I. Journal** 23/3: 10-3, 1975.

52. HOPKIN, Bart 'The Fabric Shop Toombah.' **Percussive Notes** 23/4: 47-9, 1985.

    This is a description of the construction and sound of the author's invention, the Toombah, which is a definite pitched percussion aerophone, made from cardboard tubes in the style of an old, vertically mounted xylophone.

53. HORST, Thomas 'Rewinding Yarn-covered Mallets.' **Woodwind World, Brass and Percussion** 16/3: 44-5, 1977.

54. HORST, Thomas 'Rewinding Cord-covered Mallets.' **Woodwind World, Brass and Percussion** 16/4: 41, 1977.

55. KNAACK, D.F. 'Care and Maintenance of Percussion Instruments.' **The Instrumentalist** 25: 50-3, Oct. 1970.

    Basic guidelines for the handling of the main orchestral percussion instruments.

56. KOFSKY, Frank 'The Care and Feeding of Drums.' (2 parts) **Modern Drummer** 4/5: 74-5, 89; 4/6: 42-5, 64+, 1981.
An interesting and rare article, helping the drummer to maintain his instrument and also improve and/or re-build it. The author shows in detail how to "true" the bearing edge of a drum (part 1) and other renovations and re-buildings of a drum (part 2).

57. KOFSKY, Frank 'The Care and Feeding of Cymbals.' **Modern Drummer** 5/6: 23-5. 41-2, 54, 1981.
Good advice on how to maintain and repair cymbals, including riveting a cymbal, proper suspension and repairing cracks.

58. KULB, David **Percussion Crafts: A Handbook Service Manual.** Paul Price Publication, 1979, 49 p.
The subtitle describes the book quite well: 'A how-to book featuring care and repair of standard percussion; sound effects; Latin instruments; mallet making for timpani and keyboard percussion; and making cases for sticks, beaters and mallets.'

59. LEVINE, Dave 'Drum Head Selection.' **The Instrumentalist** 33: 56-8, May 1979.
This article advises the school teacher on determining when a drum head needs changing. He points out the fact that what type of music is being played on it and what type of sound is required will influence the choice of a head. He also provides a chart of the different types of drum heads available, their tone qualities and surface finish, their recommended uses, and lists manufacturers (five U.S. brand names). A useful and thorough report on this subject.

60. MONTAGU, Jeremy 'On the Reconstruction of Medieval Instruments of Percussion.' **The Galpin Society Journal** 23: 104-114, 1970.
Montagu explains in detail (and with illustrations) how to build a tabor, and in lesser detail he discusses the reconstruction of snare drum, nakers, tambourines, triangle, cymbals, bells and beaters.

61. MONTAGU, Jeremy **Making Early Percussion Instruments.** London, O.U.P., 1976, 49 p.
In this text we find detailed guidelines on how to make authentic instruments of this period, ranging from simple to very complicated constructions.

62. MOREHEAD, Kenneth 'Forging a New Instrument.' **Percussive Notes** 21/2: 70-2, 1983.
[Detailed description of how to manufacture crotales]

63. MURPHY, James E. 'Getting the "Noise" out of your Set.' **Modern Drummer** 6/6: 100-1, 1982.
Gives practical hints and advice on corrective meassures to maintain and obtain a noise-free sound from the drum set, especially for recording purposes.

64. MYNETT, Alan 'On the Reconstruction of a Medieval Tabor.' **Early Music** 6/4: 223-7, 1973.
Reasonably detailed instructions on how to build a tabor, with critical comments by Jeremy Montagu on the instrument built by the author (Mynett).

65. McKINNEY, James 'Percussion Accessories you can make.' **The Instrumentalist** 37: 46-8, Apr., 1983.
    A useful list of accessories the average handyman could make to save money includes triangle clamps and beaters; guiro scratcher; beaters for cowbells, timpani and bass drum; sticks for timbales and snare drum; tambourines; anvil, and slapstick. Instructions are very basic, without illustrations.

66. NOONAN, J. 'The Perfect Concert Snare Drum.' **Percussive Notes** 14/1: 40-1, 1975.
    Basic questions and answers about the choice of a good instrument.

67. PAYSON, Al 'The Timpani Mute.' **Percussionist** 9/2: 46-7, 1971.
    Discussion of the use, effectiveness and construction of a timpani mute.

68. PETERS, Gordon 'Care and Maintenance of Percussion Instruments.' **The Instrumentalist** 29: 56-60, May 1975.
    A useful article on the basic maintenance and problem-prevention measures for most orchestral percussion instruments.

69. POLLART, Gene 'Some Hints on the Playing and Maintenance of Timpani.' **Woodwind World, Brass and Percussion** 21/6: 20-21, 1982.
    This article is not at all on playing technique, but a reasonable run-down on problems of maintaining a good quality instrument, including advice on pedal mechanism, proper tuning, and general maintenance.

70. POWER, Andrew 'Sound Production of the Timpani.' (2 parts) **Percussive Notes** 21/4: 62-4; 21/5: 65-7, 1983.
    This explains in acoustic and technical terms the sound qualities, based on the construction and quality of tuning devises, vibrations of the membrane, bowl shape, timpani mallets and the tuning itself.

71. PRESS, Arthur **Mallet Repair.** New York, Belwin-Mills, 1971, 24 p.
    A detailed and useful book on this subject, for anybody wishing to repair mallets (for financial advantages) or maybe manufacture mallets of one's own design.

72. RICHARDS, Emil & Celeste **Making Music in Mommy's Kitchen. Making Music around the Home & Yard.** New York, Award Music, 1974, 30 p @ .
    Two books aimed at children, to make them aware of how they can utilize everyday objects as "musical instruments". The ideas are very simple with the second book ('Home & Yard') being the more interesting one.

73. ROSEN, Michael 'How to make a Castanet Machine.' **Percussive Notes** 22/1: 75, 1983.

74. SANTOS, John 'Mounting Conga and Bongo Heads.' **Modern Percussionist** 1/3: 62-3, 1985.

75. SAWYER, David **Vibrations; Making Unorthodox Musical Instruments.** Cambridge, Cambridge University Press, 1977, 102 p.
    This book shows how to make a number of original, nice looking instruments from varying inexpensive materials like wood, cardboard,

metal, clay, bamboo, etc. The majority are percussion instruments, and seem fun to make and play.

76. SCHAFER, R.M. 'Bricolage: there is a Twang in my Trash.' **Music Educator's Journal** 66: 32-7, March 1980.
[Building percussive sound-sculptures out of old hardware.]

77. SCHINSTINE, W.J. 'How to wrap Marimba Mallets.' **Percussive Notes** 13/2: 29, 1975.

78. SLOANE, I. **Making Musical Instruments.** New York, E.P. Dutton, 1978, 159 p.
A detailed and nicely presented book on making six professional-looking instruments of high quality. The introductory chapters deal with veneers, tools, laminated shells, release form, and other related subjects. The instruments to be made are a banjo, regimental snare drum, tambourine, Appalachian dulcimer, Hardanger fiddle and a Dolmetsch recorder. All with detailed drawings, photographs, and a bibliography.

79. SOAMES, Cynthia 'Care and Repair of Percussion Mallets.' **Percussive Notes** 17/1: 52, 1979.

80. SPRINGER, G.H. **Maintenance and Repair of Wind and Percussion Instruments.** Boston, Allyn & Bacon 1976.

81. THE MUSIC TRADES (ed.) 'Rhythm Tech designs revolutionary new Tambourine.' **The Music Trades (USA)** 128: 143-4, May 1980.

82. TOBISCHEK, Herbert **Die Pauke - Ihre spiel- und bautechnische Entwicklung in der Neuzeit** Utzing, Schneider, 1977, 311 p.
This is a major work, beautifully presented, on the subject of timpani. It contains detailed, illustrated information on the many models and continuous improvements the timpani has experienced from the beginning of the 19th century onwards - so often ignored by top players of the time. The other main parts in the book are the three large chapters on how composers have utilized the timpani, from the Renaissance up to contemporary music, using many excerpts from the literature.

83. UDOW, Michael 'The Tambourine - Basic Information.' **Percussive Notes** 14/1: 30-1, 1975.
84. UDOW, Michael 'Repairing the Tambourine.' **The Instrumentalist** 30: 57-8, Jan. 1976.
These articles are very similar, with the latter one being slightly more extensive.

85. UDOW, Michael 'The Basic Construction of a Bass Drum Mallet.' **Percussive Notes** 14/2: 41-2, 1976.
Gives clear instructions (with diagrams) on how to make a beater.

86. VAN HORN, Rick 'Cleaning your Set.' **Modern Drummer** 4/5: 46-7, 1980.
Detailed advice on how (and why) to clean all parts of the drum set.

87. WICKSTROM, F. 'The do it yourself Percussionist (Wooden Rack to hold Hand Cymbals).' **Percussionist** 4/3: 149-50, 1967.

# CHAPTER 3.

## NOTATION OF CONTEMPORARY MUSIC:

### (a) Notation for Percussion.

88. BROWN, Allen 'A Survey of Notational Procedures found in Contemporary Percussion Music.' [Part 1] **Brass and Percussion** 2/5: 14-5, 20-1, 1974.

89. BROWN, Allen 'A Survey of Notational Procedures found in Contemporary Percussion Music.' [Part 2] **Woodwind World, Brass and Percussion** 15/6: 44-5, 1976.

      The author examines various notational techniques used today, in particular reference to multi-percussion music; the systems used, their good and bad points, and their successfulness in this respect. The compositions under discussion are: "Corrente" (W. Kraft), "Sextet for Brass & Percussion" (E. Siegmeister), "Couleurs Juxtaposees" (J.P. Guezec), "Elegy" (J. Rosen), "XL Plus One" (A. Etler), and "Sources III" (D. Burge).

90. CASKEL, Christopher 'Notation for Percussion Instruments.' **Percussionist** 8/3: 80-4, 1971. (Reprinted from 'Darmstaedter Beitraege zur Neuen Musik' No.9, 1965)

      In this article, translated by Vernon Martin, C. Caskel, a prominent German percussionist and author, discusses problems of notation for solo multi-percussion. He compares different systems, like traditional staff and single-line staff, and the advantages for the performer of using a logical system of symbols.

91. DE FELICE, L.A. 'Problems in Percussion Notation.' **Percussionist** 6/4: 108-112, 1969.

      Some of the basic errors in literature composers have made in percussion scoring, and how they could have been avoided.

92. FINK, Siegfried **Tablature 72.** Hamburg/London, N.Simrock, Elite Edition, 1972, 8 p.

      This is a listing (in four languages) of 61 symbols (pictograms) for the various percussion instruments and 18 symbols for the beaters. They are the choice and/or invention of the author and are intented to help unify the wealth of notation used today.

93. GALM, John 'The Need for Using Symbols in Percussion Notation.' **N.A.C.W.P.I. Journal** 46-8, Fall, 1972.

      (Not available for annotation)

94. HONG, Sherman 'Percussion Research and Studies (Alea and Graphic).' **Percussionist** 10/2: 65-8, 1972.

      Gives some examples of the freedom and advantages in aleatoric and graphic notation for the performer.

95. JAMISON, R. 'Percussion Notation.' **Woodwind World, Brass and Percussion** 17/5: 36+, 1978.
Seemingly basic, but important and often overlooked, advice for the composer/arranger in dealing with the aspects of durational notation (i.e. sustain vs. non-sustain) of percussion instruments, and the importance of clear indication of cut-off in sustaining instruments.

96. KNAACK, D.F. 'Modern Notation - It's nothing to be afraid of.' **Modern Percussionist** 1/1: 56-7, 1984-85.

97. LEACH, Joel 'The Use of Symbols in Multiple Percussion.' **Brass and Percussion** 1/2: 7-9+, 1973.
Leach points out the difficulty and danger for the performer of having to recognize similar and often contradicting symbols in percussion music, when in many cases words (or better abbreviations) would have been better.

98. McCARTY, Frank 'Notational Standards for Percussion - A Report on the Ghent Conference.' **The Instrumentalist** 29: 53-5, June 1975.

99. McCARTY, Frank 'Percussion Notation.' **Percussionist** 15/2: 49-60, 1978.
This is a report and a discussion about the results of a survey returned by c. 100 top U.S.A. percussionists, conducted by the Percussive Arts Society in 1974. A detailed questionnaire on notational problems and preferred possibilities was sent out, including questions on what kind of staff, terminology and language, notational symbology, comformity of notation with other instruments, problems of notation for decay, ornaments, rolls, score order, mallets, etc. Some of the answers should be of special interest to composers.

100. McCARTY, Frank 'Symbols for Percussion Notation.' **Percussionist** 18/1: 8-19, 1980.
In this the author tries to present a "complete collection of pictographic symbols for percussion instruments and beaters". It is a comprehensive listing of (1) 'Pictograms for Percussion Instruments', (2) 'Pictograms for Percussion Beaters', and (3) 'Application of Pictographic Symbols'. Unlike some other articles and books on this subject, only one symbol per instrument/action is chosen by the author, being his choice for various reasons given. Also included is a 'Bibliography of Percussion Symbols and Scoring.'

101. MEYER, Ramon E. 'The Notation and Interpretation of Rolls.' **The Instrumentalist** 22: 68-9, Dec. 1967.

102. O'CONNER, George 'Prevailing Trends in Contemporary Percussion Notation.' **Percussionist** 3/4: 61-74, 1966.
The three prevailing trends here in discussion are: (1) the expansion of our conventional system of notation, (2) the concept of metrical modulation, and (3) aleatoric (proportional) notation. The author points out the advantages and limitations of these systems, the "expanded system of note values" (H. Cowell, 1917), the "microrhythmic" notation (M. Colegrass, early 1960's), and the many advantages of proportional notation in allowing performers more freedom on all parameters of the performance (e.g. freedom from a rhythmic pulse). Also shows how a new graphic notation is being developed for this system.

103. O'NEILL, John 'Recent Trends in Percussion Notation.' **Percussionist** 18/1: 20-55, 1980.
   In this informative and knowledgeable paper, the author presents the reader with various possible systems for notation. He discusses their advantages and disadvantages, looking at examples from the contemporary literature, and discusses questions like the need and reasons for the variety of systems in use, their ability and intent to convey the intentions of the composer, etc. The chapters are called: (1) Introduction and Exposition of the Problem, (2) Staff Systems, (3) Line-Score Systems, (4) Determinate Systems, (5) Indeterminate Systems, and (6) Conclusion. Some of the pieces discussed and compared (re. notation) are: "Janissary Music (C. Wuorinen), "Ionization" (E. Varese), "Circles" (L. Berio), "Loops" (R. Erickson), "Zyklus" (K. Stockhausen), and "The King of Denmark" (M. Feldman).

104. PAPASTEFAN, John 'Timpani Roll Notation: Observations and Clarifications.' **Percussive Notes** 20/1: 69-71, 1981.
   Sifts through some examples from the literature and gives his recommendations for notation.

105. PERCUSSIVE ARTS SOCIETY 'Project on Terminology and Notation of Percussion Instruments.' **Percussionist** 3/2: 47-53, 1966.
   A group of Northwestern University faculty members, chaired by Gordon Peters, gives some findings and recommendations. Although this report is already 20 years of age, it still holds a lot of valid comments, especially for composers and arrangers. For example, it specifies clear layouts for scores, individual parts, points about durational notation, clarifications of rolls and embellishments, pointers on muting and muffling, and other ambiguities and problems.

106. PERCUSSIVE ARTS SOCIETY **Standardization of Percussion Notation.** Terre Haute, IN, Percussive Arts Society, 1973, 8 p.
   A short, but authoritative booklet, presenting recommendations for new notation, especially from the percussionist's angle.

107. SABLINSKIS, Paul **The Significance of Percussion in Contemporary Music between 1945 and 1970.** Masters Thesis, Univ. of Melbourne, 1982, 462 p.
   This is an extensive and thorough examination of this subject, investigating some original material, and examining the "fundamental role played by percussion in the evolution of New Music forms."
   Chapter I traces the musical background of this century up to 1945 (with special focus on percussion), and Chapter II extends this analysis of styles from 1945 to 1970. Chapter III is the major part of this thesis (pp 154-430) and analyzes four works: "Zyklus" (K. Stockhausen), "Circles" (L. Berio), "The King of Denmark" (M. Feldman), and "Persephassa" (I. Xenakis). These works represent various world-wide trends and styles with regard to structure, performance, and notation in New Music. The presentation of these analyses and findings in these areas are very detailed and often original (especially in "Persephessa").

108. SKINNER, Michael 'Percussion Time Signatures.' **Crescendo International** 14: 13, Jan. 1976.

109. STEVENS, Leigh Howard 'Musical Shorthand - A Personal Notation System (for Marimba).' **Percussive Notes** 22/4: 25-8, 1984.

110. STEVENS, Leigh Howard 'Roll and Notation.' **Percussive Notes** 19/1: 60-1, 1980.
   Deals with rolls for keyboard percussion instruments only - new notation and symbols.

111. UDOW, Michael 'Visual Correspondence between Notation Systems and Instrument Configurations.' **Percussionist** 18/2: 15-29, 1981.
   As the title indicates, the essay tries to make a point for the correlation of notation and instrumental set-up, in particular the pitch-related set-up of non-pitched instruments (e.g. drums, wood and metal instruments), and the use of so called "timbre-racks."

# CHAPTER 3.

## NOTATION OF CONTEMPORARY MUSIC:

### (b) General Notation References.

112. BOEHM, Laszle **Modern Music Notation: A Reference and Textbook.** New York, Schirmer, 1961, 69 p.
Good, basic reference book, but not up to date in percussion notation.

113. COLE, Hugo **Sounds and Signs.** London, O.U.P., 1974, 162 p. (Subtitle: 'Aspects of Musical Notation')
Although this book has no special reference to (i.e section about) percussion, it is a "thoughtful and stimulating" book (as the cover says). The author deals with many questions of purpose, evolution, success and failure of notation. It is reasonably up to date, with many illustrated examples.

114. COPE, David 'Contemporary Notation in Music.' **The Instrumentalist** 30: 28-32, May 1976.
An introduction (with examples) to the new notation symbols and techniques, with sections being: Proportional Notation, Dynamics, Articulation, Timbre, Selecting a Score, and Symbols (chart).

115. COPE, David **New Music Notation.** Dubuque, IA, Kendall/Hunt, 1976, 122 p.
The author provides clearly laid-out charts where he first explains the meaning of the needed symbol, then his recommended sign, notes the composer(s) who are already using this sign, and shows also some other composers' notational symbols meaning the same. The symbols are grouped into sections of pitch, rhythm, dynamics, articulation, and timbre (instrumental groups - including a good section on percussion). An annotated bibliography concludes this worthy book.

116. KARKOSCHKA, Erhardt **Notation in New Music.** London, Universal Edition, 1972, 183 p. (Orig. ed. in German by Moeck, 1966, "Das Schriftbild der Neuen Musik")
This is the first major collection of new notation since 1945. Part I discusses the present situation, tempered notation, suggestions for reform, and new notation.
Part II consists of 721 different symbols and signs, listed in five chapters: (1)Exact Notation, (2) Frame Notation, (3) Indicative Notation, (4) Musical Graphics, (5) Electronic. Chapters (1) to (3) are then divided into groups like: tempo, duration, pitch, intensity, new symbols for special effects (subdivided idiomatically), articulation, etc.
Part III is a selection of c. 70 musical examples with explanation of the notation used in each piece, and referred to one or more of the symbols 1 to 721.
There are sections in Part II especially for percussion notation, but many other relevant examples will be found elsewhere, and also in Part III. The

book is very informative and comprehensive for the time (1966), and in Chapter III Karkoschka gives his own comments and opinions on most examples. Unfortunately, the English edition (1972) omits three large fold-out posters which give a clear, instant summary of the 721 signs, grouped idiomatically, and thereby makes it almost impossible to evaluate and compare notational signs, especially since the author hardly gives any recommendations for symbols himself.

117. KARKOSCHKA, Erhardt 'Notation wohin?' (2 parts) **Melos** 3: 183-7; 4: 272-7, 1975. [German]
   In Part I Karkoschka claims that music has changed its notation before, and it is high time to adjust our notation system to cope with today's character of music. Among the possible new systems he recommends is his own (Equition), but he also discusses Iraj Schirmi's system, called "Topographical Notation". This considers not only all sound elements, but also gives information of an acoustical-spatial-time nature, including a special seating plan for the orchestra with instructions for each player (e.g. time-delay action).
   Part II claims that professional musicians today must be expected to learn several notation systems, and goes on briefly to give the benefits of a few, like Extented Analysis to show all components of a musical structure; and simplified "listening scores" - graphical and verbal; new notation of "sound timbre" (e.g. of one note); program-diagrams for synthesizers.

118. PERKINS, D.N. & HOWARD, V.A. 'Toward a Notation for Rhythmic Perception.' **Interface** 5/1-2: 69-86, 1976.
   This article is reasonably well described at the beginning of the introduction: "This paper analyzes the concept of rhythm in music and outlines a notation for certain aspects of rhythm perception". The following aspects of rhythm are first clarified and then illustrated with notational examples: Impulse, Pulse, Counting, Counting Notation, Clustering and Clustering Notation, Influence of the Stimulus on the Rhythmic Organization, Ambiguity and Retrospective Revision. There is also a review of Cooper & Meyer's "The Rhythmic Structure of Music" (Univ. of Chicago Press, 1960).

119. READ, Gardner 'Self-indulgent Notational Aberrations.' **The World of Music** 15: 36-49, 1973.
   A personal viewpoint and some observations on the evolution of notation (in Western music); today's (1973) notational dilemma and its reason; the often excessive importance placed on the visual aspects of graphic scores and possible reactions of performers; and a conclusive plea to composers and performers alike.

120. READ, Gardner **Music Notation.** London, Victor Gollancz, 1978, 468 p. (1st ed. publ. by Allyn & Bacon, Boston, 1969)
   This is a very useful, contemporary and comprehensive source-book for the student composer, dealing with all aspects of notation. It is divided into general and idiomatic notation, each with its traditional practice and modern innovations. Although the section on percussion gives more up-to-date details than most books on orchestration generally do, I find that it is not as good as some other sections of the book, and sometimes it may be a little confusing for the percussion student as the author endorses too many notational possibilities.

121. READ, Gardner **Modern Rhythmic Notation.** London, Bloomington, Indiana Univ. Press, 1978, 202 p.
    A more specialized book than earlier ones by the same author, but does not deal very much with totally new concepts, but rather quotes examples of conventional (if expanded) notation from the contemporary works of over 100 composers.

122. READ, Gardner **Twentieth Century Notation.** New York, The New York Public Library, 1833 p. (Microfilm)
    Not available for annotation. Gerald Warfield states in his review of this book ('Writings on Contemporary Music Notation: An Annotated Bibliography', Ann Arbor, 1976) that it documents an enormous amount of contemporary notation from several hundred compositions of our time, each properly quoted and overal sections of notational examples being explained and discussed.

123. RISATTI, Howard **New Music Vocabulary.** Urbana, University of Illinois Press, 1975, 215 p. (Subtitle: 'A Guide to Notational Signs for Contemporary Music')
    This is a similar project to Karkoschka's (see entry 'Notation in New Music' in this chapter), except that Risatti offers no comparison or personal opinions. He has collected an immense number of symbols and notational instructions, and collated them into six main chapters: (1) General Notational Material, (2) Strings, (3) Percussion and Harp, (4) Woodwinds, (5) Brass, and (6) Voice, - no electronic or piano section. Where there is more than one sign which is meant to convey the same action or instrument, the author has grouped them together, so they are easier to compare, and they are ordered (from left to right) by degree of clarity - in Risatti's opinion.
    Each chapter is clearly divided into many sub-groups, and each sign is referred to the composer and work by a simple cross-reference method at the rear of the book. He took examples from 278 compositions by 131 composers, dated from 1952 to 1972 (except for "Pierrot Lunaire", 1914, and Varese's "Offrandes", 1929). The percussion section is well represented and shows the incredible diversity of signs being used, often very illogically and contradictory - sometimes by the same composer in different works.

124. ROSENTHAL, Carl **Practical Guide to Music Notation for Composers, Arrangers and Editors.** New York, MCA Music, 1967, 86 p.

125. SHIPP, C.M. 'Standardizing Symbols.' **American Music Teacher** 17/5: 40-1+, 1968.

126. SKINNER, Michael 'Various Methods of Time Signature Notation.' (2 parts) **Crescendo International** 15: 34, Feb.; 15: 33, March 1977.

127. SMITH, Sylvia 'Scribing Sound.' **Percussive Notes** 23/3: 34-51, 1985.
    A short article, plus 17 examples from "Scribing Sound - An Exhibition of Music Notations" (1952-1984), which relies heavily on graphic and visual techniques for innovative music notation, but excludes post-scoring notation.

128. SMITH, Stuart & SMITH, Sylvia 'Musical Notation as Visual Art.' **Percussionist** 18/2: 7-14, 1981. (Reprinted in 'Percussive Notes' 20/1: 49-54, 1981)

A report on some examples of and a discussion on visually artistic (and "free") notation, which the authors conclude with a plea not to standardize new notation, in order not to "standardize patterns of thought and creativity" as well.

129. STOCKHAUSEN, Karlheinz 'Musik und Graphik.' **Darmstaedter Beitraege zur Neuen Music** 3: 5-25, 1960. [German]
A brief historic background on the graphic representation (and its development) of music is followed by discussions on several contemporary examples of compositions employing graphic notation. They include Cornelius Cardew's "Piano Piece", Maurice Kagel's "Transicion II", and the author's own "Zyklus."

130. STONE, Kurt 'Problems and Methods of Notation.' **Perspectives of New Music** 1/2: 9-31, 1963.
The author discusses four aspects of a composition (in strictly "controlled" music) to be dealt with by satisfactory notation: pitch, tempo, rhythm (and meter), and articulation. Various examples from the literature are depicted, with their benefits and problems for the performer.

131. STONE, Kurt 'New Notation for New Music.' **Music Educator's Journal** 63: 48-56, Oct.; 63: 54-61, Nov. 1976.
In the first half of Part I, the author gives a general background as to why notation in contemporary music creates so many problems, and considers some work which had been done under his direction through the "Index of New Musical Notation" at the New York Public Library Centre (Lincoln Centre).The second half pertains to new notation for vocal music. Part II discusses microtonal notation, proportional notation, clusters, indeterminate repeats, and percussion notation.

132. STONE, Kurt **Music Notation in the 20th Century: A Practical Guidebook.** New York, W. Norton, 1980, 357 p.
A major work on notation - in particular for the composer/arranger. The special chapter on percussion includes listings of abbreviations and symbols (pictograms) for instruments and beaters, which are the author's choice, out of the many different ones in use already. The book gives ranges of instruments, suggestions for notation of set-ups and percussion ensembles, and special effects.

133. STONE, K. & WARFIELD, Gerald 'Report on the International Conference on New Music Notation.' **American Society of University Composers** 9-10: 56-78, 1974-75.
Outlines the procedures and methods used at the conference to decide which new musical notation (since c. 1950) already in usage should be recommended for standardization. This includes an eight page notation questionnaire (over 1000 copies received throughout the world, including many leading composers). It also gives a sample of results, but full details are shown in another article published since (see following entry).

134. STONE, K., WARFIELD, G. & SABBE, H. (Edi.) 'Report: International Conference on Musical Notation.' **Interface** 4: 1-120, 1975.
This is a major article and a full report on this important conference, which took place at the University of Ghent in The Netherlands, from October 22-25, 1974. Apart from the usual official reports like speeches, list of participants, and criteria of selection for new notation, it gives a

detailed report of all the musical notation endorsed by the conference. This is divided into two main categories, General and Instrumental. The first section contains: (1) Pitch, (2) Duration and Rhythm, (3) Dynamics and Articulation, (4) Score Layout, Conducting and Synchronization. The second category is divided into (1) Woodwind, (2) Brass, (3) Percussion, (4) Bowed Instruments, (5) Piano, (6) Voice, (7) Electronic Music.

For our purpose the General Category and the section on Percussion are of great interest. The latter includes a table of 60 recommended symbols for various instruments and 22 symbols for mallets. Also included are ranges of instruments, modes of attack and striking, consideration of decay times, families of instruments, and special effects.

This is not a dictionary of complete notation, but a valid attempt to clarify and standardize new percussion notation - as well as for all other instruments, of course - already in use since around 1950. This undertaking has been welcomed by most percussionists, and only time will tell how helpful and successful it will be. Highly recommended reading for all musicians and composers.

135. SZENTKIRALYI, Andras 'An Attempt to Modernize Notation.' **Music Review** 34/2: 100-23, 1973.

A report, with critical comments, on various attempts to invent new staff notations with regard to pitch, duration (time units), dynamics, and the use of new symbols.

# CHAPTER 4.

## CONTEMPORARY COMPOSITION AND ORCHESTRATION

136. ADLER, Samuel **The Study of Orchestration.** New York, Norton, 1982, 560 p. (separate workbook available)

    The chapter on "The Percussion Ensemble" (pp 328-363) in this major work covers a wide range of percussion instruments, including many small hand-percussion instruments and special effects instruments. All the important playing techniques are briefly described and amply illustrated with examples from the literature.

137. ALBIN, W. 'Keyboard Percussion Mallets.' **The Composer (USA)** 8/17: 36-41, 1976-77.

    A brief discussion of the various types of mallets and their sound-producing effects. Has a detailed listing of all the keyboard mallets manufactored by Musser, Deagan, Slingerland, Bruno, Premier, Mike Balter, and Vic Firth.

138. BLATTER, Alfred **Instrumentation/Orchestration.** New York, Longman Inc., 1980, 427 p.

    Generally speaking, this is a very comprehensive and contemporary-orientated book on orchestration, and the 46-page section on percussion is no exception. The author presents clear and informative information, including most contempoary aspects of percussion sounds, techniques and notation possibilities, including extensive charts with symbols in four languages.

139. BRAZAUSKAS, P. 'Editing Overwritten Percussion Parts.' **The Instrumentalist** 38: 52+, Apr., 1904.

    Some very basic suggestions on this subject, either to help students' techniques, or to simplify textures which are too dense.

140. CACAVAS, J. **Music Arranging and Orchestration.** New York, Belwin-Mills, 1975.

    (Not available for annotation; see book review in 'Music in Education', 40/379: 133, 1976.)

141. CAMPBELL, James B. 'Percussion on the March: Contemporary Field Percussion: Arranging for Multiple Forms.' **Percussive Notes** 19/3: 32-3, 1981.

142. CAMPBELL, James B. 'Contemporary Field Percussion: Arranging for the Rhythm Section Sound.' **Percussive Notes** 20/3: 54-5, 1982.

    Adopting a jazz/rock idiom to the marching percussion ensemble.

143. CASKEL, Christopher 'Neue Klangmoeglichkeiten des Schlagzeugs.' **Melos** 31: 16-22, Jan. 1964. [German]

    In this essay the author follows the recent development of the use of percussion from simply being an orchestral colouring (19th century) to being a completely musical sound on its own. Examples discussed include Stravinsky's "L'histoire du soldat", Bartok's "Sonata for Two Pianos and Percussion", Boulez's "Le Marteau sans maitre", Stockhausen's "Groups for Three Orchestras", "Zyklus" and "Kontakte". (One should remember that C. Caskel was the first person to perform "Zyklus".)

144. COLNOT, C. 'Arranging for the Drum Corps Band.' **The Instrumentalist** 31: 24-5, June 1977.
Several idiomatic points are briefly discussed here: "emotional contour", change of tempi and meter, marching step, woodwinds, percussion adjudication, and voicings.

145. COSSABOOM, Sterling **Compositional and Scoring Practices for Percussion in Symphonies Written for Concert Band: 1950-1970.** Ph.D. Thesis, The University of Connecticut, 1981, 230 p. (Diss. Abst. 2350-A, 1981)
Eight symphonies of that period were examined and compared with existing band-scoring texts on the use of percussion in the concert band, and the author's findings were that percussion was used more extensively and less traditionally than recommended in these books.

146. DEL MAR, Norman **Anatomy of the Orchestra.** London, Faber & Faber, 1981, 525 p.
The large chapter on percussion (pp 339-430) refers mainly to examples of the orchestral repertoire. The various instruments are dicussed with regard to scoring and orchestrational application in the literature. New playing techniques and up-to-date effects are not dealt with in this survey.

147. DEUTSCH, M. 'A Primer on Latin Rhythm Instruments' (Exerpt from **How to Arrange for Latin American Instruments**).
**Downbeat** 51: 54-7, Jan., 1984.

148. DIEMER, Emma 'Writing for Mallet Percussion.' **Woodwind World, Brass and Percussion** 22/4: 10-13+, 1983.
This paper discusses the idiomatic problems and also advantages of the instruments (vibes, xylophone, marimba), how to consider melodic and harmonic directions, sustain and vibrato (vibes) vs. dryness and short sounds (xylophone), clusters, glissandi, etc., illustrated with examples from the author's own compositions.

149. GEORGE, Ron 'Research into New Areas of Multiple Percussion Performance and Composition.' **Percussionist** 12/3: 110-31, 1975.
In this worthwhile article the author presents a detailed description (illustrated with photographs and diagrams) of the new technique of building and playing a "percussion console". This type of console gives the performer a greatly extented playing area, as the instruments are mounted on heavy, adjustable stands and racks, and this results in a very compact playing area with greater control over more instruments. The space all around the performer is utilized, embracing the regions in front and above his head. Apart from a thorough explanation of how to build such a console, how to group and mount instruments, etc., the author also debates how this new "instrument" gives rise to compositions being written with these new technical and timbral possibilities in mind, which, previously, would have been impossible to execute.

150. HOLLAND, James 'Writing for Percussion.' **The Composer (London)** No.76/77: 1-2, 1982.
(For more detailed information by this author see the entry "Percussion" in Chapter 1/a.)

151. HOUSTON, Robert 'A Summary of the Percussion Writings of Stravinsky.' **Percussionist** 16/1: 9-15, 1978.

152. JACOB, Gordon **The Elements of Orchestration.** New York, October House, 1965, 216 p.

153. KENNAN, Kent Wheeler **The Technique of Orchestration.** Englewood Cliffs, NJ, Prentice Hall, 1970, 364 p. (2nd ed.; originally published 1952)
Includes fairly good, basic and reliable information on how to write for percussion instruments.

154. KETTLE, Rupert 'Composer's Corner.' **Percussionist** 6/2: 52-4, 1968.
(Not available for annotation)

155. KREUTZER, Bill 'Editing the Marching Band Percussion Part.' **The Instrumentalist** 27: 48-50, Oct. 1972.
This article, which applies especially to the writing of snare drum parts, tells how to obtain a simple, yet full and rich sound, by editing some parts, that is, either strengthening or simplifying, as necessary.

156. KUNITZ, Hans **Die Instrumentation - Teil 10: Schlaginstrumente.** Leipzig, Breitkopf & Haertel, 1978, 205 p. (In German; first published 1956)
The first thing to notice about this book is that it has no table of contents, no index, no introduction or bibliography. This might be due to the fact that it is one of a series of books on instrumentation, and contents and index might be found elsewhere. Although it has no illustrations (but a wealth of musical examples), it is a very informative book, covering all the major instruments from these seven angles and considerations:
(1) Historical Development, (2) Technical Structure (and design of instruments), (3) Sound-Generation and Notation, (4) Character of Sound (timbre), (5) Combination of Sounds, (6) Idiomatic Performance Possibilities, (7) Use in the Orchestra. In particular, points (4), (5) and (6) are very helpful and unique for the composer, and give many examples from the literature with descriptive and constructive comments.

157. KUPFERBERG, H. **A Rainbow of Sound; The Instruments of the Orchestra and their Music.** New York, Scribner, 1973, 64 p. [Very basic text]

158. LEACH, Joel 'Stravinsky and the Cimbalom.' **The Composer** No.40: 1-5, Summer 1971.
The author, a recognized expert on this instrument, gives some illustrated examples from Stravinsky's orchestrations for the cimbalom (with relevant details of performance technique).

159. LE CROY, H.F. 'Percussion Scoring.' **The Instrumentalist** 20: 70+, Sep. 1965.

160. LEPPER, K. 'Writing Effective Percussion Parts.' **The Instrumentalist** 36: 78+, March 1982.
Basic advice for the music teacher or director of concert and marching bands on simple stylistic and idiomatic guidelines for orchestration.

161. MANCINI, Henry **Sounds and Scores - A Practical Guide to Professional Orchestration.** Northbridge, Northbridge Music, 1973, 243 p. (Includes 3 records)
This is a text on the "modern orchestra" (as distinct from the symphony orchestra) and is clear and well presented. The section on percussion discusses basic notation for drums, bar percussion and timpani, and the musical style refers to popular and jazz orchestration. There is also a section on Latin instruments and basic rhythms, and a section on orchestrating for the combo.

162. MITCHELL, D. 'Percussion in the Orchestra of Henry Partch.' **Percussionist** 3/2-3: 37-8, 1966.

163. MUTCHLER, R.D. **A Guide to Arranging and Scoring for Marching or Pep Band.** Libertyville, IL, National Education Services, 1967, 75 p.

164. OTTE, A. 'Considerations for Compositions for Marimba.' **Percussionist** 11/4: 129-34, 1974.
The author claims to show a "new consciousness" of the marimba's possibilities among composers. Discusses first the use and possibilities of the "Musser" grip (four mallets), what sort of technical phrases and note-configurations can be played, followed by two excerpts from new pieces for marimba.

165. PETERS, Gordon 'Outline Guide to Percussion Orchestration.' **The Instrumentalist** 20: 69-72, June 1966.
Gives elementary advice on snare drum, timpani, mallet keyboard (ranges and mallet types), a list of accessory percussion instruments, and Latin American instruments (lists only), and some notational advice.

166. PETTY, Mark 'Contemporary Marching Percussion: Voicing for Contemporary Percussion.' **Percussive Notes** 15/3: 20-1, 1977.

167. PIRRIE, J. 'Arranging for the Rhythm Section.' **Canadian Musician** 3/1: 63, 1981.

168. PISTON, Walter **Orchestration.** London, Victor Gollancz, 1978, 477 p. (First published in 1955)
[Very limited in the area of percussion.]

169. PTASZYNSKA, M. 'Tonal Control of Indefinite Pitch Percussion Instruments.' **Percussionist** 18/1: 4-7, 1980.
Musical suggestions for the composer (re notation) and performer to improve the sound and effect of non-pitched instruments, especially in groups of similar types of instruments (e.g. 5 tom toms, 3 cymbals, etc.), by grouping them in certain intervals.

170. PRENSHAW, E.R. **Current Practices in Arranging for the Marching Band.** D.M.A. Thesis, Univ. of Texas at Austin, 1970, 254 p. (Diss. Abst. 31: 3585A-6A, Jan. 1971)

171. RAUSCHENBERG, D. 'Orchestrating for Percussion Ensemble.' **Woodwind World, Brass and Percussion** 18/1: 28-9, 40+, 1979.
The article gives basic consideration to the many available timbres within the percussion section. It also points out the physical problems of the multi-percussion performer and the composer's considerations thereof.

172. READ, Gardner **Thesaurus of Orchestral Devices.** New York, Greenwood Press, 1969, 631 p. (Originally published in 1953)
This large reference text has some useful tables for percussionists/composers: (1) nomenclature of percussion instruments and playing technique terminolgy in four languages, (2) comparative table of ranges, (3) list of abbreviations, and (4) index of notation (symbols). The section on percussion is divided into chapters on the different instruments, and each chapter lists (again in four languages) various methods of striking, dampening, tremoli, etc., and refers each instruction for actions to one or more examples of the literature, stating also page number and bar number in the relevant score. But no actual musical examples are given in the book.

173. READ, Gardner **Contemporary Instrumental Techniques.** New York, Schirmer Books (Macmillan Co.), 1976, 259 p.
This is a helpful and very informative collection of new techniques from this prolific author. It is divided into 'Generalized' and 'Idiomatic Techniques'. The 'Generalized' section discusses eight areas of new playing techniques which are applicable to most groups of instruments as a whole, whereas the 'Idiomatic' section deals with the different groups of instruments separately (e.g. brass, strings, etc.). Every technique of generating sounds is at first discussed and then referred to an often extensive list of compositions, some of them with musical notation.
In the 'Generalized' section the techniques for percussion instruments are: extended ranges, muting, glissandi, harmonics and amplification. In the separate chapter on percussion instruments (22 pages) he deals with: tuning of unpitched instruments, new areas of striking, unusual agents of attack, new methods of striking, tremoli variants, idiophone clusters, and miscellaneous effects.

174. REED, H.O. & LEACH, J.T. **Scoring for Percussion** Englewood Cliffs, NY, Prentice Hall, 1969, 150 p.
(For annotation see same entry in Chapter 1/a.)

175. RIMSKY-KORSAKOV, N. **Principles of Orchestration - With Musical Examples Drawn from his Own Work.** New York/London, Dover/Constable, 1964, 152 p & 333 p. (2 vols; Reprint of 1922 ed.; Edited by M. Steinberg, translated by E. Agate.)

176. SEBESKY, Don **The Contemporary Arranger.** New York, Alfred Publ. Co., 1974, 233 p. (Includes three 7" recordings)
A reasonable text on arranging for popular music (i.e. pop, rock and jazz), but contains only very basic information on percussion and drum set writing.

177. STEINKE, G. 'The Percussive Composer.' **Woodwind World, Brass and Percussion** 16/1: 38-9+, 1977.
Very short and basic article relating some attitude and intentions of scoring for percussion from the composer's point of view.

178. VIERA, Joe **Reihe Jazz: Vol.3. Arrangement und Improvisation.** Vienna, Universal, 1971, 50 p. [German]

179. WEBSTER, Gilbert 'On Percussion.' **Composer** No.26: 21-4, 1968.
   Contains some elementary (but good) advice by a percussionist for composers on writing percussion parts - how to avoid common problems.

# CHAPTER 5.

## INSTRUCTION AND PERFORMANCE - ORCHESTRAL INSTRUMENTS:

### (a) Snare Drum.

180. AGOSTINI, Dante **Solfege Rhythmique (5 vols.).** Bryn Mawr, PA, Theodore Presser.
The five volumes for this snare drum method are:
(1) Simple measures (64 p)
(2) Compound measures (27 p)
(3) More advanced, asymmetric exercises (32 p)
(4) More advanced, simple and compound exercises (50 p)
(5) Simultaneous independent polyrhythms (50 p)

181. ALBRIGHT, Fred **Rhythmic Analysis for the Snare Drum.** New York, Award Music Co., 1977.
A book for the advanced, with an introduction to polyrhythms, followed by 35 etudes and 26 solos, utilizing all the snare drum techniques.

182. AMEELE, David 'Focus on Snare Drum - Choosing the Right Instrument.' **Woodwind World, Brass and Percussion** 18/2: 36-7, 44-5, 1979.
This gives a detailed and useful account of the important parts of a snare drum which influence its sound: the shell, heads, snares and snare-straines, and sticks. Choice and comparison of materials, size, thickness and shape are discussed and some good advice is given.

183. BENSON, Allen **Basic Principles of the Scottish Style.** New York, Benson Publications, 1978, 17 p.
This contains exercises and examples of the Scottish style of snare drumming, notation vs. actual execution of performance, Scottish 7/8 beatings, as well as four solos and one duet by the author.

184. BENSON, Allen **Details of the Swiss Style of Drumming.** New York, Benson Publications, 1980, 25 p.
Contains all the typical elements and rudiments of this type of drumming, like the Swiss Army Triplet, Swiss rolls, the Ratafla, Millstroke, Patafla and others. Also includes an English-German glossary of terms.

185. BERKLEY, Dick 'A Practical Approach to Rudiments.' **Percussionist** 7/3: 82-7, 1970.

186. BERKLEY, Dick 'Teaching the Concert Style Roll.' [Buzz roll] **Percussionist** 9/2: 42-3, 1972.

187. BOLINGER, G.M. 'Playing the Snare Drum Musically.' **Percussionist** 12/4: 50-3, 1975.

188. BRITTON, M.W. **Crative Approach to the Snare Drum.** New York, Award Music, 1969. (2 vols.: I. Elementary, II. Intermediate)
Basic technique and musicianship is taught in this book, and some of the less common features in this text are the abundant uses of exercises and studies in duet form, and the concept of making the student sing the exercises.

189. BRITTON, M.W. 'A Good Snare Drum Grip and Seven Deadly Errors.' **The Instrumentalist** 24: 74-6, May 1970.
Explains seven faults and their prevention and cure.

190. BRITTON, M.W. 'Rudimental Families.' **The Instrumentalist** 25: 63-5, April 1971.
How to choose the most important snare drum rudiments (out of the eight families of rudiments) for modern practice and performance.

191. BRITTON, M.W. 'Developing a Good Snare Drum Roll.' **The Instrumentalist** 26: 43-4, Nov. 1971.
How to use and combine the rudimental and bounce technique to obtain an even and full sound.

192. BURNS, Roy 'The Super Soft Roll and how to develop it.' **The Instrumentalist** 26: 54+, May 1972.
Shows and discusses the "variables that affect the sound of the buzz roll", how to practise, dynamic principles, and the texture of the roll.

193. BURNS, Roy **Natural Hand Development for Drummers.** New York, Dick Grove Publication, 1978, 238 p. (Includes cassette)
An extremely thorough book on this subject, going through all the physical and musical exercises very systematically and progressively. An extension of the author's earlier book 'Practical Method of Developing Finger Control' in collaboration with Lewis Malin (see entry in this chapter).

194. BURNS, Roy & FELDSTEIN, Saul **Snare Drum Music.** New York, Alfred Publ. Co., 1976(?), 32 p.
Contains 17 solos in progressive order exploring the sound properties of the drum.

195. BURNS, Roy & MALIN, Lewis **Practical Method for Developing Finger Control.** New York, Belwin Inc., 1966, 49 p. (Original ed. Henry Adler, 1958)
A very specialized book to develop "Finger Control" in playing with snare drum sticks. After the basic playing with wrist-controlled strokes ("no bounce"), the exercises proceed to "Bounce studies", Finger Bounce, Accent Studies, Solo Studies, and also some musical studies employing the drum set.

196. CAMP, W.H. 'Rudiments must be made opposite.' **Woodwind World, Brass and Percussion** 20/1: 14-5, 1981.
Suggests the use of (memorized) rudiments to develop and perfect tone production and quality of sound, by concentrating on every physical aspect of the strokes.

197. CHAFFEE, Gary 'Sticking Patterns - A Musical Approach.' **Percussionist** 10/2: 47-9, 1972.

Very short article, which only gives food for thought to consider articulation by various types of stroke pattern.

198. CHAFFEE, Gary **Patterns (Vol. I.& II.).** Hyde Park, MA, G.C. Music, 1976, 85 p & 103 p. (Vol.I: **Rhythmic and Metric Considerations,** Vol.II: **Sticking)**
Vol.I deals with extensive rhythmic materials in many groupings, polyrhythms, mixed meters, metric modulation, etc., relating to contemporary music.
Vol.II is mainly concerned with sticking, how to use it in various musical ways and in difficult rhythmic situations. Both volumes cover intermediate to very advanced stages.

199. CIRONE, Anthony **Portraits in Rhythm - 50 Studies for Snare Drum.** New York, Belwin-Mills, 1966, 54 p.
Fifty interesting exercises, covering a wide range of rhythms and meters.

200. CIRONE, Anthony **The Orchestral Snare Drummer.** Menlo Park, CA, The Author, 1975, 44 p.
Although the subtitle reads: 'A Non-Rudimental Approach to the Teaching of Snare Drum", the author teaches and utilizes the roll, flams, drag, ruff, etc. However, the text proceeds in a clear, progressive manner in presenting reading exercises and studies from beginner to advanced level, but contains no orchestral excerpts. The author has one novel approach in suggesting tapping the foot on various (notated) parts of the beat.

201. CIRONE, Anthony (Edi.) **Master Technique Builders for Snare Drum.** New York, Belwin-Mills, 1982, 46 p.
Twenty one percussionists and drummers have combined to present drum patterns they personally endorse, with helpful hints on how to practise.

202. CLARK, Forest 'Pros and Cons of Matched Grip for Snare Drumming.' **Percussionist** 6/3: 83-5, 1969.

203. COMBS, F. Michael 'Selecting a Snare Drum Method Book.' **The Instrumentalist** 27: 50-1, Dec. 1972.

204. DAVIS, T.L. 'Rudiments - The Means, not the End.' **Percussionist** 1/1: 1-3, 1963.

205. DELECLUSE, Jaques **Initium (4 Vols.).** Paris, A. Leduc. (US Agent: Theodore Presser)
Presents extensive study and teaching exercises and etudes in four books, from elementary level through to very advanced.

206. FELDSTEIN, Sandy **Snare Drum Rudiment Dictionary.** Sherman Oaks, CA, Alfred Publ. Co., 1980, 32 p.
The cover-notes say: 'A complete reference guide containing all of the original 26 rudiments. In addition, other widely used rudimental patterns and helpful practice hints are also included.'

207. FINK, Ron 'Finger Control Applied to Percussion Performance.' **Percussionist** 9/3: 63-7, 1972.

The author urges all students and teachers to learn this technique as soon as possible after having mastered the wrist technique. He also explains the definitions of French and German grips with finger control, and with what types of snare drum and timpani techniques they can be used.

208. FROCK, G. 'A Comparative Study on Snare Drum Technique.' **Percussionist** 1/4: 1-4, 1964.
This is the follow-up to a 1963 thesis comparing the traditional and the matched grip. The conclusion and summary of the author's experiment claims that no measurable difference between the two techniques has been found.

209. GALM, John 'Snare Drum Embellishments.' **N.A.C.W.P.I. Journal** 27/1: 37-41, 1978.

210. GLASSOCK, Lynn 'The Buzz Roll.' **The Instrumentalist** 30: 68-70, Nov. 1975.

211. GOLDENBERG, Morris **Modern School for Snare Drum.** New York, Chappell & Co., 1955, 184 p.
This has been a good, basic tutor for many years now. Part I contains "study material" to develop reading, including many musical duets (e.g. for teacher and student). Part II is the so-called "Guide for the Artistic Percussionist", dealing with most non-pitched percussion instruments (individually). It has plenty of examples (including 'special effects') from the repertoire, plus 60 pages of musical examples of percussion parts and scores - mainly from the 20th century - including a full score of Varese's "Ionisation."

212. HOCHRAINER, Richard 'Drum Talk from Vienna - Embellishments.' **Percussionist** 12/4: 160-2, 1975. (Translated and reprinted from 'Das Orchester')

213. HONG, Sherman 'A Drag is not a Diddle.' **The Instrumentalist** 39: 41-4, Mar., 1985.
Debates some problems which arise for students who play in marching bands and in concert ensembles. These relate especially to the notation and interpretation of double and triple grace notes in rudiments.

214. HONG, Sherman 'Playing Rudiments Musically.' **The Instrumentalist** 39: 46-8, May, 1985.
The author recommends speaking and singing the various rudiments in musical ways (before and during execution) to improve evenness and musical expression.

215. HOULLIF, M. & PETERCSAK, J. **Contemporary Collection for Snare Drum.** Potsdam, NY, Potsdam Publications, c.1977.
The book contains seven studies and seven duets of a very advanced level, and features many aspects of contemporary styles and rhythms.

216. HOULLIF, Murray 'Developing the Snare Drum Roll.' **Woodwind World, Brass and Percussion** 22/5: 14-6, 1983.
Advocates the theory of approaching the "proper" roll by way of the "buzz" (or multiple bounce) roll right from the beginning, and recommends some exercises to teach (or study) this technique.

217. JACKSON, H.J. **An Instructional Method for Individual or Group Development of Snare Drummers.** D.Mus.Ed. Thesis, University of Oklahoma, 1968, 204 p. (Diss. Abst. 29: 1242A, Oct. 1968)
The author states in his summary that this method is aimed at both the beginner student and the (non-percussionist) band instructor, and proceeds to train the snare drummer in technical expertise and musical sensitivity. The program seems to proceed in a logical and progressive way, and recommends the use of the measured roll in nearly all cases.

218. KETTLE, Rupert 'Understanding Flams.' **Modern Drummer** 3/4: 48-9, 1979.
Teaching suggestions to help obtain a clean and easy flam technique.

219. KEUNE, Eckehart **Schlaginstrumente, ein Schulwerk: Vol.1 - Kleine Trommel.** [Snare Drum] Kassel, Baerenreiter, 1982, 150 p. (1st ed. publ. 1977)
A major series on orchestral percussion techniques. The text is in English and German (in all the three volumes), and includes some interesting illustrations and historic background of the snare drum. Exercises are progressive, clear and with good dynamic markings. From beginner's level to advanced.

220. KOONS, Randy **The Musical Snare Drum Player.** Lebanon, IN, Studio P/R, 39 p.
This contains 13 solos and five duets, ranging from intermediate to difficult, some being quite unusual and challenging.

221. LA VINE, S. 'Snare Drum Suggestions for Educators.' **Woodwind World, Brass and Percussion** 10/4: 32-3, 1977.

222. LANG, Morris **The Beginning Snare Drummer.** New York, Lang Percussion Co., 1980, 80 p.
Grouped into 30 progressive and practical lessons, each with a particular point of technical or musical interest.

223. LAROSA, Michael **Contemporary Drum Method.** Somers, CT, Somers Music, 1981, 62 p.
A consistent and progressive method, useful for private or class instruction. Highlights of the book are the duets and multiple percussion solos.

224. LAWRENCE, P. 'Understanding Ruffs and Drags.' **The Instrumentalist** 31: 62-5, Nov. 1976.

225. LEFEVRE, Guy **Le Tambour.** Paris, The Author, 1979, 90 p.
A French method book on the snare drum in the classic French tradition of drumming techniques. Part I contains all the basic exercises, flams and rolls, and Part II features control, rhythm and musical studies, French marches and solos.

226. LEIMSIDOR, Bud **Here's how to Strengthen the Drummer's Left Hand.** Miami Beach, Hansen Publications, 1966, 32 p.
Perhaps the only book dedicated to this special subject. It consists of snare drum exercises, the first part being for left hand only and containing common rhythms with dynamic markings, accents and flams. The second part is to be played with both hands, emphasizing the left hand with special stickings, and also featuring odd meters.

227. LEPAK, Alexander **50 Contemporary Snare Drum Etudes.** Windsor, CT, Windsor Music Publications, 1977.
    Deals with many different rhythms, meters and styles, also including odd and changing meters, as well as some proportional and graphic notation.

228. MAZZACANO, P.T. '2 B or not 2 B ? (proper drum stick size).' **The Instrumentalist** 25: 43-5, Dec. 1970.

229. McCORMICK, R. 'Developing Concert Snare Drum Technique.' **The Instrumentalist** 34: 72-5, Apr. 1980.
    The author feels that this area is very neglected and offers some advice for the teacher and student on how to improve this situation, including a list of recommended repertoire.

230. McKENZIE, Jack 'The Matched Grip - Yes.' **Percussionist** 1/3: 3-4, 1963.

231. MEMPHIS, Charles **The Contemporary Percussionist.** Hollywood, CA, Try Publishing Co., 76 p.
    The book contains mostly snare drum exercises, including some duets and also some drum set studies, with the aim to develop sight-reading.

232. MEYER, Ramon E. 'The Snare Drum Rudiments: Another Analysis.' **Percussionist** 1/3: 1-3, 1963.

233. MORELLO, Joe 'Finger-control in Manipulating the Sticks.' **Crescendo International** 12:37, Jan. 1974.

234. MORELLO, Joe **Master Studies.** Clifton, NJ, Modern Drummer Book Division, 1984.
    Subtitled: 'Exercises for the Development of Control and Technique'. A book on hand development and stick control, with over 800 exercises, covering accents, various types of rolls and stroke patterns, flams, endurance, dynamics, and others.

235. MORTON, James **The Virtuoso Drummer.** Pacific, MO, Mel Bay Publications, 1983, 52 p.
    A snare drum method for serious students who wish to master the instrument technically and musically. Divided into three parts: Fundamental Technique, Hand to Hand Coordination, and Ambidexterity.

236. MODERN DRUMMER (Editorial) 'The Merits of the Matched Grip.' **Modern Drummer** 1/2: 12, 1977.
    [An essay in favour of the matched grip]

237. MODERN DRUMMER (Editorial) 'A Realistic Look at the Matched Grip.' **Modern Drummer** 6/2: 22-5, 1982.
    A detailed study (from a physical and a musical point of view) of this grip, in comparison to the traditional grip, which seems to show that it has many advantages over the older one.

238. OLMSTEAD, Gary 'The Snare Drum Roll; A Discussion for the Teacher - with Emphasis on the Beginning Student.' **Percussionist** 8/2: 47-52, 1960.
    Several types of rolls are discussed, their notation, sound and purpose in musical application.

239. PERCUSSIVE ARTS SOCIETY **International Drum Rudiments.** Sherman Oaks, Alfred Publ. Co., 1985. (Includes 90 min. demo cassette by Rob Carson)

240. PERKINS, Phil **The Logical Approach to Rudimental Snare Drum.** (Vol.I. & II.)
Cincinnati, Logical Publications, 1981 (96 p each Vol.).
Vol.I is a beginner's method, teaching reading skills with a so-called "rhythmic alphabet", i.e. reading rhythmic groups as one unit, and features many dynamic exercises.
Vol.II Extends the level of rhythmic difficulty and includes basic techniques such as flams, ruffs and various rolls.

241. PETERS, Mitchell 'Detached Rolls in Snare Drumming.' **The Instrumentalist** 18: 68-70, Dec. 1963.

242. PRESS, Arthur 'Capriccio Espagnol.' **Modern Percussionist** 1/2: 54-7, 1985.
[Discusses performance aspects of the snare drum part]

243. PRESS, Arthur 'Scheherazade.' **Modern Percussionist** 1/3: 26-9, 1985.
[Discusses performance aspects of the snare drum part]

244. PRESTON, A.C. 'An Investigation into the Current Acceptance of the Matched Grip for Snare Drummer.' **Percussionist** 8/3: 99-103, 1971.

245. PULLIS, J.M. 'Developing the Rudimental Snare Drum Grip.' **The Instrumentalist** 26: 47-8, Oct. 1971.

246. ROTHMAN, Joel **Complete Drumming Technique.** New York, J.R. Publications, 1974, 256 p.
This collection of exercises has been selected from several smaller books by the same author, and deals with reading and rudimental technique development. As with many of this author's books, every new idea is exhaustively (sometimes repetitively) dealt with.

247. SCHINSTINE, W.J. 'All about Paradiddles.' **Percussionist** 2/1-2: 28-36, 1965.
Gives 336 different examples of accented paradiddles for practice, plus permutations and other variations and adaptations across uneven rhythmic groups.

248. SCHINSTINE, W.J. 'Three-way Flams.' **The Instrumentalist** 27: 47-8, Nov. 1972.

249. SCHINSTINE, W. & HOEY, F. **Basic Drum Book.** San Antonio, TX, Southern Music, 1973(?), 84 p.
As well as snare drum technique, the book covers basic theory of music. It includes solos, duets and quartets, and some bass drum and cymbal technique.

250. SHAUGHNESSY, Ed 'Finger Control in Modern Drumming.' **Percussionist** 5/3: 284-5, 1968.

251. SPALDING, Dan 'Common Errors in Snare Drum Playing.' **The Instrumentalist** 38: 42+, May, 1984.

Spalding points out some of the errors causing sound quality and balance problems, and advises on how to correct and overcome these. They include tension, mute, snares, sticks, and striking techniques.

252. SPELLISSEY, G.J. 'Roll: Sustaining Snare Drum Tones.' **Music Educator's Journal** 61: 46-51, Nov. 1974. (Reprinted in 'Percussionist' 11/4: 135-42, 1974; and in 'Modern Drummer' 1/2: 19-20, 1977)
      A discussion and short history on various ways of executing open and closed rolls, and how each type has its place in music.

253. STONE, G.L. **Stick Control for the Drummer.** Boston, Georg B. Stone & Son, 1963, 46 p. (First published in 1935)
      Simply a specialized, good practice book to develop speed and control in playing basic rhythmic figures and rudiments, which still seems to be very popular with drum teachers.

254. TUTHILL, G. 'A Look at Technique.' **Percussive Notes** 19/2: 34-7, 1981.
      Analyzes some rudiments in small details of stroke-execution, movement and control of the stick, with diagrams and recommended exercises, and also includes notation of some lesser known rudiments.

255. TUTHILL, G. 'Re-defining Rudiments.' **The Instrumentalist** 37: 48-52, May, 1983.
      A similar article to the author's earlier one on technique and rudiments (see previous entry above). Tuthill suggests here that teaching the roll, for example, is really a combination of different strokes, which should be understood and practised. They are the bounce stroke, down stroke, up stroke, and rebound-tap series of strokes (all illustrated with graphs). He recommends a series of exercises and sticking patterns to practise rolls, grace notes and flams.

256. VAN DYCK, Mark 'Rudimental Positioning for Set and Snare.' **Modern Drummer** 6/8: 100-103, 1982. (Positioning here means position of hands over the drum)

257. WANAMAKER, Jay 'P.A.S. International Drum Rudiment Proposal.' **Percussive Notes** 21/1: 74-8, 1982.
      This proposal means to extend the original 26 standard rudiments (of 1933) to a group of 40 rudiments, which would include Swiss, drum corps and other contemporary rudiments.

258. WHALEY, Garwood **Fundamental Studies for the Snare Drum.** New York, J.R. Publications, 1973.

259. WHALEY, Garwood **Primary Handbook for Snare Drum.** Fort Lauderdale, FL, Meredith Music Publ., 1981, 48 p.
      (Not available for annotation; for book review see 'Percussive Notes' 20/2: 78, 1982.)

260. WHEELER, Douglas 'Snare Drum: Tone Quality.' **Woodwind World, Brass and Percussion** 19/5: 15, 1980.
      [Points out important factors governing the sound quality.]

261. WHEELER, Douglas 'Performing the Ruff.' **Woodwind World, Brass and Percussion** 23/8: 14-5, 1984.
      Discussion on the various technical possibilities of playing this rudiment, and when to play which version.

# CHAPTER 5.

## INSTRUCTION AND PERFORMANCE - ORCHESTRAL INSTRUMENTS:

### (b) Timpani.

262. AKINS, T.N. **The Musical Timpanist.** Delevan, NY, Kendor Music, 1974, 97 p.
   This tutor is divided into 20 lessons, each one dealing with two aspects of performing: 1) intervals and tuning, and 2) technical exercises (sticking, rolls, dynamics, etc.). The book covers intermediate to advanced (4 drums) techniques quite well, but gives no preceding indications of number and pitches of drums, and notation is sometimes old-fashioned (e.g. glissandi notation is very bad).

263. AVGERINOS, Gerassimos **Lexikon der Pauke.** Frankfurt am Main, Verlag Das Musikinstrument, 1964, 105 p. [German]
   This is a dictionary (in German), which tries to cover all the terms and aspects of timpani-related matters in alphabetically ordered key-words.

264. BEGUN, Fred **Twentyone Etudes for Timpani.** Fort Lauderdale, FL, Meredith Music Publ.
   This book is advertised as containing "21 technically and musically challinging solos for 3, 4, & 5 drums". It also has recommendations on sticking, interpretation, selection of mallets and drums.

265. BENVENGA, Nancy **Timpani and the Timpanist's Art.** Gothenburg University, Dept. of Musicology: 3, 1979, 160 p. (Musical and Technical Development in the 19th and 20th Centuries)
   In this thorough, extensive and well-documented study, the author tries to show how technical development of the instrument and the development of music took parallel paths. The four main chapters are:
   I. "Technical Evolution", which divides into the main happenings on (1) the Continent, and (2) in England and the USA.
   Chapter II covers "The Evolution of the Timpani Tone", with regard to technique, sticks, heads and range.
   "The Music" is the title of Chapter III and shows (in 30 pages) how the music related to various technical improvements and also geographical differences.
   Chapter IV deals with the "Implications on modern Performance" (of older and new music). The 50 page appendix consists of 24 detailed diagrams and descriptions of machine timpani, as well as photographs and instructions for making timpani sticks.

266. BRITTON, M.W. **Timpani Tuning.** New York, Belwin-Mills, 1967, 64 p.
   The subtitle reads: "A supplementary method to develop the ability to recognize and match pitch, perceive and produce intervals, and handle the mechanical aspects of the kettles."
   This is really a general aural training and basic theory book, with applications to the timpani. The author proceeds step by step through the basics of theory (like key signatures, intervals, etc.), and then covers all the various types of scales and triads. Exercises are to be played on the

37

piano first, then to be sung, and then applied to the timpani.

267. BROWN, H.J. 'Orchestral Timpani Parts; to change or not to change?' **Percussionist** 9/1: 11-14, 1971.

268. CIRONE, Anthony **The Orchestral Timpanist.** Menlo Park, CA, The Author, 1978, 42 p.
    A beginner's method covering from two to four drums, but mostly for two. All the techniques are presented in 40 exercises and six larger etudes, but there is very little advice on tuning, no advice on mallets, and it contains no orchestral excerpts.

269. DOWD, Charles **The Well-Tempered Timpanist.** Melville, NY, Belwin-Mills, 1982. (Edi. by A.J. Cirone)
    This book contains 770 patterns and exercises for the technical development of basics, with special emphasis on cross sticking, muffling, phrasing, articulation, rolls (at all dynamic levels), intonation and staccato playing. It also includes a good section on tuning.

270. DUFF, Cloyd 'Timpanist, Musician or Technician?' **Percussionist** 6/1: 2-9, 1968.
    This stresses the importance of playing from a musical, not only a rhythmical point of view, and discusses the following points: Heads - calf vs. plastic, falseness; Sticks - variety and choice; Touch - blend with and support of other instruments, concept of sound; Muffling; Tuning - pedals, ear training; Intonation - whilst playing; also counting, interpretation and set-ups.

271. FINK, Ron 'Finger Control Applied to Percussion Performance.' **Percussionist** 9/3: 63-7, 1972.
    (For annotation see same entry in Chapter 5/a.)

272. FINK, Ron **Timpani Tuning Etudes.** Denton, TX, Fink Publ. Co., 1981, 38 p.
    Contains 16 interesting and musical etudes, ranging from two to five timpani.

273. FINK, Siegfried **Solobuch fuer Pauken.** Hamburg, Anton Benjamin, 15 p.
    A selection of nine graded timpani solos with playing instructions and musical considerations.

274. FIRTH, Vic 'Tips on Timpani.' **The Instrumentalist** 30: 49+, Apr. 1976.

275. FIRTH, Vic 'Reflections of a Timpanist.' **Percussionist** 17/2: 106-9, 1980.
    [Discussion of audition process (orchestra), choosing a teacher, and how to obtain experience]

276. FIRTH, Vic 'Symphonic Timpani Heads.' **Modern Drummer** 5/2: 36-7, 1981.
    Possible problems, and how to overcome them, of mounting new heads.

277. FRAZEUR, T.C. 'Some Thoughts on Timpani and Intonation.' **Percussionist** 6/4: 113-8, 1969.
    This article wishes to make the timpanist think and invites experimentation with the many variables of timpani sizes and types, quality and types of heads and mallets, the methods of sound production, and the effects these have on the final sound.

278. FRIESE, A. & LEPAK, A. **The Friese - Lepak Timpani Method.** New York, Henry Adler, 1954, 158 p.

      This 'Complete Method for Timpani' is in four major parts: (1) Basic Theory (just that), (2) Technique and Facts (covers all the basic techniques), (3) Intonation (a good chapter, covering intervals, scales, singing and tuning exercises), (4) Repertoire (a large chapter, presenting 19th and 20th century orchestral literature, often complete excerpts).

279. GAETANO, Mario 'Teaching the Beginning Timpani Student.' **Woodwind World, Brass and Percussion** 21/2: 34, 1982.

      Advice to the inexperienced music teacher on basic principles of timpani playing (the three grips, rolls, tuning, and sticks).

280. GOODMAN, Saul **Modern Method for Tympani.** New York, Belwin-Mills, 1948, 132 p.

      Divided into four parts: (1) Fundamentals (covers some history, elementary playing techniques, maintenance and tuning), (2) Exercises for two drums, (3) Exercises for three and four drums, (4) Repertoire for timpani (Classical to 20th century).

281. HINGER, Fred **Technique for the Virtuoso Timpanist.** Leonia, NJ, The Author, 1975, 78 p.

      The three sections of this book, a very personal one by this experienced author, are: (1) The description of Hinger's technique, (2) Short exercises and technical studies to practise this technique on two drums, (3) Several demanding etudes for 3-4 timpani, and also a listing of timpani repertoire.

282. HINGER, Fred **The Timpani Player's Orchestral Repertoire.** Hackensack, N.J, Jerona Music Corp., 1981, 72 p. (Vol.1: Beethoven Symphonies)

      The book contains the complete parts to all the nine symphonies, as well as detailed suggestions with regard to sticking, interpretation, balance, and the relation of the timpani to the orchestra.

283. HOCHRAINER, Richard **Etudes for Timpani - Vol.1, 2 & 3.** Vienna, Ludwig Doblinger, Vol.I: 1958, 40 p, Vol.II: 1967, 40 p, Vol.III: 1983, 32 p. (US Agent: Associated Music Publishers, New York)

      A good collection of very musical studies, relevant to the solo and orchestral repertoire, and many are preceded by preparatory exercises.

284. HOUSTON, Robert 'A Study of Methods used in Pitch Production of the Timpani.' **Percussionist** 8/2: 61-2, 1970.

      Report of a study (and questionnaire distributed in 1967) on this subject.

285. KASTUK, Steve 'Problems of the Student Timpanist.' **The School Musician** 52: 12+, Dec. 1980.

286. KASTUK, Steve **The Timpanist Etudes - Book 1.** Ridgefield, CT, H.K.S. Productions, 1980, 25 p.

      The 40 etudes cover some challenging material, especially relating to 20th century techniques.

287. KEUNE, Eckehart **Schlaginstrumente - Ein Schulwerk, Vol.2 : Pauken.**[Timpani] Kassel, Baerenreiter, 1977, 155 p.

      A major timpani tutor, text in English and German. Contains a brief history, basic notation and ranges, followed by technical exerises for two drums (75 pages), with etudes thereafter increasing to five timpani. Ranges from beginner to advanced, and covers all technical aspects of playing.

288. LANG, Morris **Timpani Tuning.** New York, Lang Percussion Company, c. 1983. (Includes cassette)
    This is divided into three parts: (1) intervallic exercises, (2) pitch recognition exercises, and (3) etudes and symphonic parts. Sections (2) and (3) are used in conjunction with a pre-recorded cassette, all with the intent to develop and improve hearing and tuning ability.

289. LARRICK, G.H. 'A Study of the Timpani Parts of Beethoven's Symphonies.' **N.A.C.W.P.I. Journal** 33/3: 4-19, 1985.

290. LEACH, Joel 'Questions and Answers about Timpani.' **The Instrumentalist** 23: 63-6, March 1969.
    These are possible questions from a would-be (orchestral) band instructor about preference in sizes, designs, heads and mallets; some elementary playing techniques, maintenance and repair of heads and pedals.

291. LEPAK, Alexander **Thirty Two Solos for Timpani.** Windsor, CT, Windsor Music Publications, 1981.
    Not available for annotation; a quote from the advertising material reads: "Advanced solo-etudes for the contemporary performer, covering difficult pitch, rhythm, and technical problems."

292. LUDWIG, William **Timpani Instructor.** Chicago, Ludwig Drum Co., 1957, 64 p.
    A fairly good basic tutor, but hardly gets into the 20th century at all. Covers rudiments, tuning exercises, care and tuning of instrument, with many excerpts from the orchestral repertoire.

293. MARDINLY, Georg **Etudes for the Master Timpanist.** Leonia, NJ, Charles River Music.
    The book contains 12 studies, most of them a challenge in pedaling and tuning. However, tuning hints are not given with each piece but only in charts at the end of the book.

294. MEYER, Ramon E. 'Timpani: The Creation of Silence.' **Percussionist** 12/2: 43-9, 1975.
    This explains the importance of muffling in timpani playing and the careful consideration of these five points with regard to successful muffling: (1) styles of articulation, (2) acoustics of the hall, (3) pitch, (4) duration, (5) tempo and clarity of melodic line and harmony.

295. MUELLER, Erwin Carl **A Timpani Method based on the Performance Practices of Edward M. Metzenger with an Application of these Practices to the Symphonies of Beethoven and Brahms.** D.A. Thesis, Ball State University, 1976, 439 p. (Diss. Abst. 37: 6132A-3A, Apr. 1977)

296. PAPASTEFAN, John 'Contemporary Timpani Techniques.' **Percussionist** 17/2: 75-87, 1980.
    The author discusses and gives good descriptions of new techniques, grouped into three subject areas: (a) "Agents of attack and implements

of execution", which includes many examples of new effects asked for by contemporary composers; (b) "Methods of striking", e.g. dead strokes and rim shots; (c) "Areas of striking."

297. PAYSON, Al 'Timpani Sticks.' **The International Musician** 62: 22-4, Oct. 1963.

298. PERCUSSIVE ARTS SOCIETY 'Timpani Education Report.' **Percussionist** 16/1: 35-43, 1978.
    Nineteen important and interesting questions regarding teaching and studying timpani have been given to several prominent timpanists, and their answers compiled into this report, which should prove very helpful to teachers and students alike.

299. PETERCSAK, J. 'Tuning the Timpani.' **Woodwind World, Brass and Percussion** 14/5: 42, 1975.

300. PETERS, Gordon 'Ear Training and the Timpanist.' **Percussionist** 4/2: 119-24, 1967. (Reprinted from 'The Instrumentalist' 20: 109-12, Apr. 1966)
    The author suggests and shows why we must develop an aural vocabulary, and goes on to explain various aspects of ear training: ranges of the drums, balancing heads, tuning (intervals), how to practise, tuning whilst counting, and other ideas.

301. POWER, Andrew 'Sound Production of the Timpani.' (2 parts) **Percussive Notes** 21/4: 62-4; 21/5: 65-7, 1983.
    (For annotation see same entry in Chapter 2.)

302. REMSEN, Eric 'Timpani Tuning - A much too Neglected and Misunderstood Subject.' **Percussionist** 14/2: 60-3, 1977.
    The author assumes that the instrument and the head in question are of good quality, before pointing out these two important factors of tuning: (1) the accurate mounting and tensioning of the head, and (2) the skill of the player in hearing pitch intervals and their successful transfer to the timpani.

303. REMSEN, Eric 'Editing the Timpani Parts of the Orchestral Music of the 18th and 19th Centuries.' **Percussive Notes** 21/2: 50-9, 1983.
    Discusses the need or desire of the percussionist to edit parts to suit today's instruments and performance practice (with examples from the literature).

304. SCHINSTINE, W.J. **The Developing Solo Timpanist.** San Antonio, TX, Southern Music, 68 p.
    Contains five sections in a progressive series of solos from easy to difficult. Each of the 52 solos addresses itself to a specific problem, giving special instructions.

305. SEELE, Otto **Schule fuer Pauken.** Frankfurt, Zimmermann, (?).
    [Timpani instruction method in German - Element. to intermed.]

306. SNIDER, Larry B. 'Concert Preparations for the Timpanist.' **The Instrumentalist** 31: 68-71, Dec. 1976.
    In this article the author advises on planning ahead for a performance. This includes setting-up of timpani and stick-tray, clearly marking any

changes in mallets (or instruments), tuning and conducting notes on the part during rehearsals, making a mute, and also visual aspects and mental preparations.

307. STUART, Robert 'The Timpani Roll.' **Woodwind World, Brass and Percussion** 16/3: 48-9, 1977.
Basic guidelines on how to develop a musical and even timpani roll.

308. STUART, Robert 'Rhythmic Clarity for Timpanists.' **Woodwind World, Brass and Percussion** 16/4: 38, 1977.
Explains a physical approach to obtain more clarity in playing rhythmic figures.

309. TAYLOR, Henry W. **The Art and Science of the Timpani.** London, John Baker Publishers, 1964, 76 p.
Written in 1964, it seems somewhat behind the times in attitude. Although it gives some interesting information on the acoustics, production of tone, path of sound-wave, construction of drums, "fine" hand-tuning, etc., it has almost become "historic" now with its praise for animal skins and dislike of pedal-tuned timpani.

310. TOBISCHEK, Herbert **Die Pauke - Ihre spiel- und bautechnische Entwicklung in der Neuzeit.** Tutzing, Schneider, 1977, 311 p.
(For annotation see same entry in Chapter 2.)

311. VERNON, Ronald 'Timpani Tone - The untapped Potential.' **The Instrumentalist** 31: 62,64-5, Sep. 1976.
This paper presents some considerations for obtaining a sensitive style and beautiful tone. The points made are with regard to proper striking area (on the head), choice of mallets, choice of drum for a particular pitch (which may be obtained on more than one drum), stroke technique, and good balance of head tension.

312. WELLS, Rusty 'Selecting Sticks and Mallets.' **Percussive Notes** 18/3: 77-80, 1980.
[Listing of available mallets for timpani.]

313. WHALEY, Garwood **Primary Handbook for Timpani.** Fort Lauderdale, FL, Meredith Music Publ.
Not available for annotation, but the review in 'The Instrumentalist' (36/11: 53, June 1982) recommends it as a good beginners text for two timpani. It describes the book as having a progressive presentation, logical exercises and studies for strokes and rolls. It includes tuning exercises and a selection of musical solos.

314. WHITE, C.L. 'The "Rite" Timpani Player.' **Percussionist** 8/4: 130-4, 1971.
The author explains how he managed to perform the timpani part of "The Rite of Spring" (Stravinsky) with confidence, by analyzing and writing out his own version of the part.

315. WIGGINS, B. 'Timpani Fundamentals: Rolls.' **The Instrumentalist** 37: 73-6, Oct., 1982.
Points out the differences in approaching a timpani roll from another drum roll with regard to construction of the drum and the resulting tone qualities, the speed and rhythms of strokes, basic technique of rolling from drum to drum, mallet grip, and choice of beaters.

# CHAPTER 5.

## INSTRUCTION AND PERFORMANCE - ORCHESTRAL INSTRUMENTS:

### (c) Bar Percussion Instruments.

316. ANDERSON, Dean 'Bowing Mallet Keyboard Instruments.' **Percussive Notes** 22/4: 65-8, 1984.
    Explains types of bows to use for which instruments and in what way, with dicussion of 6 examples from the literature.

317. BROWN, Allen 'Practical Four-mallet Percussion Performance.' **N.A.C.W.P.I. Journal** 27/1: 4-19, 1978.
    The author first describes the four different grips in use (the Musser, and three versions of the Cross-Grip, including the so called "Burton" grip), and then discusses the advantages and disadvantages of the above grips (with the aid of musical examples). He concludes that, (a) four-mallet technique is essential for today's music, and (b) that in most cases the best grips to use are the traditional Cross-grip or the Burton grip.

318. BROWN, Theodore D. 'Strawfiddle Antics (playing problems in the xylophone part to "Porgy and Bess").' **Percussionist** 10/4: 130-33, 1973.

319. BROWN, Theodore D. 'Four Mallet Techniques for Vibes.' **Brass and Percussion** 1/4: 10-11+, 1973.

320. BROWN, Thomas A. **The Vibe Player's Method.** La Grange, IL, Ludwig Industries, 48 p.
    A very comprehensive listing of physical techniques with good illustrations, covering up to four-mallet techniques in many styles and tempi.

321. BURTON, Gary 'Vibraharp Study: Essence and Development.' **Music Journal** 22: 35+, Dec. 1964.
    A short essay on musical possibilities of the vibraphone and some suggestions for its use.

322. BURTON, Gary **Four Mallet Studies.** Glenview, IL, Creative Music, 1968, 40 p.
    A tutor, by the then still very young author, on a subject about which he is now one of the undisputed masters. After the introduction and explanation on holding the mallets, the book has three main sections of exercises:
    (1) 119 exercises for 4 mallets in rhythmic unison and open voicings;
    (2) 18 exercises to develop independance in both hands;
    (3) 25 exercises to develop strength and control of each individual mallet.

323. BURTON, Gary 'Evolution of Mallet Techniques.' **Percussionist** 10/3: 74-82, 1973.

44

discusses general points of advantages and differences the vibraphone has over and to other types of instruments. For example, the author claims less need for regimentation in technique (due to lack of tradition); the musical advantages in particular being the ability to play chords, and the level of dexterity on the instrument; four-mallet playing (which should be taught from the very beginning^); the awareness of visual shapes related to the sound. Part 2 deals with current changes of mallet techniques, such as sticking procedures, voicing, phrasing, independence and "comping."

324. CIRONE, Anthony **The Orchestral Mallet Player.** Menlo Park, CA, The Author, 1977.
This is meant as a companion book to the 'The Orchestral Snare Drummer' and the 'Orchestral Timpanist'. It starts at beginner level and the exercises and pieces are mostly in two-mallet tradition.

325. COMBS, Joseph Carl **The Problems of Sight-Reading on Mallet-played Instruments and their Relationship to Kinesthetic Sensation.** D. Mus. Ed. Thesis, The University of Oklahoma, 1967, 73 p. (Diss. Abst. 28: 2707A-8A, Jan. 1968)
This study examines first of all the importance of kinesthetics and vision in the technique of sight-reading, which is followed by experiments in test form of (1) visual responses alone, (2) kinesthetic responses alone, and (3) both responses combined. The study then makes recommendations for improvements and needs for specific study materials for bar-percussion, and also presents some original musical material of this nature.

326. FELDSTEIN, Sandy 'The Marimba as a useful and musical Band Instrument.' **Percussionist** 2/1-2: 36-40, 1965.

327. FELDSTEIN, Sandy 'The Bell Lyra.' **Percussionist** 4/3: 147-8, 1967.

328. FELDSTEIN, Sandy 'Mallet Technique.' **Percussionist** 5/4: 333-7, 1968.
Discusses the beginner's approach to the performance of two and four part playing on one staff and/or on two staves, and either on one treble or one bass staff.

329. FRIEDMAN, David **Vibraphone Technique - Dampening and Pedaling.** Boston, Berklee Press, 1973, 60 p.
This is a rare book with explicit instructions and etudes with regard to the musical effect of dampening and pedaling on the vibraphone.

330. GAETANO, Mario 'Beginning Four-Mallet Playing.' **The Instrumentalist** 35: 66+, Jan. 1981.

331. GAETANO, Mario 'Teaching the Vibraphone.' **The Instrumentalist** 37: 40-43, Nov., 1982.

332. GARD, Ronald 'A Description of Three Percussion Keyboard Techniques Relative to the Use of Four Mallets.' **Percussionist** 15/1: 7-16, 1977.
The three techniques in discussion here are: Non-sustained, Sustained, and Independent, which are then applied in a detailed study of one composition ("Yellow after the Rain", a four-mallet marimba solo by Mitchell Peter).

333. GIBBS, Terry **The Terry Gibbs Method for Vibes, Xylophone & Marimba.** Pacific, MO, Mel Bay Publications, 1980(?), 336 p.

Rather than a "teaching method" it appears to be a large listing of all types of scales and corresponding chords. Only three pages contain melodic material, and no idiomatic techniques nor any four-mallet techniques are featured.

334. GILBERT, D.K. 'Mallet Warm-Up.' **Brass and Percussion** 2/4: 8-11, 1974.

335. GLASSOCK, Lynn 'Four-Mallet Grips.' **Percussionist** 11/1: 2-11, 1973.

This article provides a close, technical look at the three different types of grips in common use (in 1973). They are the "Musser" grip and the Cross Stick grips no.1 and no.2.

336. GOLDENBERG, Morris **Modern School for Xylophone, Marimba, Vibraphone.** New York, Chappell & Co., 1950, 132 p.

Another popular tutor by Goldenberg, containing plenty of exercises with rolls, scales and arpeggios, doublestops, rhythmic studies and 39 etudes. Also a fairly good selection of orchestral excerpts from Mozart to Russell Bennett. But there is neither idiomatic treatment of the marimba or vibraphone, nor four-mallet technique at all.

337. KEUNE, Eckehart **Schlaginstrumente - Ein Schulwerk, Vol.3: Glockenspiel, Xylophone, Vibraphone, Marimba, Tubular Bells.** Kassel, Baerenreiter, 1982, 148 p.

Another major tutor by this author, with the text being in English and German. It discusses the various (illustrated) types of wood and metal bar percussion, ranges, and idiomatic sounds. Contains extensive, progressive studies, including four-mallet etudes, as well as separate studies for various instruments. However, the vibraphone lacks instructions for pedaling and dampening.

338. KRAUS, Phil **Modern Mallet Method. (3 Vols)** New York, Henry Adler, 1959, c.180 p @ vol. (Edi. by Doug Allan; The subtitle reads: 'A progressive lesson plan, combining technique, theory and harmony, for vibes, xylophone and marimba.')

339. KRAUS, P. & FELDSTEIN, S. **Marching Bells.** New York, Henry Adler, 1965. (Subtitle: 'A complete Method for Glockenspiel, Bell Lyra, Field and Band Bells')

340. LANG, Morris **Fourteen Contemporary Etudes for all Mallet Instruments.** New York, Belwin-Mills, 1967, 16 p.

All the etudes are for two mallets only, but they are of reasonable interest and musically challenging for the student, as each one is in a different style and 20th century compositional technique.

341. LEACH, Joel 'Questions, Answers and Suggestions for Mallet Instruments.' **The Instrumentalist** 23: 63-4+, Nov. 1968.

Imaginary questions from the viewpoint of the music educator are posed and answered. Information and advice given includes the purchase of mallet instruments: sizes; wich one to buy first and second (ans.: glockenspiel and marimba); tuning of bars; which mallets to use (a list of Musser and Deagan mallets); and some basic rules for mallet playing technique.

342. MARCEL, Jorand **Cramer - Xylo (Vol.1 & 2).** Paris, Alphonse Leduc.
Contains 40 progressive etudes for xylophone (two mallets) based on the music of J.B. Cramer.

343. MEYER, Ramon E. (Edi.) **Multiple Mallet Studies for Marimba.** Huntington, NY, Ha MaR Percussion Publication.
(Not available for annotation)

344. PIMENTEL, Linda 'Evolving Solo Techniques for the Marimba.' (4 parts) **Percussionist** 10/4: 107-10; 11/1: 19-20, 1973; 11/2: 77-81; 11/3: 97-101, 1974.
The first part of this series of articles (totalling 18 pages) deals with simple strokes and common sticking patterns, which is expanded in part two into rhythmic and melodic phrasing considerations. Part three shows ways of playing the open roll (suggesting why to use unmeasured rolls most of the time), and the final part touches on the usage and technique of four mallets.

345. PIMENTEL, Linda 'Mallet Co-ordination and Flexibility Exercises.' **Percussive Notes** 13/1: 33-4, 1974.

346. PIMENTEL, Linda 'Multiple Mallet Marimba Techniques.' **Percussionist** 14/1: 1-21, 1976.
In this authoritative paper, the author explains and discusses, with reference to the literature, how to use three- to six-mallet grips, their various advantages, control of individual mallets (in a multi-mallet grip), use of rolls, and other techniques.

347. PIMENTEL, Linda **Bar Percussion Notebook - Vol.1. & 2.** Columbus, Permus Publications, 1978 & 1980, 23 p & 24 p.
Vol.1 is a good keyboard training text, developing technical and reading skills by using short pieces of music as exercises.
Vol.2 is a collection of 24 pieces in many styles.

348. PIMENTEL, Linda 'Interval Study on Mallet Instruments.' **The Instrumentalist** 36: 83-6+, Nov. 1981.

349. RAUSCH, John **Four Mallet Technique and its Use in Selected Examples of Training and Performance Literature for Solo Marimba.** D.M.A. Thesis, Univ. of Texas, Austin, 1977, 374 p. (Diss. Abst. 38: 2406A, Nov. 1977)
First of all, the four-mallet technique is investigated from four aspects: adjustment to the keyboard, types of attack and release, four-mallet grips, and sticking procedures. Then, eleven compositions for solo marimba are analyzed with regard to performance problems. Also, five teaching texts are studied to judge how effective they are in preparing the student for contemporary music, and findings on this study and recommendations on how to improve future texts are given.

350. RAUSCH, John 'Developing Interpretative Skills in Marimba Performance.' **Percussive Notes** 20/2: 54-6, 1982.
Some ideas and advice on how to play "expressively", dealing with phrasing and articulation, legato and staccato, and interpretation of articulatory patterns.

351. RAUSCH, John 'The Interpretation of Rolled Notes in Mallet Instrument Performance.' **The Instrumentalist** 36: 44-7, Feb. 1982.
   This refers in particular to the necessity of having to roll notes when required to play legato on xylophone or marimba. The aim is to avoid playing all rolls in the same manner, that is attack, release and volume. The author suggests a certain approach, understanding of interpretation, and exercises to overcome this problem. Contains some interesting musical considerations.

352. RICHARDS, Emil **Two and Four Mallet Exercises on Vibraphone and Marimba for the Advanced Player.** Hollywood, Underdog Publishing, 1979.
   The book contains seven short pieces and 500 examples with a variety of techniques, including changing meters, rhythmic groupings, chordal and melodic line concepts, mostly suitable for improving one's reading and ear training skills.

353. SAINDON, Ed 'Dampening on the Vibraphone.' **Percussive Notes** 17/1: 50-1, 1978.

354. SAINDON, Ed 'Multi-Keyboard Playing.' **Percussive Notes** 17/3: 54-5, 1979.
   Useful tips on how to play vibes, marimba and xylophone as one physical unit.

355. SAINDON, Ed 'Sticking Concept.' **Percussive Notes** 22/1: 52-4, 1983.
   Demonstrates how to adapt sticking according to musical needs and personal choice.

356. SAMUELS, David 'Musical Awareness through Mallets.' **Modern Drummer** 5/4: 68-9, 1981.
   Encouragement for drummers to get some experience in bar percussion playing to improve their musical awareness.

357. SAMUELS, David 'Musical Development.' **Modern Drummer** 5/7: 58-60, 1981.
   Channelling single-hand etudes into some musical direction and purpose.

358. SAMUELS, David **A Musical Approach to Four-Mallet Technique for Vibraphone (Vol.1).** Bryn Mawr, Theodore Presser Co., 1982.
   Very extensive coverage of basic techniques, including grip (Gary Burton), sticking, dampening and pedaling.

359. SAMUELS, David 'Relaxing your Mind and Body through Warm-ups.' [Vibraphone] **Modern Percussionist** 1/1: 40-42, 1984-85.

360. SCHAFFER, Frank 'Two-mallet Keyboard Fundamentals.' **The Instrumentalist** 35: 40-45, Apr., 1981.
   Explains the six basic two-mallet techniques to be studied: major and minor scales, chromatic scales, playing in octaves, rolls, arpeggios, and doubling techniques (double sticking). Aimed at the percussionist without keyboard background.

361. SCHLUETER, Wolfgang **Studies for Vibraphone.** Hamburg, A.J. Benjamin - N. Simrock, 1979, 44 p. (Vol.1: Elementary)

A rare and good book on this subject, with idiomatic exercises and studies especially written for the vibraphone (Text in German and English).

362. SKINNER, Michael 'Sight Reading on Tuned Percussion.' **Crescendo International** 14: 33, June 1976.

363. SKINNER, Michael 'Developing Xylophone Skills.' **Crescendo International** 16: 32, June 1978.

364. SMITH, D.L. 'Four Mallet Legato Techniques for Marimba.' **Woodwind World, Brass and Percussion** 14/5: 40, 1975.

365. SMITH, J.B. 'Mallet Keyboard Sight-Reading.' **The Instrumentalist** 37: 25-7, Mar., 1983.
Suggests an approach to make sight-reading a fast and accurate reflexive skill. The program progresses at first through perception (fast recognition), interpretation of pitches, and execution (looking ahead). Recommendations for practice are given and materials for sight-reading are endorsed.

366. STEVENS, Leigh Howard **Method of Movement for Marimba.** New York, Marimba Productions, 1979, 97 p.
This is a major technical book for the serious marimba player. The first 38 pages of this beautifully printed text discuss (in 17 chapters) the so called "method of movement", i.e. the various techniques of stickings, grips and strokes. The second part contains 590 exercises, divided into: (1) single independent strokes, (2) single alternating strokes, (3) double vertical strokes, (4) double lateral strokes, and (5) mixed strokes. The clear photographs and diagrams are also very helpful.

367. STEVENS, Leigh Howard 'Marimba Perspectives: Switch Gripping.' **Modern Percussionst** 1/2: 28-9, 1985.

368. STEVENS, Leigh Howard 'Four-Mallet Grip Needed.' **Modern Percussionist** 1/3: 30-1, 1985.
Explains and evaluates four different grips: traditionally crossed-stick, Burton, Musser, and Stevens (named after this author).

369. STOUT, Gordon 'Three Tips for Practising Marimba.' **Percussive Notes** 21/1: 71-2, 1982.
The tips in discussion are: (1) set goals when you practise, (2) learn to teach yourself, and (3) creative practice is best.

370. TILLES, Bob 'Practical Mallet Studies.' (10 parts) **Percussionist** from vol.2, 1965 to vol.6, 1968.
Short articles, but with some useful exercises:
2/3: 13-4; 2/4: 17-8, 1965. 3/4: 78-9, 1966.
4/4: 200-1; 5/1: 224-5; 5/2: 259-61, 1967.
5/3: 301-2; 5/4: 326-8; 6/1: 22-3; 6/2: 50-1, 1968.

371. WEINER, Richard 'Debussy's "La Mer": A Performer's Analysis.' **Percussive Notes** 24/1: 19-24, 1985.
Debates performance problems and musical considerations regarding the composer's (most likely) intentions for the glockenspiel part, in particular the choice of the best octave placement, choice of mallets, articulation and dynamics.

372. WHALEY, Garwood **Primary Handbook for Mallets.** Fort Lauderdale, FL, Meredith Music Publ., 1980, 48 p.

Appears to be a thorough, well-planned beginners method, which covers all the rudiments, includes progressive studies in reading, some duets, as well as student assignments to foster compositional creativity. One of the good points of the book is that it gets the student to play with four mallets right from the beginning.

373. WHALEY, Garwood **Musical Studies for the Intermediate Mallet Player.** Fort Lauderdale, FL, Meredith Music Publ.

(Not available for annotation. For book review see 'Percussive Notes' 20/3: 79, 1982.)

# CHAPTER 5.

## INSTRUCTION AND PERFORMANCE - ORCHESTRAL INSTRUMENTS:

### (d) Bass Drum and Cymbal.

374. AMEELE, David 'Focus on Cymbals - Choosing the Right Sound.' **Woodwind World, Brass and Percussion** 18/3: 36-7, 1979.
    Specific advice on how to develop an ear for a good cymbal sound, what to listen for when choosing a pair and a suspended cymbal for concert use.

375. DENOV, Sam **The Art of Playing the Cymbals.** New York, Henry Adler, 1963, 29 p. (Subtitle: 'A Complete Guide and Text for the Artistic Percussionist')
    (For a book review see 'The Instrumentalist' 18: 14, Feb. 1964)

376. ETTLESON, Steve 'Testing, Selecting & Caring for your Cymbals.' **Percussive Notes** 21/4: 48-55, 1983.
    Describes choosing and testing considerations and procedures for various types of cymbals, for sound quality and personal satisfaction.

377. HOCHRAINER, Richard 'A full sounding Cymbalbeat.' **Percussionist** 7/3: 93-5, 1970.
    A detailed description of how to obtain a beautiful sound from hand-held crash cymbals.

378. HOCHRAINER, Richard 'Die Cassa.' **Das Orchester** 25: 599-601, Sep. 1977. [German]
    Essay on the "cassa", meaning here bass drum with mounted cymbal (for one percussionist), its historic background and playing technique.

379. JOHNSON, Warren 'Techniques of Orchestral Cymbal Playing.' **Percussionist** 12/4: 153-60, 1975.
    An article covering many elementary aspects of cymbal playing. First, the suspended cymbal: various types and characteristics, necessary mallets and implements, modes of attack; second, the crash cymbals: types and playing techniques; third, the gongs and tam-tams: differentiation and basic playing.

380. KAHLE, Dennis 'Cymbal and Gong Techniques.' **The Instrumentalist** 28/10: 34-5, 1974. (Part of article 'New Directions')
    This short but informative article explains some newer techniques very well. They include "cymbal tremolo", "cymbal vibrato"; how to produce strong cymbal fundamentals, and the effect of a glissando. Also talks about the "water gong", the bowed tam-tam, and tam-tam fundamentals.

381. KAHLE, Dennis 'Some new Sound producing Techniques for Idiophones.' **Percussionist** 12/3: 87-90, 1975.
    Seven contemporary and specific cymbal techniques are clearly

demonstrated, including the use of fishing line to bring out harmonics, bowing, "cymbal tree", change of pitch, etc., and two more techniques especially for the tam-tam.

382. KING, Chris 'Tips on Cleaning Cymbals.' **Modern Drummer** 7/1: 84, 1983.

383. MASONER, B. 'The Bass Drummer.' **The Instrumentalist** 17: 83-4+, April 1963.

384. MATSON, R. 'Bass Drum.' **Percussionist** 13/3: 85-9, 1976.
    This advice is aimed at the "high school and college band director". Under discussion are: the advantages of plastic heads; usage of stands; tuning (not too tight!); and the necessity of several types of sticks.

385. McCARTY, L.L. 'The Bass Drum deserves the Attention it demands.' **Music Education Journal** 56: 77-9, Sep. 1969.
    An informative debate on the playing technique of the bass drum, in particular what type and placement of strokes (and why), types of beaters, muffling, rolls, heads and tuning.

386. McCORMICK, L.W. 'Effective Use of Cymbals.' **The Instrumentalist** 22: 75-6, Oct. 1967.

387. NEIDIG, Kenneth 'A Cymbal Symposium - with Sam Denov, Bobby Christian, Bill Crowden, and Brian Shlim.' **The Instrumentalist** 34/10: 12-5, 1980.
    In an informative interview with Sam Denov (orchestral cymbalist), Bobby Christian (percussionist/drummer), Bill Crowden (from Drums Inc.) and Brian Shlim (consultant), the points in discussion include the following: how to select a pair of crash and suspended cymbals; how one can describe a "desirable sound" in a cymbal; sound limitations of a cymbal; some common misconceptions about cymbals (including the advice not to use ordinary cleaning and polishing agents).

388. PETERS, Gordon 'Concert Bass Drumming.' **The Instrumentalist** 20: 63-71, Feb. 1966.
    This valuable article on bass drumming discusses musical attitudes, training and various detailed aspects of playing techniques. They include: playing area, the roll, muffling and muting, and notation. It also advises on the equipment, care and maintenance, tensioning of head (incl. head collar), positioning of drum, and consideration of acoustics.

389. POLLART, Gene 'Everything you always wanted to know about Crash Cymbals.' **Woodwind World, Brass and Percussion** 20/4: 3, 1981.

390. POLLART, Gene 'Concert Bass Drum Beaters.' **Woodwind World, Brass and Percussion** 20/5: 12-3, 1981.
    A detailed discussion on the desired qualities of bass drum beaters, considering shape, size, weight, and material. It includes a short bibliography.

391. POLLART, Gene 'The Care & Maintenance of Crash Cymbals.' **Woodwind World, Brass and Percussion** 20/7: 10-11, 1981.

392. VINCENT, David W. 'Even a Bass Drummer should be a Musician.' **Percussionist** 15/2: 88-91, 1978.
    [Suggestions for stand, tuning, muffling, beaters and strokes.]

393. WHEELER, Douglas 'Concert Bass Drum Beaters and Technique.' **Woodwind World, Brass and Percussion** 21/1: 18-9, 1982.

Deals really with technique only. The author divides his discussion into five clear areas: Stroke (type), Grips (two grips are discussed), Muffling - Dampening, Angles of Suspension (horizontal & vertical), and Playing Area.

# CHAPTER 5.

## INSTRUCTION AND PERFORMANCE - ORCHESTRAL INSTRUMENTS:

### (e) Other Instruments.

394. AMEELE, David 'Focus on Triangle.' **Woodwind World, Brass and Percussion** 19/1: 12-4, 1980.
William Cahn, principal with the Rochester Philharmonic Orch., gives some interesting information and helpful hints about different types of triangles and beaters, playing techniques and suspending of triangles.

395. FIRTH, Vic **Rototom Technique - 21 Progressive Studies.** New York, Carl Fischer, 1981, 40 p.
The text is in English, French, Spanish and German - which makes the introduction 16 pages long. It explains the design and operation of conventional and pedal-rototoms in conjunction with the use of timpani and/or in solo capacity. The etudes are musical, dynamic and cover a lot of ground.

396. FLAHERTY, P. 'The Crotales.' **The School Musician** 45: 8+, Oct. 1973.

397. HART, W.S. 'Tambourine Technique.' **The Instrumentalist** 17: 56-8, June 1963.
Basic instructions and advice. Points out the need for several different instruments to suit various works in the repertoire.

398. IDA, T.T. & JOZSEF **Cymbalschule.** Budapest, Editio Musica Budapest, 1958, 107 & 144 p. (School for Cymbalom; Vols. 1 & 2)
The text is in Hungarian and German. The only proper and detailed instruction books I have found on this instrument.

399. KETTLEWELL, David 'First Steps on the Dulcimer.' **Early Music** 2/4: 247-53, Oct. 1974.
This well written article gives descriptions on various aspects of this instrument. Firstly, construction (various types of bridges, strings and hammers), possible tunings, various playing positions and techniques (e.g. hammers and plucking). This is followed by information and suggestions about ensemble and repertoire possibilities, which relate especially to the area of early music.

400. KETTLEWELL, David **The Dulcimer.** Ph.D. Thesis, Loughborough University, 1976, 473 p.
This is the most extensive and thorough text on this instrument. The seven chapters deal with all aspects of construction, tunings, playing techniques, musical styles, and historical evolution of the dulcimer. Chapter III covers the history in Europe from antiquity to the Classical period. Chapter IV is devoted to the "Dulcimer in the British Isles" since 1800, and the same time period is covered in Chapter V, but pertains to other countries around the world. Here the author has collected an

enormous amount of first-hand information and experience in many places, and the authoritative text is illustrated with 270 drawings and photographs.
Chapter VI gives a good summary of the many varieties of designs, structures and usages of the dulcimer, and the appendices include a discography with examples of music from many parts of the world.

401. KNAACK, D.F. 'Techniques of Tambourine Playing.' **The Instrumentalist** 28: 58-60, Jan. 1974.
    Explains clearly various (orchestral) techniques for the tambourine player.

402. LEACH, Joel 'The Cimbalom.' **Music and Letters** 53/2: 134-42, 1972.
    The first part of the article gives some historic background on the cimbalom (the word is Hungarian, meaning dulcimer), followed by details of construction, tuning systems and beaters. The second part gives examples of the instrument's use in Hungarian compositions, and also debates briefly Stravinsky's use of the cimbalom.

403. LEVINE, Dave 'The Doubling Drummer; playing the Rock Tambourine.' **Percussive Notes** 14/3: 26-7, 1976. (Reprinted in 'Modern Drummer' 1/4:14, 1977)

404. LEVITAN, Daniel 'The Tabla as a Contemporary Chamber Instrument.' **Percussive Notes** 16/1: 34-5, 1977.
    Suggests more extensive utilization of the tabla in contemporary music, and explains basic playing technique.

405. LUCAS, Clyde **The Amazing Batom.** St. Albans, NY, The Author, 1981. (separate record available)
    First of all, a "batom" is a floor tom tom which has a pedal attached to its bottom head, creating the effect of a bass drum, thus saving space and transportation problems. The short book gives enough examples to illustrate some idiomatic possibilities this set-up allows, especially the double bass drum effect, obtained by playing the tom tom with the pedal and the right hand on the top head. These patterns can also be used on a normal drum set.

406. PAPASTEFAN, John. 'Temple Blocks and Wood Blocks.' **Woodwind World, Brass and Percussion** 22/1: 20-23, 1983.
    The author defines clearly how the two types of instruments differ (e.g. pitched and non-pitched, suitability of various mallets and sticks, construction, tone, etc.), gives some examples of their use in the literature, how not to break them, and their availability.

407. POLLART, Gene 'Effective Use of the Cowbell.' **Woodwind World, Brass and Percussion** 21/1: 15, 1982.

408. POLLART, Gene 'Anvils, Brake Drums, and Bell Plates: Their Use in the Band.' **Woodwind World, Brass and Percussion** 21/2: 4, 1982.
    Brief description of these instruments and where (or how) to obtain them. However, advice on "their use in the band" is not really present.

409. SCHICKHAUS, Karl-Heinz **Neues Schulwerk fuer Hackbrett. (3 Vols.)** Munich, Musikverlag Josef Preissler, 1978.
    [German: 'New Tutor for Hammer Dulcimer'; Part 1: "Fuer Kinder", 40

p; Part 2: "Volksmusik", 60 p; Part 3: "Klassische und moderne Originalmusik, 40 p.]

This is an excellent set of books to study the playing technique and repertoire of the chromatic "Hackbrett" (as used in Central Europe). It is written in a clear manner and suitable to be used also without a teacher. Part 1 is designed for primary school level and contains basic music theory, exercises and pieces in the style of childrens' songs and dances. Part 2 (Folk Music) has more detailed tuning instructions, added techniques and exercises and their immediate application in traditional pieces. One very good point is the chapter on improvisation. It shows how to approach its technique and the importance of improvisation in folk music (in particular on this instrument). This volume concludes with a selection of traditional European pieces. Part 3 extends the technique with idiomatic studies and presents good arrangements of pieces by composers like Mozart, Bach, Landi, and Gluck. The most interesting part is the section on new, contemporary original music for the dulcimer.

410. SCHNEIDER, Ria **Schule fuer Kastagnetten.** Frankfurt, Zimmermann, 1983(?).
[Method for castanets; text in German and English]

411. SCHULTZ, Herbert L. 'Gongs.' **Woodwind World, Brass and Percussion** 19/6: 31, 1980.
[Brief advice on the selection of a gong.]

412. WHEELER, Douglas 'The Percussionists' Chime Trees?' **Woodwind World, Brass and Percussion** 23/1: 10, 1984.

413. WHEELER, Douglas 'The Triangle: Basic Equipment and Technique.' **Woodwind World, Brass and Percussion** 20/4: 18-9, 1981.
Helpful and instructive article on this often under-estimated instrument.

414. WHEELER, Douglas 'The Cowbell.' **Woodwind World, Brass and Percussion** 22/5: 12, 1983.
Basic advice on the availability of different instruments, and some playing techniques of various types of cowbells.

# CHAPTER 5.

## INSTRUCTION AND PERFORMANCE - ORCHESTRAL INSTRUMENTS:

### (f) Limited Instrumental Surveys.

415. ALFORD, E.E. **Identification of Percussion Performance Techniques in the Standard Orchestral Percussion Repertoire.** D.M.A Thesis, The Univ. of Oklahoma, 1983, 637 p. (Diss. Abst. 45: 676A, Sep. 1984)
    A major contribution to the study of the orchestral repertoire and its performance problems. By way of survey of the audition requirements for percussionists of 27 North American symphony orchestras, the "standard" repertoire was set (if it appeared 5 times or more). Many passages from the repertoire were examined, various possible interpretations discussed, and the technical difficulties of execution debated. The study also includes a brief discussion of the orchestral (percussion) instruments, with regard to history, construction and performance techniques, and the appendices include the established "Standard Repertoire" and a listing of the complete published parts to this repertoire.

416. BIRCHER, J. 'Chamber Percussion: Approach to Musicality.' **The Instrumentalist** 26: 74-6, March 1972.
    Some very elementary considerations, mainly directed at the inexperienced music teacher, about aspects of percussion ensemble playing.

417. BLADES, James **Orchestral Percussion Technique.** London, O.U.P., 1973, 86 p. (2nd ed.)
    Tries to give an all-round basic understanding of most pitched and non-pitched orchestral percussion instruments and their playing techniques, including some 20th Century examples.

418. CENTAZZO, Andrea **Percussion - New Techniques.** Milan, Italy, G. Ricordi, 1983(?), 85 p.
    (For annotation see same entry in Chapter 1/a.)

419. CHRISTIAN, Bobby & PAYSON, Al **In the Studio - Percussion Recording Techniques.** Park Ridge, IL, Payson Percussion Products, 1980, 74 p.
    Chapter I & II (pp 7-54) are mostly a collection of contemporary charts and parts for timpani and mallet keyboards with little helpful (verbal) comments. However, the shorter chapters on Latin percussion and special effects contain some well illustrated playing techniques (especially relating to recording situations), rhythms, and particular interesting special effects with drums, timpani, and various implements played on top of pedal timpani.

420. CIRONE, Anthony & SINAI, Joe **The Logic of it all.** Menlo Park, CA, Cirone Publications, 1977, 136 p. (Subtitle: 'Professional Secrets applying Imagination to Percussion Techniques')

Although this book seems to have been prepared with loving care by the authors, it appears a little laboured and out-dated and does not quite deliver what the title indicates. For example, the first 85 pages only manage to demonstrate how to play snare drum, triangle, castanets and tam tam. This is done with the aid of an excessive number of photographs depicting the execution of playing techniques. There is a very short section on percussion instruments, but timpani and other percussion instruments are not dealt with, and there is not a single note of rudiments or rhythmic patterns. The last 30 pages contain excerpts from the Classical and Romantic repertoire with comments on performance.

421. COMBS, F. Michael 'Percussion.' **Music Educator's Journal** 62: 38-41, Oct. 1975.
    The author offers some guidelines for music teachers in selecting percussion instruments for high school students. This includes sticks and mallets, snare drum, cymbals, timpani and bar percussion.

422. FAIRCHILD, F. 'Percussion Instrument Recommendations for the Schools.' **The Instrumentalist** 32: 85-9, Oct.; 32: 67-8+, Nov. 1977.

423. FAULMAN, Roger **The Junior Percussionist.** Chicago, Ludwig, 1977, 76 p.
    A beginner's text designed to teach snare drum techniques and bar percussion instruments simultaneously, applying a treble staff and a single line (for the snare drum) together.

424. FINK, Siegfried **I like Percussion.** Frankfurt, Zimmerman, 1974, 64 p. (Subtitle: 'Percussion Course for Self Instruction, with the Assistance of Bernd Kremling')
    An instruction book which tries to teach a little bit in all the basic areas of percussion: snare drum technique (but rudiments are not listed), and other instruments like bass drum, cymbals, Latin American instruments, the drum set, timpani, special effects, bar percussion, and multi percussion. Each subject is only dealt with very briefly as the book consists of only 64 small pages (18 by 18 cm), including many photographs. The accompanying record contains 19 short examples of the above areas of percussion.

425. FINK, Siegfried **Studies for "I like Percussion."** Frankfurt, Zimmermann, c.1975.
    This is a complementary book of 143 studies for the instruction book 'I Like Percussion' by the same author (see listing above).

426. FIRTH, Vic **Percussion Symposium.** New York, Carl Fischer, 1966, 46 p. (Subtitle: 'A Manual defining and illustrating the Complete Percussion Section')
    Gives a basic, illustrated overview of a reasonable selection of instruments and their playing techniques.

427. GALM, John 'Drumset and Timpani - What do they have in common?' **N.A.C.W.P.I. Journal** 23/3: 39-42, 1975.
    (For annotation see same entry in Chapter 5/a.)

428. LEVINE, Dave 'Drum Tension and Muffling Techniques.' **The Instrumentalist** 32: 56-9, June 1978.

429. LEVINE, Dave 'Drum Head Selection.' **The Instrumentalist** 33: 56-8, May 1979.
(For annotation see same entry in Chapter 2.)

430. McKINNEY, James 'Substitute Percussion Instruments.' **The Instrumentalist** 34/12: 41-2, 1980.
Suggests some down to earth substitutes for a number of basic percussion instruments.

431. MOORE, Stephen S. **Percussion Playing.** London, Paxton & Co., 1959, 89 p.

432. PARTCH, Harry 'Barbs and Bradsides' (An edited transcription of a series of lectures given by Harry Partch between 1950 and 1970; transcribed by Danlee Mitchell) **Percussionist** 18/3: 7-15, 1980.
The paper is divided into these three parts: (1) Ritual and Corporeality, (2) Building Instruments, and (3) Intonation.

433. PETERS, Gordon 'Un-contestable Advice for Timpani and Marimba Players.' **The Instrumentalist** 33: 67-70, Dec. 1978.
Some seemingly elementary, but actually helpful advice and hints to overcome technique and performance problems. Timpani: proper foot placement, stick choice (e.g. should have round head) and grip, rolls and strokes, articulation, tuning, expression, etc. Marimba: foot placement, grip, tempo, editions (of music), cause of wrong notes, and more.

434. PTASZYNSKA, M. 'Tonal Control of Indefinite Pitch Percussion Instruments.' **Percussionist** 18/1: 4-7, 1980.
(For annotation see same entry in Chapter 4.)

435. RICHARDS, Emil **Emil Richards' World of Percussion.** Sherman Oaks, CA, Gwyn Publishing Co., 1972, 94 p.
(For annotation see same entry in Chapter 1/a.)

436. UDOW, Michael 'An Interview with Karlheinz Stockhausen.' **Percussive Notes** 23/6: 4-47, 1985.
This interview took place in Ann Arbor on March 8, 1984, where Stockhausen was in residence at the time. The discussion centres around the specific percussion instruments which the composer requires for some of his works. The main works discussed in detail were: "Lucifer's Dance", "Gruppen for three Orchestras", "Zyklus", "Kontakte", "Musik im Bauch", "Katinka's Chant for Lucifer's Requiem", "Inori", and others. Requirements for specific and unusual instruments are described, their performance techniques, timbral characteristics, and compositional background of some pieces. It includes 26 pages of "preface pages" (from scores), indicating and illustrating his specific interest and concern for the quality of the, often extensive, percussion sounds in his music.

437. WILDMAN, Louis **Practical Understanding of the Percussion Section.** Boston, Humphries, 1964, 86 p.

CHAPTER 5.

INSTRUCTION AND PERFORMANCE - ORCHESTRAL INSTRUMENTS:

(g) Multi-Instrumental Techniques.

438. BAKER, Donald R. 'Multiple Percussion Techniques.' (2 parts) **The Instrumentalist** 31: 75-9, April; 31: 74-8, May 1977.
This article is written in connection with an earlier one by J.R. McKinney ('The Instrumentalist' Jan. 1977, "Play a Multiple Percussion Solo"). It deals mainly with the approach, preparation and technical set-up problems of instruments for the music to be played. It also gives advice on grip, mallet technique, rehearsal suggestions and final performance.

439. BALDWIN, James 'Multipercussion in Chamber and Solo Music.' **Percussionist** 5/3: 286-9, 1968.

440. BROWN, Steven 'A Study in Multi-Percussion Setup Design.' **Percussive Notes** 21/2: 35-7, 1983.
Discussion of physical problems with multi-percussion.

441. BURNS, Roy & FELDSTEIN, Saul **Adler's Percussion Solo Series.** New York, Henry Adler, 1966,.
Bk.1 Elementary Solos (12 p)
Bk.2 Intermediate Solos (15 p)
Bk.3 Advanced Solos (16 p)
This is a good series of books, presenting altogether 19 solos of good variety. The individual line system of notation is used here, which is easy to read, timbres of instruments are explored and more odd time signatures are used than in other similar books.

442. BURNS, Roy & FELDSTEIN, Saul **Drum Set Music.** New York, Alfred Publ. Co., 1971, 48 p.
As the subtitle says: 'A progressive collection of solos that explore the tonalities and musical properties of the drum set.' Each of the 12 solos in 3/4, 4/4, and 5/4 is discussed in detail and has preparatory exercises to point out the musical characteristics and problems.

443. CHEADLE, R.D. **A Bibliography of Multimedia Solo Percussion Works with an Analysis of Performance Problems.** D.A. Thesis, Univ. of Northern Colorado, 1983, 185 p. (Diss. Abst. 44: 2919A+, Apr. 1984)
The content is divided into five groups, which are: (1) tape, (2) dance, (3) graphics, (4) narration, and (5) any combination of media. The entries give all the relevant details, as well as a summary of performance problems. The author explains that the problems were based on the score, and include his comments on the set-up, balance, grip, stroke-types, notation and media synthesis.

444. COFFIN, James **The Performing Percussionist. (Vol. 1 & 2)** Oskaloosa, IA, C.L. Barnhouse Co. 1974(?).

Vol.1 is a beginner's method of basically snare drum technique, but utilizes multiple percussion solos for technical and musical supplimentation. Vol.2 has extented multiple solos and a section on musicianship.

445. COFFIN, James **Solo Album.** Oskaloosa, IA, C.L.Barnhouse Co., 1982.

Contains 16 solos, 5 easy, 6 medium and 5 advanced ones; including set-up diagrams, from solo drum to multiple percussion.

446. DELP, Ron **Multipitched Rhythm Studies for Drums.** Boston, Berklee Press, 1973.

(For a book review see 'Brass and Percussion' 2/1: 19, 1974.)

447. FELDSTEIN, Saul 'Multiple Percussion Playing.' **The Instrumentalist** 23: 68-71, Oct. 1968.

This is aimed at the beginner percussionist. Technical and musical considerations are pointed out in multiple percussion playing, and several examples in two and three parts are demonstrated.

448. FELDSTEIN, Saul **Multiple Percussion Music.** New York, Alfred Publ. Co., 1970, 32 p.

The subtitle describes the book quite well: 'A progressive collection of solos that explores the tonalities and musical properties of various percussion instruments'. There are 18 solos in a variety of meters and styles, ranging from two to five instruments, useful for beginner to intermediate player.

449. FITZ, Richard 'Notes from a Percussionist.' **Music Journal** 33/10: 12-3, 1975.

A brief essay on the necessity for today's percussionist to have multiple skills, demonstrated by three examples: C. Wuorinen's "Speculum Speculi", D. Martino's "Notturno", and L. Berio's "Circles."

450. FRASER, Julia **The Multiple Percussionist.** Oskaloosa, IA, C.L. Barnhouse Co., 1983.

This contains fifteen solos for percussionist, including set-up recommendations, instrument glossary and helpful hints on mallets and other preparations.

451. GEORGE, Ron 'Research into New Areas of Multiple Percussion Performance and Composition.' **Percussionist** 12/3: 110-31, 1975.

(For annotation see same entry in Chapter 4.)

452. GOLDENBERG, Morris **Studies in Solo Percussion.** New York, Chappell & Co., 1968, 72 p.

This is one of the best, constructive and progressive collections of pieces I have seen, which teaches the student the ability of solo-multi-percussion playing. It shows the lay-out of instruments and uses simple traditional staff notation. There are seven pieces for two drums, three for three drums, and 16 good pieces for four to thirteen instruments, which, apart from the author's compositions, include other composers like W. Kraft and R. Rodney-Bennett.

453. LAMBERT, James **Multiple Percussion Performance Problems as Illustrated in Five Different Works Composed by Stockhausen, Smith-Brindle, Colgrass, Dahl and Kraft between 1959 and 1967.** D.M.A. Thesis, The Univ. of Oklahoma, 1983, 107 p. (Diss. Abst. 44: 2921A-2A, Apr. 1984)

     The author classifies three categories of performance problems related to multi-percussion: (1) notation, (2) placement of instruments, and (3) movement. The five different works were chosen to illustrate different combinations of these possibilities: number of players, make-up of instrumentation, and these formats of compositions: (1) multiple percussion solo, (2) concerto style (with percussion ensemble accompaniment), (3) percussion ensemble, and (4) multiple percussion with another instrument. These works were analyzed and used to illustrate the above factors: "Zyklus" (K. Stockhausen), "Orion M.42" (Smith-Brindle), "Fantasy Variations" (M. Colgrass), "Duettino Concertante" (I. Dahl), and "Suite for Percussion" (W. Kraft).

454. LEVINE, Dave 'The Auxiliary Percussionist: what to play and where to play it.' **Percussive Notes** 16/3: 44-5, 1978.

     Some advice on various possibilities of using auxiliary instruments in the area of swing, rock, Latin, and similar music.

455. MATTINGLY, Rick 'Complete Percussionist - Donald Knaack.' (On the performance of M. Duchamp's "The Bride stripped bare by her Bachelors, even") **Modern Drummer** 5/8: 66-7, 1981.

456. McKINNEY, James 'Play a Multiple Percussion Solo.' **The Instrumentalist** 31/1: 54-7, 1977.

     The author gives ten points of advice to the percussionist approaching a multiple solo for the first time, plus a selected list of pieces.

457. MEYER, Ramon E. 'Percussion Ensemble Floor Plans.' **The Instrumentalist** 21: 63-5, Jan. 1967.

458. MEYER, Ramon E. 'Stage Arrangement for the Percussion Ensemble.' **Percussionist** 14/1: 22-5, 1976.

459. NEUHAUS, M. 'Zyklus.' **Percussionist** 3/1: 6-12, 1965.

     Neuhaus points out the necessity of finding the optimum position for each of the instruments used in order to create ONE instrument upon which the performer can then improvise. Describes some details of how the author solved set-up and mounting problems of instruments.

460. SAINDON, Ed 'Multi-Keyboard Playing.' **Percussive Notes** 17/3: 54-5, 1979.

     Useful tips on how to play vibes, marimba and xylophone as one physical unit.

461. SENN, Dan 'Standard Performance Practice, Soundsculpture and Scrapercussion.' **Percussive Notes** 21/6: 23-45, 1983.

     The author (and composer) describes some of the methods he has used to discourage the use of "standard performance practice" in the performance of his compositions, that is, in the context of his Scrap Percussion and Sound-sculpture Music. His Scrapercussion installations (or sculptures) are made from old pieces of industrial or domestic origin, and the sounds are obtained from these in the performance.

462. WHEELER, Douglas 'The Problem of Balance for the Multiple Percussionist.' **Woodwind World, Brass and Percussion** 20/1: 11, 1981. [A very basic - and not very helpful - discussion on these problems.]

# CHAPTER 5.

## INSTRUCTION AND PERFORMANCE - ORCHESTRAL INSTRUMENTS:

### (h) Marching Band Percussion.

463. BENSON, Allen **Basic Principles of the Scottish Style.** New York, Benson Publications, 1978, 17 p.
This contains exercises and examples of the Scottish style of snare drumming, notation vs. actual execution of performance, Scottish 7/8 beatings, as well as four solos and one duet by the author.

464. BENSON, Allen **Details of the Swiss Style of Drumming.** New York, Benson Publications, 1980, 25 p.
Contains all the typical elements and rudiments of this type of drumming, like the Swiss Army Triplet, Swiss rolls, the Ratafla, Mill-stroke, Patafla and others. Also includes an English-German glossary of terms.

465. BENSON, Allen 'An Introduction to the Swiss Rudiments and their Notation.' **Percussionist** 17/3: 140-48, 1980.
This article relates especially to the marching band. It explains several rudiments with their Swiss notation and their corresponding American and French notation, as well as the so-called Wintzer (graphic) Code. Included is a selected bibliography on this subject.

466. BRIDWELL, B.D. 'Marching Percussion Rehearsal Techniques.' **The Instrumentalist** 39: 71-4, Aug., 1984.
Discusses the various components making up a rehearsal and their individual importance and techniques. Includes pointers regarding warm-ups, timing exercises (and patterns), selection of target, learning new music, and some recommended method books.

467. BUCK, Robert **Precision Marching Percussion Ensemble Method.** Sherman Oaks, CA, Alfred Publ. Co., 1979(?) 32 p & 62 p. (Student and Teacher edition)
These two books should be used together; the teacher's copy includes equipment, technical development and arranging, and the student's book pertains to individual training of snare drum, timp-toms, bass drum, timpani, cymbals and keyboard percussion.

468. CAHIL, Michael **Developing Corps Style Percussion.** Milwaukee, Hal Leonard Publishing Co.
22 basic ensemble exercises, based on the rudiments, with training hints.

469. COMBS, F. Michael 'University Marching Band Drum Cadences.' (2 parts) **The Instrumentalist** 28: 69-71, Nov.; 28: 65-9, Dec. 1973.

470. DE LUCIA, D.F. 'The Corps-influenced Marching Percussion Section.' **The Instrumentalist** 31: 29-31, June 1977.

471. DE LUCIA, D.F. 'Ensemble Warm-up Exercises.' [2 parts] **Modern Percussionist** 1/3: 48-53,; 1/4: 48-9, 1985.

472. DE LUCIA, D.F. **Building a Championship Drumline.** Milwaukee, Hal Leonard Publ. Co.

473. DONNELLY, Jeff 'Swiss Rudiments.' [10 examples] **Percussive Notes** 16/2: 52-3, 1978.

474. DURRETT, Ward 'Percussion Staging Made Basic.' **Percussive Notes** 20/3: 46-8, 1982.

475. FELDSTEIN, Sandy **Alfred's New Band Method. (2 vols.)** Port Washington, NY, Alfred Publishing Co., 32 p @ vol.
(Not available for annotaion; see book review in 'Percussive Notes' 15/3: 29, 1977.)

476. GALM, John 'A Study of Rudiments used in Foreign Military Drumming Styles.' **Percussionist** 2/1-2: 10-27, 1965.
Lists, describes and compares briefly the American system with the following ones: German, Dutch, Swiss, Scotch and French; includes bibliography and four detailed comparison charts of rudiments.

477. HONG, Sherman & HAMILTON, Jim **Percussion Section: Developing the Corps Style.** Hattiesburg, MS, Eagle Press, 80 p.
This book has a lot of basic information and helpful ideas for organizing and improving the performance of the percussion section, as well as technical exercises and illustrations.

478. HOUSTON, Robert 'Multiple Percussion on the March.' **The Instrumentalist** 32: 32-5, May 1978.

479. LE CROY, H.F. **Percussion Techniques in Original Music for Bands.** Ph.D. Thesis, Univ. of Southern Mississippi, 1978, 195 p. (Diss. Abst. 39: 5201A, March 1979)
Quote from 'Dissertation Abstracts': "Purpose of study: (1) to examine percussion techniques and musical requirements in selecting original music for bands, (2) to examine selected method books as to their effectiveness presenting those techniques, (3) to develop appropriate instructional materials as dictated by the findings of the research."

480. MAZUR, Ken 'Advanced Rudimental Training Technique.' **Percussive Notes** 18/3: 45-9, 1980.
A quote from the article: "The purpose of this article is to inform the percussionist as to techniques now used to train performers in the advanced stages of rudimental drumming."

481. MAZUR, Ken **The Technique & Mechanics of Competitive Rudimental Snare Drumming.** St. Clair Shore, MI, The Author, 350 p.
This is a most comprehensive collection of (advanced) exercises, covering all rudimental variations, including Swiss and Chinese, variations on buzz rudiments, visual specialities, and individual competition training techniques, with several solos.

482. McCORMICK, L.W. 'Improving your Marching Band Drum Section.' **The Instrumentalist** 21: 77-8+, Sep. 1966.

483. POLLART, Gene 'Selecting Drum Heads for your Band.' **Woodwind World, Brass and Percussion** 20/2: 14-5, 1981.

484. RAPP, Will **Marching Percussion Method - an Ensemble Approach.** New Berlin, WI, Jenson Publications. (Includes score and 5 books, limited edition)
   (Not available for annotation. For book review see 'Percussive Notes' 19/1: 59, 1980.)

485. RAPP, Will 'The Evolution of the Multi-Toms.' **Percussionist** 17/3: 132-9, 1980.

486. SANFORD, F. 'Today's Field Percussion.' **The Instrumentalist** 29: 50-3, June 1975.

487. SNIDER, Larry B. 'Marching Tonal Percussion.' **The Instrumentalist** 28: 59-62, Sep. 1973.

488. SNIDER, Larry B. **Developing the Corps Style Percussion Section.** Oskaloosa, IA, C.L. Barnhouse Co., 1980, 32 p.
   Contains 20 exercises for this instrumental group, designed to help develop various techniques. Also included are illustrations, tuning instructions and general recommendations.

489. SPALDING, Dan 'The Evolution of Drum Corps Drumming.' **Percussionist** 17/3: 116-31, 1980.
   The subtitle of this lengthy article reads: 'A brief history of rudimental drumming in America from the music of the Continental Army to the modern junior drum and bugle corps.' Includes large bibliography.

490. VICKERS, S. 'Drum Corps.' **The Instrumentalist** 31: 26-8, June 1977.

491. VOGEL, L. 'Marching Mallet Percussion.' **The Instrumentalist** 35: 48-51, May 1981.
   Basic description of typical construction, weight, and range of the main instruments (i.e. bells, xylophone, marimba, and vibes of the Deagan and Musser ranges), and very basic advice on scoring and playing techniques.

492. WANAMAKER, Jay **Corpse Style Snare Drum Dictionary.** Sherman Oaks, CA, Alfred Publ. Co.
   Not available for annotation. The book review in 'Percussive Notes' (21/5: 72, 1983) describes it as having detailed listings of the various rudiments used in corps style percussion, but also gives some practice patterns with short solos, as well as special effects. It comes in a convenient pocket-size (eleven by four and a half inches).

493. WANAMAKER, Jay (and others) **Championship Auxiliary Units.** Sherman Oaks, CA, Alfred Publ. Co., 256 p.
   The book contains a 76-page section entitled "Contemporary Marching Percussion Ensemble", which has good references to care and tuning of percussion equipment, organization, basic grips and strokes, and also possible visual effects in the drumline.

494. WANAMAKER, Jay **Contemporary Corps Style Cadences.**
**Corps Style Warmups.** Sherman Oaks, CA, Alfred Publ. Co., 1982.
    Each of the two books is scored for xylophone, bells, snare drums, multiple toms, four bass drums, four cymbals, and some other percussion instruments.

495. WANAMAKER, Jay 'Technique Tips for Marching Mallets.' **The School Musician** 58: 8+, Nov., 1983.

496. WHITE, Andy 'Scottish Pipe Band Rudiments.' **Modern Drummer** 6/3: 92-3, 1982.

# CHAPTER 6.

## INSTRUCTION AND PERFORMANCE - POPULAR AND ROCK MUSIC:

497. APPICE, Carmine **Realistic Double Feet.** New York, Alfred Publ. Co., 1976(?) 40 p.
    The book has 12 sections, each being a series of one bar patterns followed by a solo exercise.

498. APPICE, Carmine **Realistic Rock.** New York, Robbins Music, 1979, 65 p. (first ed. 1972)
    Good, progressive tutor for teaching rock rhythms from beginner to the more advanced. Good, clear notation and presentation, combined with logical design of advancing exercises, together with many effective rhythms, made this a very popular and useful book.

499. BALDWIN, James 'The Drumset.' **Percussionist** 6/2: 64-8, 1968.

500. BECK, J.H. **A practical Approach to the Drum Set.** New York, MCA Music, 1967, 48 p.

501. BELLSON, Louis **The Musical Drummer.** New York, David Gornston, 1950.
    The subtitle reads: 'A basic method for concert, band, orchestra, and dance drumming.'

502. BELLSON, Louis **Jazz Rock Beats.** Hollywood, Try Publishing Co., 1970, 13 p.
    Although the book contains 118 rhythmic patterns, many are very repetitive and too similar, and there are no helpful comments or advice at all.

503. BELLSON, Louis 'How to develop a Choir of Drum Sounds.' **Downbeat** 45: 56-7, Nov. 2 1978.
    Basic advice on tuning a drum set and some rhythmic patterns (as recorded by the author).

504. BELLSON, Louie **The All New Louie Bellson Drummers Guide.** New York, Camerica Publications, 1979, 52 p.
    The first part consists of several rock, new contemporary Latin, funk, and fusion rhythms, some exercises, all put together in no obvious order (and no index). The second part contains drum charts taken from his recording "Louie Bellson and his Big Band - 150 MPH."

505. BENN, Billy **Drummer's "Clubdate" Handbook.** New York, Award Music, 1974, 35 p.
    This book lists 56 basic short rhythms to various dances, with a further 49 variations, all listed in alphabetical order. The author wishes to avoid "unmusical" faking of rhythms, but many seem to be just that. Rhythms include ethnic orientated beats (like Greek, Jewish, Irish, Italian, etc.)

and such great dances as the "Society Beat", the "Hokey-Poke", the "Alley Cat Rhythm" and the "Peabody."

506. BENNETT, Dick **Method for the Drum Set.** Palisades Park, NJ, Beacon Music, 1969,.

507. BREITHAUPT, Robert 'Drumset Application of Ted Reed's "Syncopation".' **Modern Drummer** 5/6: 76-7, 1981.
Several ideas for applying one of the most popular drum set-teaching books still in use (first published in 1958), in the areas of swing, Latin and rock.

508. BURNS, Roy & FARRIS, Joey **Studio Funk Drumming.** Fullerton, CA, Rhythmic Publications, 1981(?).
Presents many usable rhythms in this genre, in groupings of commercial funk, New Orleans rhythms and funk style, Reggae, fusion funk, and funk rhythms in unusual time signatures. Also explains the click track, the funk snare drum, and tuning the drum set for this style of music in live and recording situations.

509. BURNS, Roy & MALIN, Lewis **Practical Method for Developing Finger Control.** New York, Belwin Inc., 1966, 49 p. (Original ed. Henry Adler, 1958)
A very specialized book to develop "Finger Control" in playing with snare drum sticks. After the basic playing with wrist-controlled strokes ("no bounce"), the exercises proceed to "Bounce studies", Finger Bounce, Accent Studies, Solo Studies, and also some musical studies employing the drum set.

510. CENTAZZO, Andrea **La Batteria: Stili, Protagonisti e Tecniche.** Padora, Italy, Franco Muzzio & Co., 1981.
This informative and unique book commences with a good outline of the origin and development of the drum, in particular with the contemporary drumset. In the second part we find references to great jazz and rock personalities, including biographies, examples of styles and techniques, well illustrated and with examples of charts and music. Part three consists of technique and study material, including tuning and maintenance advice, and setups for various styles. Also included are an annotated bibliography of teaching methods, discography and an Italian-English dictionary.

511. CHAFFEE, Gary **The Independent Drummer.** New York, Alfred Publ. Co., 1976, 64 p. (Subtitle: 'Elementary to Intermediate Independence')
The approach is systematic and well thought out with the aim to develop the independence of the player, and hopefully increase musical awareness.

512. CHAFFEE, Gary **Patterns - Vol.III** Hyde Park, MA, G.C. Music, 1980, 53 p. (Subtitle: 'Time Functioning-Patterns')
This aims to develop better independence and coordination in relation to jazz and rock playing. It has some interesting and original material on independence, "linear phrasing", and hi-hat and bass drum exercises.

513. CLAYTON, R.B. 'Polyrhythmic Patterns for the Snare Drummer.' **Percussionist** 9/4: 94-7, 1972.

514. COMPTON, Rick 'Developing Rock Independence.' **Woodwind World, Brass and Percussion** 19/6: 8-10, 1980.
     Suggests a series of progressive exercises to improve independence, which are especially aimed at the percussionist/drummer inexperienced in rock music, and points out features of rock styles.

515. COMPTON, Rick 'Playing Creative Drums to Disco.' **Woodwind World, Brass and Percussion** 20/2: 21-3, 1981.
     Is in the same vain as the previous article, but concentrates on the idiomatic style and rhythms of Disco drumming.

516. CONNELL, J. **The Different Drum Book.** 92 Hollis Ave., Toronto, The Author, 1977.
     Advanced text for the jazz/rock drummer wanting to expand his knowledge and freedom for fills and solos, and within even and odd meters.

517. CORNIOLA, Frank **Rhythm Section Drumming.** Melbourne, The Author, 1985, 138 p.
     This is an interesting and original book, insofar as it compares and relates the drum patterns with and to the bass player's line. As the subtitle suggests: 'A handbook for musical togetherness between drums and bass'. The first five chapters present a good selection of contemporary rhythms in rock, funk, Latin rock, and odd times, as well as corresponding bass lines. In Chapter VI these are put to musical use in ten full-scale arrangements for both instruments. The bass lines have been written by Rob Little, Pasquale Monear, Steve Morgan, and Alex Pertout.

518. DARACA, J. **Conga Drumming - Disco, Soul, Raggae, Rock.** Ontario, CA, Congeros, 1980. (Also avail. with cassette)
     A good thorough beginner's text. The first part teaches the basic technique, background and tuning. In the second part various rhythms, strokes, exercises for development, and charts are presented. Also includes a good discography, and a recorded cassette of the text's examples is also available.

519. DAWSON, Allan & DE MICHAEL, Don **A Manual for the Modern Drummer.** Boston, Berklee Press, 1962, 116 p. (Subtitle: 'Analysis of Stylistic and Technical Problems')
     This comprehensive instruction book is aimed at the intermediate student and is divided into three sections:
     (1) 'The Fundamentals', that is the individual parts (cymbal, left hand, etc.) and how to put it all together.
     (2) 'Dance Band Drumming'; covers basic dance rhythms.
     (3) 'Jazz'; deals with various aspects of jazz, like double time, odd time, independence, drum solos, and more, including a short description of the styles of thirteen famous jazz drummers (with musical examples).

520. DI CENSO, D. **A Practical Workbook for the Modern Drummer.** Randolph, MA, The Author, 1977.
     A fairly comprehensive book in the area of possible combinations and correlations of rudiments and their application to the drum set, playing rock, jazz and Latin.

521. DOBOE, Chet **The Rock Drumming Workbook.** Hempstead, NY, The Author, 1978, 20 p.
Although a slim book, containing just 48 different rhythms, it offers many possibilities due to various suggested routines and their musical nuances.

522. DOBOE, Chet **The Funk Drumming Workbook.** Hempstead, NY, The Author, 1978, 60 p.
Tries to develop personal ideas within the student, as well as present a great number of new rhythmic ideas for this style. Section I describes the concept (open hi-hat sounds), Section II is the "Idea Section" (4-bar patterns), and Section III shows the application in song form.

523. DOBOE, Chet **The Funk Drumming Idea Series - Bk.1.** Hempstead, NY, The Author, 1978, 20 p.
Presents a large number of new rhythmic ideas and patterns (to the book listed above).

524. DOBOE, Chet **Funk Sambas.** Uniondale, NY, The Author, 1983.
(Not available for annotation)

525. DOBOE, Chet **The Hand Feet Book.** Uniondale, NY, The Author, 1983.
Aims to increase co-ordination, all in one-bar exercises in 4/4.

526. ELIAS, S. 'For Recording Session and Show Drummers only (how to mark Charts).' **Percussive Notes** 14/3: 23-4, 1976.

527. ELLIS, Stanley 'Accents on the Hi-Hat.' **Modern Drummer** 7/7: 94-5, 1983.
Examples of how bass figures and drum phrasing can work together.

528. ENGLE, Jim **All Kinds of Rock.** Hollywood, Try Publishing Co., 1979, 53 p.
Consists of 53 cymbal patterns, 53 snare drum patterns, and 53 bass drum patterns, which can be interfaced in various ways.

529. ENGLE, Jim **The Spirit of Independence.** Hollywood, Good Time Publishing Co., 1979, 24 p.
Not available for annotation. Eddie Davidson says in his review ('Percussive Notes' 16/3: 57, 1980) ".....this book is a good introduction to rock and jazz independence - beginning to intermediate level").

530. ENGLE, Jim **Big Time: A Study in Big Band Drumming and Drum Beats of the World.** Hollywood, CA, Good Time Publ. Co., 40 p.
The three sections of this book range from intermediate level to advanced. The first part deals with short chart examples (one or two bars) and how to interpret them. The second part applies these ideas to larger and complete charts, including fills and solos, in various styles of rock, jazz and Latin. The last section is a reference of various dance beats, as well as patterns from Africa, Greece, Poland, Austria, Scotland and other countries.

531. FAMULARO, D. & RICCI, J. **Drum Set Duets.** N. Merrick, NY, Drum Center, 1983, 43 p. (Optional audio cassette available)
Good practice material for two intermediate to advanced students (or teacher and student) to practise contemporary popular rhythms. The cassette can be used for a single student to play the opposite part to the tape.

532. FINK, Ron **Drum Set Reading.** New York, Alfred Publ. Co., 1974.
    [Intermediate Reading Method]

533. FISH, Scott K. 'The Pros: On Bass Drums.' **Modern Drummer** 7/4: 18-21,
    86-9, 1983.
        An interesting article on a subject which seems to have many angles to
    it. Twelve well-known drummers present their experience and give
    advice on tuning, size, heads, pedals and playing technique.

534. FISH, Scott K. 'The History of Rock Drumming.' (5 parts) **Modern
    Drummer** from 6/4 to 6/8 1982.
        An extensive article on the development and changes in style and
    who's who in rock drummers since 1950. The titles of the five parts are:
    (1)  'The Blues Influence'; 6/4:18-21, 84-91, 1982.
    (2)  'The Country influence'; 6/5: 16-9, 62-5, 1982.
    (3)  'The Sixties'; 6/6: 18-21, 88-93, 1983.
    (4)  'The Sixties' (Pt.2); 6/7: 20-3, 96-100, 1982.
    (5)  'The Final Chapter'; 6/8: 16-9, 70-5, 1982.

535. FORTE, Nick 'Understanding Rhythm.' (10 parts) **Modern Drummer** 6/2,
    1982 to 7/2, 1983.
    'Quarter Notes' 6/2: 54-6, 1982.
    'Eigth Notes' 6/3: 46-8, 1982.
    'Sixteenth Notes' 6/4: 38-42, 1982.
    'Double Stroke Rolls' 6/5: 58-60, 1982.
    'Whole Notes and Half Notes' 6/6: 36-8, 1982.
    'Dotted Notes' 6/7: 44-7, 1982.
    'The Eigth-Note Triplet' 6/8: 32-4, 1982.
    'The Sixteenth-Note Triplet' 6/9: 34-6, 1982.
    'The Quarter-Note Triplet' 7/1: 32-3, 1983.
    'Half-Note Triplet' 6/8: 28+30, 1983.
    Each part explains the rhythms in theory (including other aspects like
    dynamics and phrasing), then gives reading exercises for the snare drum,
    followed by drum set exercises and patterns, and concludes with an
    extensive drum solo.

536. FRANCO, Joe 'Double-Bass Concepts: Hand-Foot Combination Patterns.'
    **Modern Drummer** 8/10: 86-7, 1984.

537. FRANCO, Joe **Doublebass Drumming.** Farmingdale, NY, Music Ink, 1984.

538. GANDUGLIA, Jim **Comprehensive Drum Set.** Lebanon, IN, Studio 224,
    1978, 31 p.
        This book also covers some aspects not always found in other drum set
    books, like notational elements and counting (useful for studio work),
    discussion of various grips, position for the feet, and stress control of the
    four limbs.

539. GARIBALDI, David 'Developing Hand/Foot Coordination.' **Modern
    Drummer** 3/5: 36-7, 1979.

540. GARIBALDI, David 'Odd Rock.'(2 parts) **Modern Drummer** 4/2: 32; 4/3:
    32, 1980.

541. GARIBALDI, David 'A Practical Application of the 5 Stroke Roll.'
    **Modern Drummer** 4/4: 32-3, 1980.

Shows a number of applications of this roll to the drum set in popular music.

542. GARIBALDI, David 'Converting those Old Rhythms.' (2 parts) **Modern Drummer** 5/2: 32-3; 5/3: 36-7, 1981.
This article concerns itself with exploring and developing the "shuffle" rhythm in several new varieties, including the "shuffle-funk", combined with Afro-Cuban "Nanigo", and odd-time shuffle extensions.

543. GARIBALDI, David 'Concept for two Drum Sets.' **Modern Drummer** 5/4: 34-7, 1981.
Some ideas for suitable rhythms and how to spread these advantageously for two drummers (in the one band).

544. GARIBALDI, David 'A Practical Application of Swiss Army Triplets.' **Modern Drummer** 5/5: 36-7, 1981.

545. GARIBALDI, David 'Modular Rock.' **Modern Drummer** 5/6: 32-3, 1981.
Thirty short, but interesting and useful, rhythmic modules to combine and practise for developing technical and stylistic facilities.

546. GARIBALDI, David 'Future Sounds.' **Modern Drummer** 5/8: 80-1, 1981.
Several good ideas to increase musicality in the sound of rock rhythms by avoiding ever-repetitive sounding of certain instruments.

547. GROSSMAN, Norman **The Complete Book of Modern Drumming.** New York, Amsco Music, 1975.
(Not available for annotation; for book review see 'Jazz Forum' No.34: 66, Apr. 1975.)

548. GROSSMAN, Norman **Norman Grossman's Book of Drum Styles. Norman Grossman's Book of Drum Techniques.** New York, Amsco Music, c.1977, 127 p & 87 p.
These two books are intended to assist the music teacher and drummer with a number of problems of teaching and performance of percussion instruments and music. The book on drum styles covers many rock, jazz and Latin influences, as well as reading studies, notational and interpretative advice.

549. GUERIN, John **DRUMS Jazz+Rock=.** Sherman Oaks, Gwyn Publishing Co., 1971, 24 p.
This book introduced some progressive ideas at the time (1971), like "Jazz-Boogaloo", "Cross Time", "Afro Bossa Nova". Very advanced, but the manuscript is difficult to read.

550. HOULLIF, Murray **Today's Sounds for Drumset.** Delevan, NY, Kendor Music, 32 p.
The book gives basic patterns for three areas of set playing: rock, jazz (swing), and Latin American. Especially suited for the percussionist or musician wanting to add the drum set to his instrumental technique.

551. HOULLIF, Murray **The Fusion Drummer.** New York, Alfred Publ. Co., 16 p.
This is a quote from a book review in 'Percussive Notes' (19/3, 1981): "A short, but useful book, containing 52 jazz-rock fusion beats.....in the style of Steve Gadd, H. Mason, B. Cobham, and others.....".

552. HOULLIF, Murray **Contemporary Drum Set Solos.** New York, Kendor Music, 1981.
This is a collection of eight solos in various styles, from swing to funk, most of them demonstrating a sensitive and musical approach.

553. HUGHES, Harry U.K. **Rock Drumming.** London, The Premier Drum Co., 1970, 29 p.
This book includes examples by Ginger Baker, Clive Bunker, Ric Lee and Carl Palmer. It offers a few different original ideas and some good, useful odd-time rhythms.

554. HUMPHREY, Paul **No.1 Soul Drums.** Sherman Oaks, Gwyn Publishing Co., 1970, 23 p.
Behind the slightly silly title hide some very practical examples of different rock styles, usually not found in most books. For example, Country & Western, Nashville, Acid Rock, Gospel and 12/8 Blues. Also some information on studio work and facsimile of recorded drum parts.

555. HURLEY, Mark 'Improving your Drumming with Video.' **Modern Drummer** 9/7: 18-21, 74-9, 1985.
Good advice and examples of how to utilize the rather new aspect of video cassettes and/or your own video camera to improve your skills, including a list and description of available cassettes for drummers.

556. JEX, Anthony **Rhythm Techniques for the Rock Drummer.** Sydney, The Jay Projects, 1980, 81 p.
Features a large collection of rock rhythms, grouped in note-value sections, like eights, sixteens, and triplets - all in 4/4 meters.

557. JONES, Philly Joe **Brush Artistry.** London, The Premier Drum Co., 1968, 16 p.
One of the very few books I have seen which explains different rhythms (to be played with brushes on the snare drum) properly and successfully - with music, diagrams and photographs.

558. KEENAN, Mark 'Rock Perspectives - A Study in Styles.' **Modern Drummer** 1/3: 17, 1977.
Very brief examples each of the styles of C. Appice, H. Mason, S. Gadd, B. Columby and D. Garibaldi.

559. KERRIGAN, Chuck **The Art of Rock Drumming.** Johnston, PA, The Author, 52 p.

560. KERRIGAN, Chuck **Progressive Steps to Freedom on the Drum Set.** Pacific, MO, Mel Bay Publications.
The book's two subtitles 'Four Limb Musical Interpretation' and 'A Systematic, Musical Approach to Complete Four Limb Mastery', give a good indication of its purpose. Divided into three sections: eigth-note, eigth-note triplet, and sixteenth-note syncopations.

561. KINNEY, D. **Rock Socks.** Staten Island, NY, W.D. Kinne, 1977.

562. KIRK, Willis **Brushfire.** San Francisco, R & D Publications, c.1981.
An informative and instructive book for playing with brushes, useful from beginner's to advanced levels, and includes seven interesting solos.

563. LA FEMINA, Ralph **Melody and Harmony on the Drum Set.** Patchogue, NY, The Author, 99 p.

This contains many innovative ideas and concepts, including the objective of enabling the drummer to adapt any music to the drum set. It is divided into three sections:
(1) "Theory", which includes aspects of pitch, overtones, loudness, timbre, and compares the drum set to other instruments.
(2) "Melody", which deals with scales and melodic exercises on the drum set, including the range for the set and concept of phrasing.
(3) "Harmony", which talks about bass lines, harmony (two to five voices) and chords.

564. LAMBERT, Joe **Drum Improvising Studies for Jazz and Rock.** Pacific, MO, Mel Bay Publications, 1978.

The six sections of the book include eight- and twelve-bar exercises, jazz-rock fills, coordination etudes and extended improvisations.

565. LAMBERT, Joe 'Second Line Drumming.' **Percussive Notes** 19/2: 26-8, 1981.

"Second Line" drumming originated in the old New Orleans marching jazz bands. Here it is demonstrated how to apply it on the drum set in today's rock and funk music.

566. LATHAM, Rick **Advanced Funk Studies.** Dallas, TX, The Author, 1981. (Also avail. with two cassettes)

This text aims to give insight into today's funk and fusion music; with relevant exercises, transcriptions of rhythms by well-known drummers (e.g. Steve Gadd, James Mason, and others), and ten well written solos.

567. LATHAM, Rick 'Latin Rock Patterns.' **Modern Drummer** 6/3: 94-5, 1982.

Shows some of the style and patterns used by the drummer Steve Gadd.

568. LAUREN, Michael **Welcome to Odd Times.** New York, Why Not Music, 62 p.

In this book for advanced students, subtitled 'An Approach to Mental and Manual Dexterity in Odd Meters for the Drum Set', the meters utilized are 5/8, 5/4, 6/8, 7/8, 9/8, 11/8, 13/8 and 15/8. It gives warm-up exercises, various stickings, sub divisions of meters and numerous applications for funk and rock rhythms. It also includes a discography.

569. LEBLOND, G.F. **The Hip-Pocket Guide to Basic Drum Beats.** Portland, West-Gate Press, 1982.

Handy, basic reference guide to dance beats, Latin American (the Cha Cha and the Rhumba are missing), and many forms of rock beats.

570. LEVINE, Dave 'Guide to Drumset Tuning.' **Modern Drummer** 8/2: 22-5, 84-9, 1984.

An extensive survey, with findings and recommendations on the choice of heads and their corresponding sound characteristics. It explains how to tune the various drums to suit different heads; musical aims and situations (e.g. live vs. recording work); the pros and cons of muffling; "trouble-shooting" of the drum sound; and some information on the use of heads and systems of tuning of several top drummers.

571. LUCAS, Clyde **The Amazing Batom.** St. Albans, NY, The Author, 1981. (separate record available)
(For annotation see same entry in Chapter 5/e.)

572. MAGADINI, Peter 'Reading at the Drum Set.' **Percussionist** 8/2: 53-60, 1970.
Points out the different sorts of problems in reading at the drum set compared to snare drum repertoire and orchestral parts. Examples are given on the sometimes strict vs. the loose interpretation of concert and drum set music, depending on the style. Often a large amount of details and improvisations are left to the drummer to fill in, who must understand various styles of music to be able to do this satisfactorily.

573. MAGADINI, Peter **Learn to play the Drum Set - Vols.1. & 2.** Milwaukee, Hal Leonard Publ. Corp., 1980 & 1982.
Book 1 includes basic setting up, tuning, and musical notation, as well as a variety of contemporary rhythms in popular music.
Book 2 continues with reading exercises, various jazz styles on cymbal and hi-hat, funk drumming, fusion, Latin, solos and bass drum control.

574. MASON, David 'Percussion Colors.' (2 parts) **Modern Drummer** 8/4: 42-4,; 8/5: 50-2, 1984.
This interesting article deals with the following hand instruments: cowbell, tambourine and Afuche (in Part I), and shakers, maracas, claves and sleigh bells (in Part II). It suggests how to integrate and add these instruments to the drum set.

575. MAZUR, Ken 'Rudimental Set Drumming.' **Modern Drummer** 4/4: 74+76, 1980.
The author tries to show how to create good texture, coordination and consistency with the aid of rudiments.

576. McCAUSLAND, L.S. 'Show Drumming.' **Percussionist** 5/2: 244-53, 1967.
This insight-giving essay points out the many abilities and attributes a show drummer should possess. They include the knowledge of all styles of music and drumming; the ability to play all the percussion instruments; consideration for the best possible set-up and choice of sticks; the "art" of proper marking of the charts and mastering page turns; the ability to sight-read well, and simplify if necessary; to improvise sound effects in supportive work; and he should be a strong, deliberate player with good control of tempo, rhythms, and yet very flexible and alert.

577. MELIGARI, Bill **Doubledrum: A Double Bass Drum Text.** Wayne, NJ, Meligari Music Publications, 63 p.
An extensive workbook on this specialized subject, systematically and progressively working towards the interaction between double bass and the jazz and rock cymbal patterns.

578. MICHAELSON, J.M. 'The creative Show Percussionist.' **The Instrumentalist** 32: 91-2, Apr. 1978.
Points out the necessity for the percussionist to use logic and creative thinking in preparation for a performance. This includes the best possible physical set-up of instruments, selection of mallets best suited, editing parts, and tuning of instruments.

579. MICHAND, Ray **Applied Independence for the Drum Set.** Santa Clara, CA, The Author, 81 p.
This text is especially concerned with playing independent drum phrases against various ride cymbal patterns.

580. MOREY, C. **Times are Changing, Drum Study Book for the Contemporary Drummer.** New York, Kendor Music, 1969, 36 p.
Presentation of an array of basic drum patterns for a wide variety of styles and rhythms.

581. MORGAN, Graham 'Graham Morgan talks about Steve Gadd.' **Jamm** 34-6, Feb. 1978.
One of Australia's best drummers discusses here the style and current technique of Steve Gadd - one of America's most sought after studio drummers. The author also presents several of his transcriptions, taken from Steve Gadd's recordings.

582. MORGENSTEIN, Rod 'An Approach for Playing in Odd Time.' (3 parts) **Modern Drummer** 8/1: 78-9; 8/2: 78-80; 8/3: 48-9, 1984.
Part I deals with 7/8 exercises, which are expanded in Part II, and Part III discusses some 7/8 and 7/4 examples by well known drummers on record.

583. MORTON, James **Anthology of Rock Drumming** Pacific, MO, Mel Bay Publications.
Not available for annotation. Here is a quote from the publisher's advertising material: "Penetrating study into the popular and varied drum styles found from early to contemporary rock. A thoroughly researched and well written text."

584. MORTON, James **Killer - Fillers.** Pacific, MO, Mel Bay Publications. 1980. (Optional cassette avail.)
Not a very innovative book, but useful to the student wishing to practise and improve his ideas for 'drum-fills'. Several rhythms are shown to be used in different ways around the set, the last few pages being more inventive and inspiring.

585. MORTON, James **Fusion Drum Styles.** Pacific, MO, Mel Bay Publications, 1982.
A collection of contemporary drumming styles, including Reggae, funk, Latin, jazz-rock fusion and odd time. The book has an inspiring introduction, explaining the demand, the role, musicianship and coordination of today's drummer, as well as some patterns in the style of popular drummers like S. Gadd, T. Williams, B. Cobham, J. de Johnette, and others.

586. MOYLAN, David 'Towards Ambidexterity.' **Modern Drummer** 7/4: 44-8, 1983.
Several exercises and ideas towards developing ambidexterity, e.g. playing ride-cymbal lead with either hand, and other useful applications.

587. NORINE, William **Virtuoso Studies for the Drum Set.** Boston, Berklee Press, 1979, 124 p.
A book for the advanced drummer/percussionist. The first section contains preparatory studies in coordination, whilst the second part consists of 18 fugues in many different styles and rhythms, some being

very suitable as performance pieces. I feel that the more commonly used 5-line staff notation for the drum set would have been better than the sometimes unnecessarily contrived 2-line notation and symbols.

588. NORINE, William **Four-Way Fusion for the Modern Drummer.** Boston, Berklee Press, 1982.
The reading of the progressive studies in this book is very difficult due to the complex, if consistent, notation invented by the author. Relates to contemporary styles, including odd meters.

589. PAISTE DRUMMER SERVICE **Profiles of International Drummers, Percussionists, Musicians, presented by Paiste Cymbals Gongs.** Nottwill, Switzerland, Paiste Drummer Service, 1975,. (2nd ed.)
This collection gives a short biography of 256 drummers and percussionists (from various parts of the world), including the equipment and set-up they use and a discography.

590. PALMER-HUGHES, Willard **How to play Rock and Roll Drums.** New York, Alfred Publ. Co., 1965.

591. PAYNE, Jim **Funk Drumming.** Pacific, MO, Mel Bay Publications, 1983, 156 p. (separate cassette available)
A comprehensive, well presented book on this subject. It covers many aspects of the varying influences of Latin, blues and rock on the funk-drumming style, and gives many examples and variations. A useful cassette is also available, one part demonstrating eleven different styles, the other part is recorded without drums for the drummer to play along with.

592. PERKINS, Phil **The Logical Approach to Rock Coordination.** Cincinnati, Logical Publications, 1981.
This is Vol.III in a series of books, the first two dealing with snare drum only (see Perkins, 'The Logical Approach to Snare Drum', Chapter 6.), and brakes down coordination problems on the drum set into small blocks of exercises.

593. PERRY, Charlie 'Basic Brushes.' **Modern Drummer** 3/6: 16-7, 64+, 1979.
Short but informative article on some brush techniques.

594. PETACCIA, Roberto 'Rock & Jazz Clinic: Ambidexterity.' (2 parts) **Modern Drummer** 5/7: 72-3; 5/8: 38-40, 1981.
The author suggests considering the concept of physical balance (of the body) in order to fully understand ambidexterity. Part I focuses on "ambidexterity in the context of time keeping", and Part II analyzes it in the "context of soloing and sound exploration."

595. PETACCIA, Roberto 'Rock Big Band.' (2 parts) **Modern Drummer** 5/9: 42; 6/1: 72-3, 1982.
Some basic considerations and techniques suitable for this less common combination (i.e big band and rock drumming) are presented.

596. PICKERING, John **The Drummer's Cookbook.** Kirkwood, MO, Mel Bay Publications, 1972, 72 p.
This well presented book gives around 700 (!) varieties of rock rhythms for the more advanced player, also some solos, but only in 4/4 time. The book encourages and gives ideas for rhythmic improvisation and creativity.

597. PICKERING, John **Mel Bay's Stage and Band Drummer's Guide.** Kirkwood, MO, Mel Bay Publications, 1976, 96 p.
  The subtitle reads: 'A Guide to Reading Contemporary Drum Charts'. In this, the author has collected and explained many types of drum charts and chart notations, trying to prepare and train the drummer for any type of working situation (with regard to reading) which might arise.

598. PIEKARCZYK, James **The Drum Set Exerciser.** Northbrook, IL, Opus Music, 1978. (Subtitle: 'Intermediate to advanced Hand/Foot Coordination Exercises')
  Not available for annotation, but the review in 'Percussive Notes' (17/1: 36, 1978) reports that the book claims in the introduction that it should "develop arm endurance, foot coordination, cymbal control and total melodic endurance."

599. PITZEN, Tracy & KEYS, Michael **Introductory Drum Set Independence.** Peoria, IL, MDST., 1978, 53 p.

600. PORCARO, Joe **Odd Times - A new Approach to Latin, Jazz and Rock, Applied to Drum Set.** Hollywood, Try Publ. Co., 1970, 48 p.
  The book contains many cymbal patterns, reading exercises and drum patterns in many styles, all in a variety of odd meters.

601. PRESS, Arthur 'The Double-Stick Grip.' **Woodwind World, Brass and Percussion** 16/3: 46-7, 1977.
  A very brief demonstration of a quasi three-stick grip for the drum set, that is two sticks in the right and one in the left hand.

602. RAYNOR, Joe **Drumming Ideas in Focus.** San Antonio, Southern Music, 1978, 24 p.
  The book is written to help the drummer in developing stick control, coordination and speed.

603. REED, Ted **Progressive Steps to Syncopation for the Modern Drummer.** Clearwater, The Author, 1958, 60 p.
  This seems to be one of the most popular books for beginner students of the drum set still in regular use despite its age. It teaches the mastery of simple syncopation (to be played with hands only), whilst the feet keep the time (4/4). But it can be applied in other, more interesting, ways by the more advanced student.

604. ROBSON, Paul 'What Drum Head do I Choose?' **Canadian Musician** 1/2: 36-7, 1979.
  Should be a helpful article for drummers who are concerned about improving the tone of their drums. It defines the characteristics of the many different drum heads available.

605. ROBSON, Paul 'Tuning your Drum Set.' **Canadian Musician** 1/3: 53+, 1979.
  A basic set of instructions on how to tune the drum set, and also muffling possibilities for the bass drum.

606. ROGERS, Dennis **Solo Studies for the Drum Set.** San Antonio, TX, Southern Music. (3 vols.)
  These books present 26 solo studies all together, each one being based on one of the rudiments - at the intermediate to advanced level.

ROTHMAN, Joel: It should be pointed out to the reader that this prolific author has the unusually large number of about 100 (!) published method books on the market, most of them in the subject area of rock and jazz styles. As almost expected, many of these are rather shallow and repetitive, and only a small selection is listed here, some of the larger works being a selected compilation of different smaller texts.

607. ROTHMAN, Joel **The Rock and Roll Bible of Coordination.** Fort Lauderdale, FL, J.R. Publications, 1968, 80 p.
    The subtitle says it all: "For true believers. Here's where it was, where it's at and where it's going."

608. ROTHMAN, Joel **The Complete Rock Drummer.** Oneonta, NY, Swift-Dorr, 1973, 536 p.
    An unusually large text on this subject, containing an enormous number of studies, patterns and ideas, all ordered fairly logically into eight sections. From basic beats to special "feels" of slow-rock; on to 12/8 feels (section 3) and variations of the shuffle (section 4). Section 6 deals with many odd rhythms like 3/4, 5/4, 7/4, 5/8, 7/8, etc., and the following part gives insight into two-bass drum technique. The last chapter completes the book with an extensive treatment of "fills" and "breaks". The book covers from intermediate to very advanced levels, and the main intention of the author is "upon developing an overall coordinative facility", which in turn should enable the drummer to play whatever he would like to (theoretically anyway).

609. ROTHMAN, Joel **Basic Drumming.** Fort Lauderdale, FL, J.R. Publications, 160 p.
    This was recommended in 'Percussive Notes' (23/1: 76, 1984) as one of the best beginning books for drummers, covering all rudiments as well as basic popular music drumming.
    The six sections are: (1) basic rhythms, (2) rolls, (3) basic sticking patterns, (4) basic rock drumming (40 pages, covering many beats and meters), (5) basic jazz patterns (less complete than rock section), (6) various dance rhythms of all kinds.

610. ROTHMAN, Joel **Everything you always wanted to know about Drum Technique but were afraid to try.** New York, J.R. Publications, 1976, 160 p.
    This extensive book consists of ten sections which include rudimentary exercises, stick control, dynamics, roll control and odd groupings of rolls.

611. ROTHMAN, Joel **How to Play Drums.** Chicago, Albert Whitman & Co., 1977, 48 p.
    A rather unusual drum tutor aimed at the young child wanting to learn drums. The advice and instructions are mostly verbal (as in a story-book style), it covers the very basic approach to the drum set (with "cute" drawings), and advice on how to continue on.

612. RUKA, John **Disco Drums.** Milwaukee, Limited Publishing, 1976.
    This book features the technique of playing the left hand on the hi-hat and the right on snare drum and tom toms. Covers many styles and examples, including the Hustle, Bump, Salsa, Funk and Reggae.

613. RUMBLEY, J.E. 'Techniques and Equipment for the Studio Percussionist.' **Woodwind World, Brass and Percussion** 17/2: 28-9, 1978.

Basic advice regarding attitude, presentations, considerations about equipment, and recording techniques (for popular music).

614. RYAN, Lloyd **The Complete Drum Tutor.** London, Duckworth, 1981, 80 p.
Contains six chapters of often interesting and good material for study and moves from beginner to a fairly advanced stage at a fast tempo. Includes basic reading exercises, drum rudiments, typical rhythms of rock and jazz, studio drum parts, drum duets and trios, and some odd time signatures.

615. SAVAGE, J. **The Art of the Drummer.** King's Lynn, Norfolk, The Author, 1978.

616. SAVAGE, Steve **Drummer's Workbook.** New York, Consolidated Music Publishers.
(Not available for annotation; for book review see 'Modern Drummer' 6/2: 50, 1982.)

617. SCHINSTINE, W. & HOEY, F. **Drum Set Tunes.** Pacific, MO, Mel Bay Publications, 26 p.
This is a collection of 24 solos, moving progressively from very easy to difficult. However, apart from explaining symbols of music, there are no instructions or guidelines for the student.

618. SCIARRINO, J. & DE LOS REYES, W. **Salsa Rock.** Sherman Oaks, CA, Alfred Publ. Co., 1978, 24 p. (Subtitle: 'A Complete Guide for Blending the Drum Set with the Latin Rhythm Section')
Four different groups of rhythms are dealt with: Salsa Disco Rhythms, Nanigo Rhythms, Cuban Carnival Rhythms, and Odd Time Signatures (3/4, 5/4, 7/4). In each grouping there are several ensemble "Latin Patterns" given (between 2-5 players), which can be combined with any of the many corresponding drum set patterns listed. In conclusion there are also some Rhythm Section Patterns (piano, bass & guitar), to be used with previously given rhythms.

619. SCIBETTA, Charles **Chartbook for Today's Drummer.** New York, Post Publishing Co., 1980(?).
This book presents 17 different drum charts in several different styles, allowing the student to use his own imagination for interpretation and fills to practise with.

620. SHAUGHNESSY, Ed 'The Thinking Drummer.' [cymbal technique] **Downbeat** 36: 36+, 6.Feb. 1969.

621. SMITH, Allan **Drumming - Right On.** Melbourne, Eastern Suburbs School of Drumming, 1983, 52 p.
Covers a wide range of exercises and styles, from the basics of setting-up, tuning, to intermediate independence, but the "58 Lessons" are not in a logically ordered, progressive lay-out. Simple reading exercises are mixed up with disco beats, and rudiments mingle with Latin rhythms, which makes it difficult to use as an effective teaching aid.

622. SOFIA, Sal 'Linear Coordination.' [Jazz and rock] **Modern Drummer** 6/2: 64-8; 6/3: 66-9, 1982.
The author says that "linear coordination means harmoniously dividing a rhythm on different parts of the drum set, to be played by hands and

feet in a uniform straight pattern". He shows how basic patterns can be divided and combined in many ways for better independence and greater variety of sounds.

623. SOFIA, Sal 'Rudiments - Inspiration for Innovators.' (2 parts) **Modern Drummer** 6/5: 34-5; 6/6: 80-1, 1982.
Shows how to utilize rudiments on the drum set in an innovative way for contemporary styles; how to break them down and apply in a musical context.

624. SOFIA, Sal **Traps: A Rudimentary Approach.** Brooklyn, NY, The Author, 1982, 187 p.
Sofia tries to show in this book how to develop a personal, contemporary style, based on the application of the 26 American rudiments to the drum set. The text includes basic theory, reading exercises, chart reading, ear training, coordination, and other drum set techniques.

625. SOFIA, Sal 'Hi-Hat Techniques in different Styles.' **Modern Drummer** 7/1: 58+61, 1983.

626. SOFIA, Sal 'Sound Phrasing.' (2 parts) **Modern Drummer** 7/3: 64-6; 7/4: 90-2, 1983.
The article concerns itself with ways how to develop new sounds and ideas, at first in short simple cells, and then applying it to full bars.

627. SOFIA, Sal **The Omni of Drum Technique.** New York, Sal Sofia Publications, 344 p.
S.K. Fish comments on this book "...that it teaches you to think" ('Modern Drummer' 6/2: 50, 1982). This text is of advanced standard, covering development of drum fills, "independence through linear thinking", improvisation, coordination, cross-accenting, etc., but is rather costly.

628. SYRIAN, Joe 'Double Bass Drum Fills.' [Rock] **Modern Drummer** 6/7: 50-1, 1982.

629. TAYLOR, John 'Contemporary Rhythms.' [cymbal] **Crescendo International** 18: 36, June 1980.

630. THERHOFF, F. **Dictionary of Dance Rhythms.** London, Bosworth, c. 1965.

631. THIGPEN, Ed **Sound of Brushes.** Copenhagen, Ed Thigpen/Action Reaction. (Includes cassette)
As there is no standard and satisfactory notation for brush work, the author utilizes a great deal of photographs, together with his personal explanations. When the book is used in conjunction with the included recording, it must be one of the best available on the subject of brush techniques.

632. VIDER, Sam **The Best Drum Rhythms Ever Written.** Carlstadt, NJ, Lewis Music Publ. Co., 1983, 177 p.
The book is divided into three parts: Rock, Latin, and Miscellaneous Rhtyhms, with the rock section being very detailed (including odd-time signatures and funk), the Latin part covering most commonly known

rhythms, and the miscellaneous part having also odd-time rhythms, jazz waltz, marches, as well as Italian, Jewish, Rumanian, Moroccan and Bulgarian rhythms. The title will be hard to live up to, but the text is well printed, each page containing from six to twelve patterns, and there is a lot of information for the all-round drummer.

633. VOGEL, Ken **Melodic Solo Encounters.** Pacific, MO, Mel Bay Publications, 1981, 48 p. (Cassette optional)
Contains eighteen solos and a special discussion on particular sounds available from the drum set. Many musical styles and rhythmic ideas are present, with plenty of suggestions regarding the author's intentions and structure of the pieces.

634. WALKER, Steven **Analytic Drum Tuning.** Indianapolis, The Author, 39 p.
Good, basic information on tuning and muffling the drum set, considering all the variables which can influence the sound of the instruments.

635. WHISTLER, Harry **Rubank Advanced Method - Drums.** Chicago, Rubank, 1966,.

636. XEPOLEAS, J. & NUNES, W. **Studies for the Contemporary Drummer.** Miami Beach, Hansen House, 1983. (Includes record)
A good, basic and up to date beginner's book, providing material in the areas of rock, Latin and jazz rhythms and studies. It also allows and encourages the student to combine and improvise his own patterns, which is demontrated further on the recording accompanying the book.

637. ZAIL, Kenny **Commercial Rock Drumming.** Melville, NY, Belvin-Mills, 1982.
Not available for annotation, but this is how it is advertised in music journals: "Develop independence and coordination using stylistic rock beats of the commercial rock industry."

# CHAPTER 7.

## INSTRUCTION AND PERFORMANCE - JAZZ MUSIC:

### (a) Drum Set Technique.

638. BAILEY, Colin **Bass Drum Control.** Hollywood, Try Publishing Co., 1964, 32 p.
Progressive exercises for the right foot, not applied to any particular style, but generally to improve technique and independence.

639. BAILEY, Colin **Modern Jazz Solos.** Hollywood, Try Publishing Co., 1970, 28 p.
A graded, progressive selection of 'nice', musical and playable solos, ranging from 4-bar solos for snare drum to 32-bar solos for the complete drum set.

640. BELLSON, Louis **Jazz Rock Beats.** Hollywood, Try Publishing Co., 1970, 13 p.
(For annotation see same entry in Chapter 6.)

641. BELLSON, Louis 'How to develop a Choir of Drum Sounds.' **Downbeat** 45: 56-7, Nov. 2 1978.
Basic advice on tuning a drum set and some rhythmic patterns (as recorded by the author).

642. BELLSON, Louie **The All New Louie Bellson Drummers Guide.** New York, Camerica Publications, 1979, 52 p.
(For annotation see same entry in Chapter 6.)

643. BREITHAUPT, Robert 'Drumset Application of Ted Reed's "Syncopation".' **Modern Drummer** 5/6: 76-7, 1981.
Several ideas for applying one of the most popular drum set-teaching books still in use (first published in 1958), in the areas of swing, Latin and rock.

644. BURNS, Roy 'New Orleans Rhythms and Southern Funk.' **Downbeat** 51: 62-3, Oct., 1984.
Gives several musical examples of this style of drumming.

645. BURNS, Roy & FARRIS, Joey **Studio Funk Drumming.** Fullerton, CA, Rhythmic Publications, 1981(?).
(For annotation see same entry in Chapter 6.)

646. BURNS, Roy & FELDSTEIN, Saul **Drum Set Music.** N.Y., Alfred Music, 1971, 48 p.
(For annotation see same entry in Chapter 5/g.)

647. CENTAZZO, Andrea **La Batteria: Stili, Protagonisti e Tecniche.** Padora, Italy, Franco Muzzio & Co., 1981.
(For annotation see same entry in Chapter 6.)

648. CEROLI, Nick 'Driver's Seat: Fills.' [2 parts: Basic & Big Band] **Modern Drummer** 9/3: 80-2,; 9/4: 96-9, 1985.

649. CHAFFEE, Gary 'Stickings.' (2 parts) **Modern Drummer** 5/8: 34-6, 1981; 6/1: 38-9, 1982.
A re-examination of basic and alternative sticking possibilities with special consideration for contemporary music. Part 2 applies this concept to play "rock time" and "Latin time feels."

650. CHAFFEE, Gary **Patterns - Vol.III** Hyde Park, Mass., G.C. Music, 1980, 53 p. (Subtitle: 'Time Functioning-Patterns')
(For annotation see same entry in Chapter 6.)

651. CHAPIN, Jim **Advanced Techniques for the Modern Drummer.** New York, The Author, 1972,. (Two vols. combined in the 1972 ed.; vol.1 first published in 1948.) Vol.I: "Coordinated Independence as applied to Jazz and Be-Bop," Vol.II: "The Open End."
This still proves to be a very innovative, useful and intelligent tutor, despite its age. New contemporary cymbal patterns were added in 1972 to the old 'swing-style' rhythms (in handy window overlay pages), and it is for the more advanced students to help them gain independence.
See also the article by Rick Mattingly (with interview of Jim Chapin) for further interesting insight and background to this famous book: "Jim Chapin - Father of Independence", in 'Modern Drummer' 5/7: 25-6, 40+, 1981.

652. COMBE, Stuff **Anleitung zur Improvisation fuer Schlagzeug.** Mainz, B.Schott, 1974, 31 p. [German]
Basic tutor in German ('Guide to Improvisation for Drums'), sometimes a little inconsistent, aimed at the intermediate level and the 'swing style' of jazz.

653. COMPTON, Rick 'Developing Jazz Feel and Independence.' **Woodwind World, Brass and Percussion** 19/5: 16-8+, 1980.
Aimed at percussionists and/or drummers inexperienced in jazz playing and the problems of gaining a relaxed independence. Suggests several progressive exercises to "free the limbs" and improve musical perception.

654. CONNELL, J. **The Different Drum Book.** 92 Hollis Ave., Toronto, The Author, 1977.
Advanced text for the jazz/rock drummer wanting to expand his knowledge and freedom for fills and solos, and within even and odd meters.

655. DAHLGREN, Marvin **Off the Record - Famous Drum Solos by Joe Morello.** Chicago, Jamor Publications, 1966, 45 p.
The first part of the book contains reading exercises in 4/4, 3/4, and 5/4. The five long solos are preceded by specially written exercises. They are: "Sound of the Loop", "Shortnin' Bread", "Shim Wa", "Far more Drums", and "Watusi Drums."

656. DAWSON, Allan & DE MICHAEL, Don **A Manual for the Modern Drummer.** Boston, Berklee Press, 1962, 116 p. (Subtitle: 'Analysis of Stylistic and Technical Problems')
(For annotation see same entry in Chapter 6.)

657. DE JOHNETTE, Jack & PERRY, Charlie **The Art of Modern Jazz Drumming.** New York, Long Island Drum Centre Publ. Division, 1979, 120 p. (2nd Edi. 1984)
This is perhaps the most comprehensive, original and up-to-date book on jazz drumming techniques. It is divided into three sections, which are quoted here:
Book I: The concepts, principles, elements, and techniques of modern jazz and allied forms of drumming (jazz-rock, fusion), some of which are applicable to rock.
Book II: The triplet-eighth rhythmic-tonal patterns used in jazz, played between the two hands and feet.
Book III: The four-way independent coordination in playing the rhythmic-tonal punctuations and figures in jazz.

658. DI CENSO, D. **A Practical Workbook for the Modern Drummer.** Randolph, MA, The Author, 1977.
(For annotation see same entry in Chapter 6.)

659. DOBOE, Chet **The Funk Drumming Workbook.** Hempstead, NY, The Author, 1978, 60 p.
(For annotation see same entry in Chapter 6.)

660. DOBOE, Chet **The Funk Drumming Idea Series - Bk.1.** Hempstead, NY, The Author, 1978, 20 p.
(For annotation see same entry in Chapter 6.)

661. ELLIS, Stanley 'Big Band Fills: A two-handed Approach.' **Modern Drummer** 7/1: 96-8, 1983.
Examples of how to take common big band figures and try to play fills around these figures in various ways.

662. ENGLE, Jim **Big Time: A Study in Big Band Drumming and Drum Beats of the World.'** Burbank, CA, Good Time Publ. Co., 40 p.
(For annotation see same entry in chapter 6.)

663. ENGLE, Jim **The Spirit of Independence.** Hollywood, Good Time Publishing Co., 1979, 24 p.
(For annotation see same entry in Chapter 6.)

664. GIGER, Peter **Neue Schlagzeugschule.** Kabisrain, The Author, 1974, 36 p. [German; translation: 'New School for Drum Set']
A tutor for the advanced player with some jazz experience. Although this seems a slight book, it contains a great amount of accent and syncopation studies, rhythmic ideas and possible combinations thereof in a choice of phrasing and méter. The author does not teach styles and "typical patterns", but rather aims to improve the player's vocabulary of more refined rhythms and controlled dynamics, and to inspire new rhythmic textures with this presentation of progressive, and often very difficult, studies.

665. GIUFFRE, Jimmy **Jazz Phrasing and Interpretation - Percussion.** New York, Associated Music Publishers, 1969, 57 p.
This is a rather interesting and more unusual book for the aspiring jazz player. There are three parts: The first one is divided into seven chapters, trying to slowly build up the student's understanding and awareness of certain characteristics in jazz playing: (1) Feeling Time, (2)

The Downbeat, (3) The Off-Beat, (4) Establishing the Tempo at the Beginning of the Phrase, (5) Maintaining Drive throughout a Complete Phrase, (6) Studies, and (7) The Student Interpreds.Part two continues on a more advanced and musical level with: (1) Musical Considerations, (2) An Approach to practising the Exercises, (3) Group Playing. Part three concludes with very advanced and extended exercises.

666. GROSSMAN, Norman **The Complete Book of Modern Drumming.** New York, Amsco Music, 1975.
     (Not available for annotation; for book review see 'Jazz Forum' No.34: 66, Apr. 1975.)

667. GOODWIN, Simon 'Adjusting for softer Drums.' **Modern Drummer** 7/4: 72-7, 1983.
     Good advice for choosing, adjusting, and tuning the drumset for a good quality sound, yet remaining at a lower dynamic level.

668. GUERIN, John **DRUMS Jazz+Rock=.** Sherman Oaks, Gwyn Publishing Co., 1971, 24 p.
     (For annotation see same entry in Chapter 6.)

669. HERRICK, Joey **Contempoary Drum Solos.** Northridge, CA, Flat Five Music Products, 1979, 40 p.
     This book contains nine solos by Buddy Rich, Louie Bellson, Billy Cobham, Ed Shaughnessy, Shelly Manne, John Guerin, Harvey Mason, Lenny White, Alphonse Mouzon. However, there are no comments offered, and not even the titles are given by the author. There is only a list of nine records given where, one assumes, these solos can somewhere be found.

670. HOCHRAINER, Richard 'Der Orchesterstimmer.' **Das Orchester** 18: 410-12, Sep. 1970. [German]
     A thoughtful essay on the tendency of the tuning pitch in the orchestra to "creep up", and how the timpanist should help to prevent this and not aid it.

671. HOULLIF, Murray **The Fusion Drummer.** New York, Alfred Publ. Co., 16 p.
     (For annotation see the same entry in Chapter 6.)

672. HOULLIF, Murray **Contemporary Drum Set Solos.** New York, Kendor Music Inc., 1981.
     (For annotation see the same entry in Chapter 6.)

673. HUMPHREY, Ralph **Even in the Odds.** Oskaloosa, IA, C.L. Barnhouse Co., 88 p.
     This text on odd meters is clearly conceived and presented, and divided into two major parts: Part I "Time patterns for the drum set", which falls into three sub-sections: quarter notes, eigth notes and 'extending the rhythmic phrase', using the Indian way of counting in syllables. Part II is called "Accent patterns and sticking combinations" and follows the original ideas of Part I.

674. JONES, Philly Joe **Brush Artistry.** London, The Premier Drum Co., 1968, 16 p.
     (For annotation see same entry in Chapter 6.)

675. KERRIGAN, Chuck **Syncopated Rhythms for the Contemporary Drummer.** Pacific, MO, Mel Bay Publications, 1982, 100 p.
Contains a comprehensive list of syncopated rhythms in 3/4, 4/4, & 5/4, which can be combined and used in many ways, but they are strictly a set of unrelated exercises.

676. KERRIGAN, Chuck **The Key to Drum Polyrhythms.** Pacific, MO, Mel Bay Publications, 1983.
This book presents 44 polyrhythms, beginning with 2:3 and finishing with 9:8. Each exercise is broken down to fundamentals, and is followed by drum set applications in progressive form, i.e. adding instruments. Seems a good reference text.

677. KERRIGAN, Chuck 'Expanding the Paradiddle.' (3 parts) **Modern Drummer** 8/3: 86-7,; 8/4: 108-9,; 8/5: 88-90, 1984.
From basic exercises, the rhythms are expanded and stretched into polyrhythms (i.e. part (1) exercises, part (2) expanded rhythms, part (3) polyrhythms).

678. KERRIGAN, Chuck 'Jazz Patterns in 5/4.' **Modern Drummer** 8/9: 94-5, 1984.

679. KERRIGAN, Chuck 'Jazz Rhythms in 7/4.' [15 examples] **Modern Drummer** 9/1: 66-8, 1985.

680. KERRIGAN, Chuck 'Solo Ideas for Hi-Hat.' (3 parts) **Modern Drummer** 9/4: 76-7,; 9/5: 84-5,; 9/6: 86-9, 1985.
Part (1) has 24 exercises, part (2) 19, in order of progressive difficulty, and part (3) contains four solos.

681. KETTLE, Rupert 'Roach vs. Rich; A Notated Analysis of two Significant Modern Jazz Drumming Styles.' **Downbeat** 33: 19-22, March 24, 1966.

682. KETTLE, Rupert 'Krupa: A Musical Perspective.' **Modern Drummer** 3/5: 24-5, 1979.
[Three musical examples of his playing]

683. KLAUBER, Bruce 'Krupa and the Small Groups: A Lesson in Individuality and Swing.' **Modern Drummer** 3/5: 20-1,59, 1979.

684. KOFSKY, Frank 'Elvin Jones, Pt.1: Rhythmic Innovator.' **Journal of Jazz Studies** 4/1: 5-24, 1977.

685. KOFSKY, Frank 'Elvin Jones, Pt.2: Rhythmic Displacement in the Art of Elvin Jones.' **Journal of Jazz Studies** 4/2: 11-32, 1977.
The first part of the article consists mainly of a biographical and musical background of Elvin Jones, whereas the second part deals with the technique of "rhythmic displacement", which, the author says, should not be confused with polyrhythms. Kofsky analyzes several examples of Jones' rhythmic work with John Coltrane's group, which is recognized as very innovative in jazz drumming.

686. KRUPA, Gene **Gene Krupa Drum Method.** New York, Robbins, 1966.

687. LAMBERT, Joe **Drum Improvising Studies for Jazz and Rock.** Pacific, MO, Mel Bay Publications, 1978.
(For annotation see same entry in Chapter 6.)

688. LAUREN, Michael **Welcome to Odd Times.** New York, Why Not Music, 62 p.
     (For annotation see same entry in Chapter 6.)

689. LEPAK, Alexander **Control of the Drum Set.** Windsor, CT, Windsor Music Publications, 1978, 104 p. (Subtitle: 'Phrasing for the Soloist - Advanced Studies')
     This advanced text is divided into these nine sections:
     (1) coordination drills, (2) phrasing in 4/4, (3) phrasing in 3/4, (4) rock, (5) phrasing in compound time, (6) changing meters equalling 16 quarter notes, (7) phrasing with odd groupings, (8) phrasing in 5/4, 6/4, 7/4, 11/4, (9) changing meters.

690. LEWIS, Mel & DE ROSA, Clem **It's Time for the Big Band Drummer.** Delevan, NY, Kendor, 1978, 47 p. (Subtitle: 'Based on recorded materials of the Thad Jones/Mel Lewis Jazz Orchestra')
     This innovative book is divided into three sections:
     (1) 'Equipment', covering detailed tuning, playing and practising the different parts of the set.
     (2) 'Technique', which gives details on terminology in jazz and musical examples from recordings (e.g. riffs and fills).
     (3) 'Reading', the main section, which discusses chart reading with musical interpretation hints, using drum parts from the T. Jones/M. Lewis library.

691. MAC NEIL, E. **Drumming in a Big Way.** London, Island Music, 1978.
     (Not available for annotation; for book review see 'Melody Maker' 53: 38, July 22., 1978.)

692. MAGADINI, Peter 'Reading at the Drum Set.' **Percussionist** 8/2: 53-60, 1970.
     (For annotation see same entry in Chapter 6.)

693. MAGADINI, Peter **Poly-Cymbal Time.** Phoenix, Briko Publishing, 1975. (Note new publisher 1984: Belwin-Mills, Melville)
     The introductory message includes "... deals with the mental and physical phenomenon of learning to improvise and execute polyrhythms at the drum set". The book covers coordination for the four limbs, utilizing the ratios 4:4, 4:2, 6:4, 3:4, 5:4, 7:4, 4:3, 2:3. It is laid-out in a clear, progressive style, also allowing for some improvisation. A jazz record is also available, called "Polyrhythm", which features rhythms found in this book.

694. MAGADINI, Peter 'Jazz Drummer's Workshop: Polyrhythms.' **Modern Drummer** 2/1: 20, 1978.

695. MAGADINI, Peter **Learn to play the Drum Set - Vols.1. & 2.** Milwaukee, Hal Leonard Publ. Corp., 1980 & 1982.
     (For annotation see same entry in Chapter 6.)

696. MANNE, Shelly **Let's play Drums.** New York, Experience Music, 1974, 67 p. (Not available for annotation.)

697. MARTIN, Randy 'Creative Hi-Hat.' **Modern Drummer** 8/11: 36-8, 1984.
     [Variations on the accents of the 2nd and 4th beats.]

698. MAY, Gordon 'Melodic Solo Construction.' **Modern Drummer** 6/5: 94-7, 1982.
   This stresses the importance and shows the advantage of being aware of the melodic line in a musical piece, especially in order to be able to construct a "melodically oriented" solo.

699. MINTZ, Billy **Different Drummers.** New York, Amsco Music Publ. Co., 96 p. (Includes record)
   (For annotation see same entry in Chapter 6.)

700. MODERN DRUMMER (Ed.) 'The Great Jazz Drummers: 1900-1980.' (4 parts) **Modern Drummer** 4/3: 16-20+; 4/4: 16-9, 51-5; 4/5: 22-5+, 1980; 4/6: 20-3+, 1980-81.
   An extensive article, well-illustrated with photos and many musical examples. It covers the background and drumming styles from the early New Orleans drummers right through to the percussionists of the late 1970's.

701. MOLENHOF, Bill 'The musical Drummer: The Blues.' **Modern Drummer** 8/7: 70-2, 1984.
   In trying to make the drummer understand the musical basis of the blues, the author hopes to improve the musical quality of the drumming.

702. MOORE, Gene 'Cross Sticking for the Drumset.' **Modern Drummer** 5/3: 54-6, 1981.
   Some useful exercises and ideas for cross sticking, using snare drum, small and large tom toms.

703. MORTON, James **Killer - Fillers.** Pacific, MO, Mel Bay Publications, 1980. (Optional cassette avail.)
   (For annotation see same entry in Chapter 6.)

704. MORTON, James **Fusion Drum Styles.** Pacific, MO, Mel Bay Publications, 1982.
   (For annotation see same entry in Chapter 6.)

705. NESBITT, Jim **Inside Buddy Rich.** Delevan, NY, Kendor Music, 1984.
   The book is a detailed study of Buddy Rich's technique and style, with many close-up analyses of his drum techniques and many solo transcriptions from recordings, as well as illustrations and interviews.

706. NORINE, William **Virtuoso Studies for the Drum Set.** Boston, Berklee Press, 1979, 124 p.
   (For annotation see same entry in Chapter 6.)

707. NORINE, William **Four-Way Fusion for the Modern Drummer.** Boston, Berklee Press, 1982.
   (For annotation see same entry in Chapter 6.)

708. PERRY, Charlie 'Jack de Johnette advises young Drummers.' **Jazz Forum** No.47: 58-60, 1977.

709. PETACCIA, Roberto 'Rock & Jazz Clinic: Ambidexterity.' (2 parts) **Modern Drummer** 5/7: 72-3; 5/8: 38-40, 1981.
   (For annotation see same entry in Chapter 6.)

710. PICKERING, John **Mel Bay's Stage and Band Drummer's Guide.**
Kirkwood, MO, Mel Bay Publications, 1976, 96 p.
(For annotation see same entry in Chapter 6.)

711. PICKERING, John **Studio/Jazz Drum Cookbook.** Pacific, MO, Mel Bay
Publications, 95 p.
This text aims to improve the musical concept and increase
independence, by stressing exercises not only together (i.e. on the drum
set), but also in isolation for the four limbs.

712. PORCARO, Joe **Odd Times - A new Approach to Latin, Jazz and Rock,
Applied to Drum Set.** Hollywood, Try Publ. Co., 1970, 48 p.
(For annotation see same entry in Chapter 6.)

713. PORTER, Lewis 'A Historical Survey of Jazz Drumming Styles.' (2 parts)
**Percussive Notes** 20/3: 42-3, 70+; 21/3: 46-7, 78, 1982.

714. ROTHMAN, Joel 'Using the Bass Drum in Modern Drum Solos.'
**Percussionist** 4/1: 95-7, 1966.

715. ROTHMAN, Joel 'Playing Drum Solos in 3/4 Meter.' **Percussionist** 4/4:
196-9, 1967.
Several examples are explained to help drummers develop 3/4 solos in
swing style, with the main consideration being the phrasing of the solo.

716. ROTHMAN, Joel 'Fills into Offbeat Rhythmic Figures.' (2 parts) **Brass
and Percussion** 1/3: 10-1; 1/4: 16-7, 1973.
This two-part article shows various possibilities of how to approach
and execute a fill which is based on the first two beats of a 4/4 bar being
played as eigth note rest, followed by a dotted quarter note. They are
either played with 1/8 note triplets or with a 12/8 feel.

717. ROTHMAN, Joel **The Complete Jazz Drummer.** New York, J.R.
Publications, 1974, 510 p.
(Not available for annotation.)

718. ROTHMAN, Joel 'Cutting into Two-measure Rhythmic Figures Phrased
in Three.' **Percussive Notes** 14/3: 30, 1976.

719. ROTHMAN, Joel **3,5,7,9 Jazz.** New York, J.R. Publications, 1976, 62 p.
Gives basic cymbal (and/or hi-hat) beats and bass patterns, and then
combines these in many snare drum variations in 3/4, 5/4, 7/4, 3/8, 5/8,
and 7/8 ("9" appears as a multiple only).

720. ROTHMAN, Joel **Easy Drum Solos for Jazz Coordination.** Fort
Lauderdale, FL, J.R. Publications, 1983(?), 33 p.

721. RYAN, Lloyd **The Complete Drum Tutor.** London, Duckworth, 1981, 80 p.
(For annotation see same entry in Chapter 6.)

722. SEE, Cees **Reihe Jazz 4: Das Schlagzeug im Jazz.** Vienna, Universal
Edition, 1971, 35 p. [German; Editor: Joe Viera.]
This short book means to give an introduction to the way the jazz
drummer's role has changed from mainly playing time, to playing a
bigger part in helping to create all the various aspects of a piece. But it
really just gives basic exercises in the main rhythmic configurations and
some shifting-meter "feels."

723.  SHAUGHNESSY, Ed **New Time Signatures in Jazz Drumming.** New York, Henry Adler, 1966, 39 p.
      In the first part of the book the author introduces many time signatures, shows how to play them in various ways on the drum set, mixing them in numerous combinations. They include 3/4, 5/4, 7/4, 7/8, 9/4, and 6/8. The second part is meant to develop musical sight-reading ability for all types of time signatures in any working situation.

724.  SIMS, R.A. **Fundamentals of Jazz Drumming.** Fullerton, CA, Centerstream Publications,. (Vols 1. & 2.)
      In a total of 120 pages the author has combined some good detailed material to use for practice and to obtain understanding of coordinated independence which is necessary for the jazz drummer.

725.  SOFIA, Sal 'Linear Coordination.' [Jazz and Rock] **Modern Drummer** 6/2: 64-8; 6/3: 66-9, 1982.
      (For annotation see same entry in Chapter 6.)

726.  SOFIA, Sal 'Hi-Hat Techniques in different Styles.' **Modern Drummer** 7/1: 58+61, 1983.

727.  SOFIA, Sal 'Sound Phrasing.' (2 parts) **Modern Drummer** 7/3: 64-6; 7/4: 90-2, 1983.
      (For annotation see same entry in Chapter 6.)

728.  SOPH, Ed 'Basic Brush Technique.' **Modern Drummer** 3/1: 32-3, 1979.

729.  SOPH, Ed 'Fundamental Studies for Ride Cymbal Technique.' (2 parts) **Modern Drummer** 3/5: 34-5, 56; 3/6: 38-9, 1979.
      The author suggests physical changes (of the body) to aid this technique.

730.  SOPH, Ed 'Developing a Musical Approach.' **Modern Drummer** 3/6: 38-9, 1979.
      Defines some ideas on how to adapt one's drumming to a musical (melodic) phrase.

731.  SOPH, Ed 'Double Time Coordination.' **Modern Drummer** 4/2: 34-5, 1980. [Basic examples.]

732.  SOPH, Ed 'Foundation Studies for Big Band Fills.' **Modern Drummer** 7/12: 96-7, 1983.

733.  STELLA, Angelo **Fill-ins for the Progressive Drummer.** Wilkes-Barre, PA, The Author.
      Comprises 164 jazz fills, mostly of two-bar length, and most of them in the swing-era style.

734.  SYRIAN, Joe 'Unusual Phrasing.' **Modern Drummer** 7/8: 90-1, 1983. [Phrasing in one meter whilst playing in another]

735.  THIGPEN, Ed 'The Beauty of Brushes.' **Modern Drummer** 6/7: 88-9, 1982.
      Brief, but good, descriptive explanations of several rhythms and techniques.

736. THIGPEN, Ed 'Time and its Nuances.' **Modern Drummer** 7/6: 30-4, 1983.
     Debate on "keeping good time", and exercises to help develop this
     concept.

737. THIGPEN, Ed **Sound of Brushes.** Copenhagen, Ed Thigpen/Action
     Reaction. (includes cassette)
     (For annotation see same entry in Chapter 6.)

738. ULANO, S. 'Swingigng the Jazz Band - Initial Steps for the Drummer.'
     **Music Educator's Journal** 62: 84-8, Nov. 1975.
     Advice for the non-percussionist teacher (or orchestral percussionist)
     on some basic ideas, styles and rhythms for the student drummer.

739. VIERA, Joe **Reihe Jazz: Vol.1. Grundlagen der Jazzrhythmik.** Vienna,
     Universal, 1982, 51 p. [German; revised 7th Edition. Translation: 'The
     Fundamentals of Jazz Rhythm.']

740. WEBER, Glenn 'Reading of a Lead Trumpet Part.' [Big Band] **Modern
     Drummer** 7/9: 102-3, 1983.

741. XEPOLEAS, J. & NUNES, W. **Studies for the Contemporary Drummer.**
     Miami Beach, Hansen House, 1983. (Includes record)
     (For annotation see same entry in Chapter 6.)

742. ZIGMUND, Eliot 'Trading Phrases.' **Modern Drummer** 7/3: 48-52, 1983.
     Good hints and exercises for the drummer to practise and develop this
     jazz tradition.

# CHAPTER 7.

## INSTRUCTION AND PERFORMANCE - JAZZ MUSIC:

### (b) Bar Percussion Instruments.

743. BURTON, Gary 'The Art of Comping.' **Downbeat** 50: 52-3, Jan., 1983.

744. DELP, Ron **Vibraphone Technique - Four Mallet Chord Voicing.** Boston, Berklee Press, 1975, 60 p.
   Mainly deals with different ways of playing (inverting and spacing) chords of the popular and jazz music literature.

745. DELP, Ron 'Vibes - Voicing - Comping.' **Woodwind World, Brass and Percussion** 15/1: 38-9+, 1976.
   Discusses the basic techniques and references for close and open positions in chord changes.

746. DELP, Ron 'Vibes Harmonizing a Melody.' **Woodwind World, Brass and Percussion** 15/5: 50-1, 1976.

747. GIUFFRE, Jimmy **Jazz Phrasing and Interpretation - Percussion.** New York, Associated Music Publishers, 1969, 57 p.
   (For annotation see same entry in Chapter 7/a.)

748. MOLENHOF, Bill 'Developing a Vibe Arrangement.' **Percussive Notes** 22/1: 47-50, 1983.
   The author demonstrates how to work up an arrangement of a standard ("Wave", by Carlos Jobim), in order to improve vibes technique and knowledge of harmony.

749. SAINDON, Ed 'Accompaniment in Jazz Vibe Solo Playing.' **Percussive Notes** 17/2: 56-7, 1979.
   Informative article with references to dynamics, pedaling, melody vs. voicing, rhythm, guide tones, tension in voicing, stride accompaniment, and other ideas.

750. SAINDON, Ed 'Improvisation.' (2 parts) **Percussive Notes** 18/1: 68-9, 1979; 18/2: 54-6, 1980.
   Part I deals with ideas like: tension-resolve, stable/unstable notes, lines outlining voicings, pentatonics, motives and shapes. Part II extends these ideas and covers in more detail the upper structure triads and alterations.

751. SAINDON, Ed 'Vibe Comping.' **Percussive Notes** 18/3: 66-9, 1980.
   Shows various comping concepts in twelve examples from different jazz recordings.

752. SAINDON, Ed 'Vibe Workshop: Chord Solos.' **Percussive Notes** 19/2: 59-60, 1981.

Illustrates some good possibilities of playing jazz tunes as chord solos (e.g. "Over the Rainbow", "Spring is here", and "Misty").

753. SAINDON, Ed 'Vibe Workshop - Solo Playing.' **Percussive Notes** 21/1: 82-4, 1982.

754. SAINDON, Ed 'Spicing up a Standard.' (part 1) **Percussive Notes** 23/2: 54-9, 1985.
    Deals with various aspects of total "harmonic concepts for the vibes player."

755. SAMUELS, David **A Musical Approach to Four-Mallet Technique for Vibraphone (Vol.1).** Bryn Mawr, Theodore Presser Co., 1982.
    Very extensive coverage of basic techniques, including grip (Gary Burton), sticking, dampening and pedaling.

# CHAPTER 8.

## PERCUSSION IN FOLK MUSIC.

756. CARTER, Dorothy 'The Ancient, Ageless Psaltry and Hammered Dulcimer.' **Sing Out** 27/4: 28-30, 1979.
Basic article with a brief description of the (author's) instruments and two musical examples of arrangements she plays.

757. CLINE, Dallas (Edi.) **How to Play Nearly Everything.** New York, Oak Publications, 1977, 63 p.
A delightful collection of ten chapters (by ten different authors) on the playing techniques, and sometimes construction, of such 'high-brow' instruments as the bones, kazoo, and more. Of special interest to the percussionist are these rare set of instructions:
(1) 'How to Make and Play the Bones' (Sue E. Barber, pp 6-17).
Very detailed instructions; rhythms, articulation, technique, and bibliography.
(4) 'How to Make Music on a Handsaw' (Charles Blacklock, pp 27-35).
Clear, illustrated instructions on this rare art, and plenty of advice.
(6) 'How to Make and Play a Washboard' (Peter Menta, pp 40-4).
Gives some historical background on this dying skill, playing instructions, and discography.
(9) 'How to Play the Spoons' (Barbara Mendelsohn, pp 50-57).
Explains in detail the one- and two-finger methods, beats, roll, and various rhythms, special "hot licks", and discography.
(10)'How to Make and Play the Bodhran' (Dan Milner, pp 58-63).
Basic information only in this chapter on the music, instructions on building the drum, and how to play it.

758. DAHLIG, Piotr 'Drums and Drumming in Folk Music in Poland.' **Percussive Notes** 22/3: 68-76, 1984.
Covers historic information, description of some instruments, with illustrations, and musical examples of some dances.

759. DELGADO, Mimi Spencer **Zils - The Art of Playing Finger Cymbals.** Forest Knolls, CA, Jazayer Publications, 1977, 57 p.
This original booklet gives detailed instructions on the wearing of and the caring for finger cymbals, their basic playing strokes, notation and exercises. The main part of the text consists of many interesting rhythms as found in the Middle East, including Arabia, Turkey, Persia and Greece.

760. DRIVER, N. 'Bones and Bodhrans.' **English Dance and Song** 40/1: 14-5, 1978.
A short article on the bones (or clappers), relating their early history, recommended materials and playing technique. The second part deals with the bodhran (Irish single-headed drum) in a similar manner.

761. FOX, L.M. 'The Bodhran.' **The Galpin Society Journal** 24: 104, July 1971.

762. IDA, T.T. & JOZSEF **Cymbalschule.** Budapest, Editio Musica Budapest, 1958, 107 & 144 p. (School for Cymbalom; Vols. 1 & 2)
(For annotation see same entry in Chapter 5/e.)

763. KETTLEWELL, David 'That's what I call a Striking Sound - The Dulcimer in East Anglia.' (2 parts) **English Dance and Song** 36/2: 50-2; 36/3: 96-7, 1974.
Deals with the history, construction, players, and music of the dulcimer in this area of Britain.

764. KETTLEWELL, David **The Dulcimer.** Ph.D. Thesis, Loughborough University, 1976, 473 p.
(For annotation see same entry in Chapter 5/e.)

765. LYON, Nancy 'The Mighty Goatskin Drum: The Irish Bodhran.' **Sing Out** 27/4: 2-7, 1979.
A few words about the "dim history" of this instrument are followed by basic playing instructions and descriptions of several types of tunes and their rhythms.

766. PICKOW, Peter **Hammered Dulcimer.** New York, Oak, 1979, 111 p.
This concerns itself in detail with the diatonic (as distinct from the chromatic) instrument only, which has an asymetrical design with two bridges (bass and treble bridge). The author gives advice on tuning, hammers, scales, chords and modes, and presents a large number of dance tunes, classical, country and 'ragtime' pieces, and other traditional melodies from Great Britain and the U.S.A. They have a good background introduction and are notated in traditional staff notation as well as in a specially devised tablature notation.

767. PINTER, E. 'The Hungarian Dulcimer.' **New Hungarian Quarterly** 20/76: 217+, 1979.

768. RECK, David **Music of the Whole Earth.** New York, Charles Scribner's Sons, 1977, 545 p.
This is an unusual, complex and fascinating book, covering a great amount of information about all types of old and new musics and instruments from around the world. The percussionist or composer will find a great deal of relevant information and insight into many aspects of musical traditions, but he will either have to read the whole book, or look up various subjects in the comprehensive cross-index.

769. SCHICKHAUS, Karl-Heinz **Neues Schulwerk fuer Hackbrett. (3 Vols.)** Munich, Musikverlag Josef Preissler, 1978.
[German: 'New Tutor for Hammer Dulcimer'; Part 1: "Fuer Kinder", 40 p; Part 2: "Volksmusik", 60 p; Part 3: "Klassische und moderne Originalmusik, 40 p.]
(For annotation see same entry in Chapter 5/e.)

770. RUSTIN, Terry 'Teach-in: Spoons.' **Sing Out** 22/4: 17-8, 1973.
Teaches the reader how to adjust spoons and grip for "personalized fit", and how to practise the basic beats, the roll and the trill ("super spooning").

771. SUCH, David 'The Bodhran: The Black Sheep in the Family of Traditional Irish Musical Instruments.' **The Galpin Society Journal** No.38: 9-19, 1985.

The essay covers the historical development of the bodhran, its construction, playing technique, and today's general attitude towards this instrument.

772. TRICKET, E. 'Teach-in: Hammered Dulcimer.' **Sing Out** 21/4: 18-9, 1972.

773. VAN DER MEER, J.H. **Das Hackbrett, ein alpenlaendisches Musikinstrument.** Herisan/Trogen, Schlaepfer, 1975, 72 p. [German]
This book mainly deals with the history, development and today's practice of the "Hackbrett" (hammer dulcimer) in the traditional music of Switzerland.

774. VLASAK, V. 'History and the Present: Percussion Instruments in the Musical Life of Czechoslovakia.' **Woodwind World, Brass and Percussion** 24/3: 22-4, 1985.

# CHAPTER 9.

## GENERAL MUSICIANSHIP, TEACHING METHODS AND REFERENCES OF SPECIAL INTEREST TO PERCUSSION.

775. ADAIR, Yvonne **Music through the Percussion Band.** London, Boosey & Hawkes, 1952, 225 p.
   The subtitle of the book is: 'A comprehensive scheme of work from the early stages, with games and exercises for playing, listening, reading and conducting.'

776. ALBIN, W. **The Development of Video-taped Instructional Units for Teaching Selected Aspects of Mallet-played, Latin American, and Accessory Percussion Instruments.** D.M.E. Thesis, Indiana University, 1979, 463 p. (Diss. Abst. 40: 4462A-3A, Feb. 1980)
   The author's aim of this study was to develop teaching materials on video tape for the complementary assistance of students in learning percussion instruments, especially where a professional specialist is not available. The three groups of instruments in the study were: 1) Xylophone and marimba, 2) Latin American instruments (maracas, guira, claves, cowbell), and 3) accessory percussion (triangle, tambourine and cymbals). Extensive studies and performance tests found that the aids were very successful, especially when used privately by students, less so when in a class environment.

777. BELLSON, L. & BREINES, G. **Modern Reading Text in 4/4.** New York, Belwin-Mills, 1966, 91 p. (Henry Adler, 1963)
778. BELLSON, L. & BREINES, G. **Odd Time Reading Text.** New York, Belwin-Mills, 1968, 130 p.
   Both of these books are very good for improving one's sight-reading, especially in the area of syncopation. They range from beginner standard to very advanced and are especially suitable for percussionists.

779. BIRCHER, J. 'Chamber Percussion: Approach to Musicality.' **The Instrumentalist** 26: 74-6, March 1972.
   Some very elementary considerations, mainly directed at the inexperienced music teacher, about aspects of percussion ensemble playing.

780. BLADES, James **Drum Roll.** London, Faber & Faber, 1977, 275 p.
   This autobiography, subtitled "A Professional Adventure from the Circus to the Concert Hall", discusses the author's 50 years of percussion work, including many photographs, stories and descriptions of experiences, instruments, and more.

781. BRENNER, Tim 'How to Publish your own Drum Book.' **Modern Drummer** 6/2: 36-41, 1981.
   Detailed advice about such a venture, including manuscript, layout, copyright, costing, advertising, etc.

782. BROWN, Theodore D. 'Tuning the Drums.' **Brass and Percussion** 2/3: 9-10, 1974.

783. CARROLL, D.W. **Development and Evaluation of a Programmed-like Text with Accompanying Audio-Cassette Tapes as an Ancillary to Elementary Beginning Snare Drum Classes.** PH.D. Thesis, Kent State Univ., 1983, 335 p. (Diss. Abst. 44: 2702A, March 1984)

784. CHENOWETH, Vida 'Musicianship.' **Percussionist** 9/2: 48-9, 1971. (Reprinted from 'Percussionist' 1/4, 1963)

785. CLARK, Forest 'A Logical Approach to Teaching the Roll.' **Modern Drummer** 1/3: 24-5, 1977.
[Advice for the drum teacher]

786. COMBS, F. Michael 'University Marching Band Drum Cadences.' (2 parts) **The Instrumentalist** 28: 69-71, Nov.; 28: 65-9, Dec. 1973.

787. DELP, Ron 'Preparing the Student for Chart Reading.' **Percussionist** 11/2: 52-6, 1974.

788. ELLIS, Don (and others) **The New Rhythm Book.** North Hollywood, CA, Ellis Music Enterprises, 1972, 101 p. (Includes record)

789. FINK, Ron 'Finger Control Applied to Percussion Performance.' **Percussionist** 9/3: 63-7, 1972.
(For annotation see same entry in Chapter 6.)

790. FINK, Siegfried 'Percussion in the Teaching of Music.' **Percussionist** 8/1: 2-11, 1975. (Reprinted and translated from 'Musik und Bildung' 5: 378-84, Jul./Aug. 1973)

791. FINK, Siegfried 'The Necessity and Feasibility of Percussion Instruction in Music Schools.' (Translated by C.N. Wolfe) **Percussionist** 13/2: 58-66, 1976.
Refering mainly to West Germany, it discusses this subject in headings of: aquisitions and composition of instruments, literature and sources, use and performance practice, and pedagogical considerations.

792. FLETCHER, G. 'Effects of other Musical Elements upon Rhythmic Stress Perception.' **Percussionist** 10/4: 113-7, 1973.

793. FORTE, Nick 'Understanding Rhythm.' (10 parts) **Modern Drummer** 6/2, 1982 to 7/2, 1983.
'Quarter Notes' 6/2: 54-6, 1982.
'Eigth Notes' 6/3: 46-8, 1982.
'Sixteenth Notes' 6/4: 38-42, 1982.
'Double Stroke Rolls' 6/5: 58-60, 1982.
'Whole Notes and Half Notes' 6/6: 36-8, 1982.
'Dotted Notes' 6/7: 44-7, 1982.
'The Eigth-Note Triplet' 6/8: 32-4, 1982.
'The Sixteenth-Note Triplet' 6/9: 34-6, 1982.
'The Quarter-Note Triplet' 7/1: 32-3, 1983.
'Half-Note Triplet' 6/8: 28+30, 1983.
Each part explains the rhythms in theory (including other aspects like dynamics and phrasing), then gives reading exercises for the snare drum,

followed by drum set exercises and patterns, and concludes with an extensive drum solo.

794. FORTE, Nick 'Odd Time Signatures.' **Modern Drummer** 7/4: 30-2, 1983. [Basic examples, including a snare drum solo.]

795. GAETANO, Mario 'Teaching Rhythmic Superimposition.' **N.A.C.W.P.I. Journal** 32/2: 15-8, 1984-85.

796. GALM, John 'New Ideas for Clinics.' **The Instrumentalist** 22: 82-5, Jan. 1968.
Reports on and suggests ideas for themes and subjects to be used in 'clinics' for percussionists at high school level.

797. GALM, John 'Creative Warm-ups.....Steps to Improvisation.' **N.A.C.W.P.I. Journal** 25/3: 54-6, 1977.
The author encourages the use of other styles, outside jazz, to draw from for ideas of improvisation, and gives an example originating from an East Indian rhythmic system to be used for percussive practice.

798. GILBERT, D.K. 'Organizing the Percussion Section.' **The Instrumentalist** 24: 64-6, Dec. 1969.

799. GILBERT, D.K. 'How and when to teach the Rolls.' **The Instrumentalist** 31: 100-2, Mar. 1977.

800. GILBERT, D.K. 'Class Percussion in the University - Its Function.' **Woodwind World, Brass and Percussion** 17/3: 30-1, 1978.

801. GOLDSTEIN, M. 'The Gesture of Improvisation: Some Thoughts, Reflections and Questions regarding Percussion Music.' **Percussionist** 21/3: 18-24, 1983.

802. GOODWIN, Simon 'Adjusting for softer Drums.' **Modern Drummer** 7/4: 72-7, 1983.
Good advice for choosing, adjusting, and tuning the drumset for a good quality sound, yet remaining at a lower dynamic level.

803. HIEBERT, C.W. 'A New Approach to Reviewing Percussion Ensemble Literature.' **Percussionist** 10/1: 29-32, 1972.
This article suggests the use of a chart to help assess a new composition for percussion ensemble with these headings: (1) Instrumentation, (2) Instruments (specific - availability - substitution), (3) Notation, (4) Physical Set-up, (5) Technical Difficulties, (6) General Performance Problems. The article is aimed at high school level.

804. HINDEMITH, Paul **Elementary Training for Musicians.** London, Schott & Co., 1969, 237 p. (2nd Ed.; Original Ed. by AMI, 1946)
This constructive and extensive training manual is ideal for the percussionist. The ear training (intervals and sight-singing) is especially important for the timpanist, and the rhythmic exercises are perfect to be utilized to gain independence for the drummer's hands and feet. From beginner to very advanced level.

805. HOCHRAINER, Richard 'Der Orchesterstimmer.' **Das Orchester** 18: 410-12, Sep. 1970. [German]

A thoughtful essay on the tendency of the tuning pitch in the orchestra to "creep up", and how the timpanist should help to prevent this and not aid it.

806. HOCHRAINER, Richard 'The Viennese Timpani and Percussion School.' **Percussionist** 17/2: 88-102, 1979.
[Paper read at the PAS International Convention in New York, Oct. 1979]

807. HOCHRAINER, Richard 'The Beat.' **Percussionist** 16/2: 56-65, 1979.
The author tries to express the combined importance of the technical ability and (resulting) musical quality of a single percussion stroke ("... it is lifting, accelerating and relaxing").

808. HOLLY, R. 'Preparing for Percussion Auditions.' **The Instrumentalist** 38: 62+, Nov. 1983.

809. HONG, Sherman 'Entrancing Performance through Imagery.' **The Instrumentalist** 22: 103-5, May 1968.

810. HONG, Sherman 'Naturalness in Hand Position.' **Percussionist** 8/1: 1-4, 1970.
This article pleads for "naturalness" in hand position when holding the sticks - whichever type of grip one may be using.

811. HOULLIF, Murray 'Mallet Percussion Instruments: Their Value and Use in the Public School (includes list of ensemble works).' **Percussive Notes** 21/5: 47-8, 1983.

812. HOUNCHELL, R. 'A Comprehensive Outline for the Teaching of Rhythmic Reading.' (2 parts) **Percussionist** 6/1: 20-4; 6/2: 55-60, 1968.
The article is divided into 16 suggested lessons, with simple meters (based on four units) in part (1), and 6/8, 9/8, & 12/8 meters in part (2). The author groups the exercises into what he calls "typical, basic sounds" of each meter. However, the article is hardly comprehensive.

813. HURLEY, Mark 'Improving your Drumming with Video.' **Modern Drummer** 9/7: 18-21, 74-9, 1985.
(For annotation see same entry in Chapter 6.)

814. KEEZER, R. 'Experiments in Elementary Percussion Education.' **Percussionist** 6/2: 37-9, 1968.
The author claims success in a less common approach to elementary percussion teaching [note: 1968]. One aspect was the simultaneous introduction of snare drum and bar percussion instruments ("it made the student more musical and feel more important"), another being the matched grip.

815. KENEN, A.L. 'An Electronic Music System for the Modern Drum Teacher.' **Percussionist** 12/4: 132-5, 1975.
The author advocates and explains the use and components of a music system to improve the teaching of drums. Basically, a sound source is played over headphones to the student (this may include a "click track" from a metronome), who can play along, and both sounds, the original and his, are recorded together for replay.

816. KETTLE, Rupert 'Polyrhythm Practice.' **Percussive Notes** 19/3: 40-2, 1981.
Basic ideas of 2:3, 4:3, 5:3, 7:3, 3:4, 7:4, 5:4, 3:5, 4:5, but rather sloppy manuscript.

817. LEACH, Joel **Percussion Manual for Music Educators.** New York, Henry Adler, 1964, 93 p.
A text aimed at the student who wishes to become a music teacher and wishes to know the basics of all the main percussion instruments. Snare drum techniques (incl. rudiments), timpani and mallet instruments take up most of the pages. Some very basic information is also given on several hand-percussion and Latin American instruments, and it includes many illustrations.

818. LA FEMINA, Ralph **Melody and Harmony on the Drum Set.** Patchogue, NY, The Author, 99 p.
(For annotation see same entry in Chapter 6.)

819. LAMBERT, James 'Melody in Rhythm for Percussionists.' **N.A.C.W.P.I. Journal** 27/3: 8-12, 1979.
In this short essay Lambert aims to demonstrate the advantage for the percussionist to think melodically as well as rhythmically. This can be practised by first singing the percussion part, even in the case of non-pitched instruments by first writing a melodic sketch representing drums, cymbals, etc. This then should be sung again together with physical wrist movements, but without mallets.

820. LANG, M. & SPIVAK, L. **Dictionary of Percussion Terms.** New York, Lang Percussion, 1978, 123 p.
This handy little dictionary contains an alphabetical listing of terms (used in the orchestral repertoire) in German, French, Italian and Spanish, with the occasional African, Asian and Latin American reference. The appendix covers the range of mallet instruments, Russian phrases, abbreviations, and special musical expressions from the literature.

821. LARSON, Randal 'Teaching Mallet Percussion.' **Woodwind World, Brass and Percussion** 23/4: 16-7, 1984.
Advice for the music teacher on beginner's problems unique to mallet percussion, and some specific exercises are recommended.

822. LEFEVER, M. 'The Percussionist's Obligation to the Music Director.' **Percussionist** 6/2: 39-41, 1968.

823. MAGADINI, Peter **Musician's Guide to Polyrhythms - Vols.1 & 2.** Hollywood, CA, Try Publishing Co., 1968, @ vol. 29 p. (Editor: Wanda Sykes)
Vol.1 contains four sections: 3:2 (or 6:4), 3:4, 5:4, solos. It is useful for the percussionist wishing to practise these rhythms. Vol.2 continues with a further seven sections: (5) 7:4, (6) 11:4, (7) 13:4, (8) Exercises combining 7, 11, & 13; (9) Solo Exercises from 7, 11, & 13; (10) Solo Exercises from Vols. 1 & 2; (11) Polyrhythmic Time Signatures. However, some of the explanations on how to count the rhythms (i.e. against the main pulse) are not very clear at all - especially in Vol.2.

824. MASONER, E.L. 'Playing Percussion Musically.' **The Instrumentalist** 25: 65-6, June 1971.
The author is looking towards more musical percussion playing with reference to pitch (although this article refers to playing the drum), phrasing and articulation, dynamics and finesse.

825. McCORMICK, L.W. 'Rudimental Drummer or Percussionist - Can we be both?'
**Percussionist** 1/2: 3-4, 1963.

826. McKENZIE, Jack 'Some Performance Problems of Contemporary Percussion Composition.' **Percussionist** 2/4: 1-6, 1965.
Two "problems" are discussed here: "metrical modulation" and "odd rhythmic groupings". In the first instance examples are given from the music of Ben Johnston ("Knocking Piece") and Michael Colgrass (use of Micro-rhythmic notation). In the second part the author recommends and explains a teaching method for odd groupings by "placing numbers in a formula", which seems a complicated explanation for lowest common denominator.

827. MILLER, William 'Getting your Drum Book published.' **Modern Drummer** 9/4: 22-5, 1985.
Practical and helpful advice on this subject, with reference to authors and publishers.

828. OLSON, Rees 'A Beginning Percussion Class.' **The Instrumentalist** 23: 88-93, Sep. 1968.
Aimed at the music teacher, and giving advice on preparing and executing classes for children. It includes selection of teaching material and students, some snare drum technique and ensemble playing ideas.

829. PAYSON, Al 'Motivating young Percussion Students.' **Percussive Notes** 13/2: 21-2, 1975.

830. PAYSON, Al & McKENZIE, Jack **Percussion in the School Music Program.** Park Ridge, IL, Payson Percussion Products, 115 p.

831. PEARMAN, M. 'Percussion in the Classroom.' **Percussionist** 5/2: 262-6, 1967.
[Is relevant to study and teaching of rhythm.]

832. PERCUSSIVE ARTS SOCIETY 'Timpani Education Report.' **Percussionist** 16/1: 35-43, 1978.
(For annotation see same entry in Chapter 5/b.)

833. PETERMAN, T. 'The Importance of Improvisation in the Percussion Education.' **Woodwind World, Brass and Percussion** 17/3: 32-3, 1978.
Constructive advice for the teacher on giving the student some creative freedom and incentive to improvise.

834. PETERS, Gordon 'Percussion Instruction Methods by Computer.' **The Instrumentalist** 32: 41-4, Jan. 1978.
This report talks about a program in percussion instruction available world-wide through the PLATO Music Project at the University of Illinois. This CAI system (computer-assisted instruction) is not there to replace the teacher, but to assist him. There is a variety of instrumental

areas available in the program, and the lessons mostly take the form of tests with scores of results given.

835. PETERS, Gordon, AMES, T. & WICKSTROM, F.A. 'Expert Advice for Percussion Students.' **The Instrumentalist** 34/10: 17-9, 1980.
As the title suggests, some all-round advice by these three experienced percussionists on the following topics: grip, rolls, rhythm, versatility of the percussionist, timpani, snare drum, mallet percussion, accessories, and additional books.

836. PETERS, Mitchell 'Factors in Percussion Tone Quality.' **The Instrumentalist** 21: 114-6, Apr. 1967.
Argues for the necessity of considering the tone quality of percussion instruments to be as important as for any other type of instrument. The quality of the tone is dependent on the quality of the instrument itself, its condition and tone color, as well as the type of sticks and mallets, and the manner in which the instrument is struck.

837. PIMENTEL, Linda 'The Tonality-based Problems of the Percussion Student.' **Percussionist** 16/2: 73-93, 1979.
As part of a Ph.D. thesis, the author discusses in this thought-provoking paper: (1) the reasons for the existence of the lack of understanding of, and ability to perform, basic melodic and harmonic material on bar percussion instruments; (2) the reasons for other problems, such as lack of basic skills in ear training, timpani tuning, identifying musical texture, lack of knowledge of musical history, etc. The author then debates existing and proposed courses of action that will improve this situation.

838. POLLART, Gene 'An Insight into Historical Literature Adaptable to Percussion.' **Percussionist** 8/2: 65-71, 1970.
Pollart points out why the percussionist should play other music, not origially written for percussion. He discusses some of the musical styles, and provides a selected list of music from the Renaissance to the Impressionist period, suitable for solo or ensemble work.

839. PRESBYS, Scott 'Polyrhythms: Past, Present and Future.' **Percussionist** 9/2: 38-42, 1972.
Despite the impressive title of this article, it is only a short essay on a few examples of early Western rhythms and some advice for the percussionist to learn these "polyrhythms", which are actually odd meters in my opinion.

840. PRESTON, A.C. **The Development and Evaluation of Selected Instructional Materials for Teaching Percussion Instruments in the Beginning Band Class.** Ed.D. Thesis, University of North Carolina, Greensboro, 1975. (Diss. Abst. 37: 1446A, Sep. 1976)
[Mainly relevant to North Carolina]

841. PRESTON, A.C. 'The Development and Evaluation of Selected Instructional Material for Teaching Percussion.' **Council for Research in Music Education Bulletin** No.56: 15-20, Fall 1978.

842. PRIOR, Glen 'Understanding Rhythm.' (3 parts) **Modern Drummer** 1/1: 11+; 1/2: 26; 1/3: 26, 1977.
A short series of basic articles explaining rhythmic notation for the beginner.

843. RAUSCH, John 'Teaching Quintuplets and Septuplets.' **The Instrumentalist** 39: 81-4, Apr. 1985.

844. ROBSON, Paul 'Odd Time Signatures (for Percussion).' **Canadian Musician** 2/2: 52, 1980.

845. ROBSON, Paul 'Percussion: Development of Time.' **Canadian Musician** 3/1: 57, 1981.

846. SALMON, J.D. 'Percussion Education in Question and Answers.' **Percussionist** 1/3: 7-10, 1963.

847. SAVAGE, Steve **Rhythm: Notation and Analysis; Elements of Jazz and Pop.** New York, Consolidated Music Publishers.
Not available for annotation. According to a book review in 'Modern Drummer' (3/4: 40, 1979), it is a guide and reference book on rhythm, relevant to jazz and pop, which starts from the beginning and includes exercises on notation, tempo, meter, syncopation, polyrhythms and other aspects.

848. SCHINSTINE, W.J. 'Motivation in Percussion Teaching.' **Percussionist** 15/3: 149-55, 1978.
[Excerpts from a speech given at the P.A.S. Second National Conference.]

849. SCHINSTINE, W.J. (Edi.) 'Percussion in the Schools.' **Percussive Notes** 21/5: 44-55, 1983.
This is a collection of five short papers by differnt authors:
(1) C.S. WALLACE 'Teaching Children to become Total Percussion Players.'
(2) M. HOULLIF 'Mallet Percussion Instruments; Their Value and Use in the Public School.'
(3) S. HONG 'Developing Snare Drum Rolls.'
(4) F.A. WICKSTROM 'A Curriculum for College-bound Percussionists.'
(5) A.J. CIRONE 'The Percussion Method Class.'

850. SCHNEIDER, Walter C. 'Organizing a Percussion Ensembble.' **The Instrumentalist** 34: 34-6, May 1980.
Basic advice on how to plan and organize a percussion ensemble, with a list of possible substitute instruments, and a recommended selection of pieces for junior high school level.

851. SCHULTZ, Herbert L. 'Dictation: A Means of Developing Drummers who can Read.' **Woodwind World, Brass and Percussion** 18/5: 32-3, 1979.
The author relates his personal observation of percussion students often lagging behind the other players in the orchestra in sight-reading ability, and suggests some preventive measures to be incorporated into the teaching process to improve this situation.

852. SEWREY, James 'A Pedagogical Approach to the Teaching of Mallet-played Percussion.' **The School Musician** 36: 8+, Jan. 1965.

853. SHAW, Albert C. **The Development and Evaluation of a Programmed Learning Approach in Teaching Elements of Snare Drum Technique.** Ph.D. Thesis, Indiana University, 1971, 344 p. (Diss. Abst. 32: 4049A, Jan. 1972)

854. STONE, G.L. 'Technique of Percussion.' **International Musician** 64: 24-5, July 1965.

855. TERRY, Keith 'Body Music.' **Percussive Notes** 23/1: 50-7, 1984.
    The author has combined various ways of using the body as a percussion instrument, and explains his theories and techniques, including clapping, slapping, stepping and vocalizing.

856. TILLES, Bob 'Keyboard Percussion in High School - A Message to the Instrumental Music Director.' **Percussionist** 4/2: 116-8, 1967.

857. TONER, D.T. 'The Percussion Section Leader.' **Woodwind World, Brass and Percussion** 23/7: 21-4, 1984.
    Toner makes the point that a percussion section leader's role is quite different from other principal players. He claims that a "good percussion section leader must be a technically advanced and sensitive musician, an inspired teacher, and must possess high levels of organizational, analytic, interpersonal, and leadership skills", and illustrates various points of his statement, especially the organizatory aspect of it (with diagrams and charts).

858. WELLS, J.R. **An Educational Model for Developing Comprehensive Musicianship through the Study and Performance of Selected 20th Century Compositions for Marching Band.** Ed.D. Thesis, Columbia University, 1974, 195 p. (Diss. Abst. 35: 3314A, Dec. 1974)

859. WHALEY, Gary 'The Percussion Ensemble; A Vehicle for Teaching Comprehensive Musicianship.' **Woodwind World, Brass and Percussion** 15/2: 47, 1976.

860. WHALEY, Gary 'Guide to the Private Percussion Lesson.' **The Instrumentalist** 30: 75-7, March 1976.
    A selected bibliography with brief annotations of instruction and study books.

861. WHITE, Larry 'Fortissimo to Pianissimo - A Percussionist's Dilema.' **The Instrumentalist** 39/7: 62-3, 1985.
    The author gives sensible and helpful advice on how to overcome this problem ("ff" to sudden "pp") in a variety of situations with certain sticking techniques and other physical preparations.

862. ZYSKOWSKI, W. 'Developing a Sense of Dynamic Sensitivity (for Percussion).' **Woodwind World, Brass and Percussion** 14/1: 29-30, 1975.

# CHAPTER 10.

## PERCUSSION IN HISTORY:

### (a) Development of Instruments and Instrumentation.

863. BENVENGA, Nancy **Timpani and the Timpanist's Art.** Gothenburg University, Dept. of Musicology: 3, 1979, 160 p. (Musical and Technical Development in the 19th and 20th Centuries)
    (For annotation see same entry in Chapter 5/b)

864. BLADES, James 'The Orchestral Instruments of Percussion.'
    In BAINES, Anthony **Musical Instruments through the Ages,** London, Penguin Books, 1961, 383 p. (revised in 1969)
    This chapter on percussion is only 22 pages and the survey is rather limited compared with the rest of the book.

865. BLADES, James 'Percussion Instruments of the Middle Ages and Renaissance.' **Early Music** 6/1: 11-8, 1973.
    The subtitle reads: "Their history in literature and painting". Reference is made to the various instruments as the subtitle promises.

866. BLADES, James **Percussion Instruments and their History.** London, Faber & Faber, 1974, 509 p. (1st ed. 1970)
    (For annotation see same entry in Chapter 1/a.)

867. BLADES, James **A Checklist of Percussion Instruments in the Edingburgh University Collection of Historical Musical Instruments.** Edingburgh, Reid School of Music, Edingburgh Univ., 1982, 24 p.

868. BLADES, James & MONTAGU, Jeremy 'Capriol's Revenge.' **Early Music** 6/2: 84-92, 1973.
    In a question-and-answer-type article the authors (mainly J. Montagu) explain how to make one's own percussion instruments for Early Music, problems and solutions.

869. BLADES, James & MONTAGUE, Jeremy **Early Percussion Instruments from the Middle Ages to the Baroque.** London, O.U.P., 1976, 77 p.
    The first part of the book (written by J. Blades) gives a historic background of the instruments, their development and musical use, whereas the second part (written by J. Montagu) deals mainly with advice and discussion about the actual playing techniques, presented in chronological order of periods.

870. BOWLES, Edmund 'Nineteenth Century Innovations in the Use and Construction of the Timpani.' **Journal of the American Musical Instruments Society** 5-6: 74-143, 1980-81. (Reprinted in 'Percussive Notes' 19/2: 6-75, 1982)
    With many illustrations and detailed examples from the literature

throughout the whole of the century, the author traces the development of timpani design and improvements to this instrument during that time.

871. BROWN, Theodore D. 'The Bass Drum Pedal: In the Beginning.' **Percussive Notes** 21/2: 28-32, 1983.
A history of the first bass drum pedals of the last century and their subsequent early development (incl. original old drawings).

872. CABA, G.C. **United States Military Drums; 1845-1865: A Pictorial Survey.** Harrisburg, Pennsilvania, Civil War Antiques, 1977, 145 p.

873. CHAPMAN, Clifford 'The Development of Mallet Keyboard Percussion from the late 18th through the early 20th Centuries.' **Percussionist** 12/2: 54-64, 1975.
This study refers mainly to the history of these instruments within the orchestral situation.The first part traces xylophones (and marimba) and Glockenspiel (chimes) back to the time before Mozart's "The Magic Flute", while part two stretches from "The Magic Flute" to Stravinsky's "Petrushka."

874. CLARK, W.J. 'The World's First Piano.' **Clavier** 14/1: 38-41, 1975.
Describes the piano and the hammered dulcimer, especially in reference to the Santur of the Persian musician A.B. Farabi (c. 9th century) and its further development.

875. ENGLAND, W. 'The History of the Xylophon and the Marimba.' **Percussionist** 8/3: 85-93, 1971.

876. FARMER, Henry **Handel's Kettledrums.** London, Methuen, 1951, 109 p. (Limited ed.)
Discusses various aspects of percussion instruments in British military music of the 17th and 18th centuries.

877. FINGER, G. 'The History of the Timpani.' **Percussionist** 11/3: 101-6, 1974.
Very basic and sketchy article.

878. GEIRINGER, Karl **Instruments in the History of Western Music.** New York, Oxford Univ. Press, 1978.

879. HARDING, J.R. 'The Bull-Roarer in History and Antiquity.' **African Music** 5/3: 40-2, 1973-74.

880. HOLDSWORTH, C. 'The Drum Kit; its Evolution.' (3 parts) **Crescendo International** 11: 39, Aug.; 11: 39, Sep.; 11: 39-40, Oct. 1972.

881. HOWELL, S. 'Paulus Paulirinus of Prague on Musical Instruments.' **Journal of the American Musical Instruments Society** 5-6: 9-36, 1980-81.
Scholars of early music should find some items of interest with regard to early percussion instruments. The article describes (and translates) part of the section on musical instruments of "Liber virginti artium" (1459-1463), which the author claims to be the first literal description of contemporary instruments in use at that time.

882. HOWLAND, Harold 'The Vibraphone: A summary of historical observation with a catalogue of selected solo and small ensemble

literature.' **Percussionist** 15/1: 20-40, 1977.
This continues the earlier article by Jaquelin Meyer on the early development of the vibraphone ('Percussionist' 13/2: 38-47, 1976), with observations on the Deagan instruments (1927-1941) and the contribution of Clair Omer Musser, followed by developments since 1945, and an extensive catalogue of literature as well as a bibliography.

883. JACOB, I.G. 'The Constructional Development of the Marimba.' (4 parts) **Percussionist** 11/1: 31-5, 1973; 11/2: 72-6, 1974; 11/3: 121-7, 1974; 11/4: 145-52, 1974.

884. KIRBY, Percival Robson **The Kettledrums.** London, O.U.P., 1930.

885. LAMBERT, James 'The Development of the Timpani through the Baroque Era.' **Percussionist** 10/3: 42-6, 1972.

886. LARRICK, G.H. 'Percussion: its Status from Antiquity to the Modern Era.' **Percussionist** 6/2: 42-9, 1968.

887. LEACH, Joel 'The Dulcimer.' **The Consort** No.25: 390-5, 1968-69.
A basic, illustrated article on the history of this instrument, including some tuning examples.

888. LEVINE, Dave '1957-1982: A Perspective of Drumset Percussion and the Plastic Drumhead.' **Percussive Notes** 20/2: 41-8, 1982.
An article depicting the development of the instruments (with the discussions centering on the drum head), as well as a historical summary of styles, famous players and their contributions to the various musical styles.

889. MEYER, Jaqueline 'Early History and Development of the Vibes.' **Percussionist** 13/2: 38-47, 1976.
[Covers the development of the instrument from 1916 to 1936.]

890. MILLER, Ben F. 'A brief History of the Cymbal from Antiquity to the Renaissance.' **Percussionist** 11/2: 46-51, 1974.
This essay gives information on the history of the design and use of cymbals in the ancient times in Mesopotamia and Egypt, Israel, Greece and Rome, India and Tibet, China and Japan, and also Europe in the Middle Ages and Renaissance.

891. MONTAGU, Jeremy **The World of Medieval and Renaissance Musical Instruments.** Newton Abbot, David & Charles, 1976, 136 p. [Contains only very little on percussion instruments.]

892. MONTAGU, Jeremy **The World of Baroque and Classical Musical Instruments.** Newton Abbot, David & Charles, 1979, 136 p.
This only offers a small amount of information on, and some illustrations of, percussion instruments.

893. MONTAGU, Jeremy **The World of Romantic and Modern Musical Instruments.** Newton Abbot, David & Charles, 1981, 136 p.
The chapter on percussion instruments (pp 107-121) has a brief introduction on the evolution of percussion in the 19th century, and then details the development of individual instruments and their orchestral uses into the 20th century. The timpani receives a reasonable coverage

(5 pages), with the rest of the instruments (including keyboard percussion and accessory instruments) sharing the remainder of the illustrated pages.

894. MUNROW, David **Instruments of the Middle Ages and Renaissance.** London, O.U.P., 1976, 97 p.
Contains just six pages on percussion instruments, but includes excellent photographs and drawings.

895. PIMENTEL, Linda 'The Aristocracy of the Manufactured Marimbas.' **Percussive Notes** 21/1: 61-4, 1982.
A short history of manufacturers, types, constructions and characteristics of marimbas over the years.

896. READ, Danny 'The Evolution of the Drum Set.' (2 parts) **Modern Drummer** 5/8: 18-21, 1981; 6/1: 26-9,68+, 1982.
In this well-illustrated article we can follow the development of the complete drum set in Part 1, and Part 2 portrays the evolution of the individual components separately (i.e. snare drum, bass drum, tom toms, cymbals, hi-hat, pedal and drum heads).

897. RUGG, M. 'Early Californian Dulcimers.' [hammered dulcimers] **Frets** 2: 62, Feb. 1980.

898. SACHS, Curt **The History of Musical Instruments.** New York, W.W.Norton & Co., 1940, 505 p.
A major pioneering work on history, but limited application to percussion instruments.

899. SCHNEIDER, Walter C. 'Percussion Instruments of the Middle Ages.' **Percussionist** 15/3: 106-17, 1978.
This authoritative paper aims to "review existing information, present additional information, and suggest possible playing techniques". It discusses the tabor, some larger military drums, Naggara (clay drums, and forerunners of the timpani), tambourine, Brummtopf (modern Cuica), cymbals, triangle, wooden instruments (incl. xylophone), and also has a bibliography.

900. SOEBBING, H.W. 'The Development of the Snare Drum.' **Percussionist** 2/3: 4-7, 1965.

901. TANNIGEL, F. & PEINKOFER, K. 'Vom Ur-kult bis zum Percussion Ensemble; Werden und Wesen des Schlagzeuges.' (3 parts) **Das Orchester** 28: 487-92, June; 28: 697-701, Sep.; 29: 333-8, Apr., 1980+1981. [German]
This three-part series gives an authoritative if condensed overview of the development of percussion instruments from their first appearance up to the present. In the first part we read about the most common uses in the cultures of Babylon, the early Chinese, Japanese, in India and Indonesia, and Africa. It also defines how Western composers utilized some of these instruments. Part two follows the evolution of percussion in Western Art music from the Middle Ages to early Stravinsky, with special reference to Berlioz, early jazz drumming, Debussy, and the Turkish influence.
Part three deals with the rise of percussion in the 20th century, how various composers have utilized it in their music, and the different Non-

Western influences of instruments and techniques on our "Art" music. Examples thereof include E. Satie, D. Milhaud, the early use of ethnic percussion by C. Orff, the work of E. Varese, O. Messiaen, P. Boulez, K. Stockhausen, the influence of jazz (R. Liebermann), and others.

902. WHITE, C.L. 'Tympani or Timpani?' (Origin of the instruments and their names) **Percussionist** 9/3: 67-70, 1972.

# CHAPTER 10.

## PERCUSSION IN HISTORY:

### (b) Development of Performance Practices and Techniques.

903. ALTENBURG, J.E. **Versuch einer Anleitung zur heroisch-musikalischen Trompeter - und Paukenkunst.** Leipzig, Deutscher Verlag fuer Musik, 1972, 156 p. (Facsimile of 1795 ed.)

904. ALTENBURG, J.E. **Trumpeters' and Kettledrummers' Art.** Nashville, Brass Press, 1974, 168 p. (English ed.; reprint of 1795 ed.)
    Contains an interesting - if very brief - chapter on timpani playing of the time (1795).

905. ARBEAU, (?) **Orchesography.** New York, Dover Press, 1967. (first publ. 1588)
    This is a translation (by Evans) of this French book (originally published in 1588 ) and contains the earliest known method for drummers.

906. ASHWORTH, Charles **New and Complete System of Drumming.** Williamsburg, VA, Drummer's Assistant, 1966.
    This is an edited reprint (by Georg Carroll) of the original title, and was the first military drum method in the U.S. (see also J.K. Galm, 'Percussionist' 7/2: 47, 1969).

907. BENVENGA, Nancy 'Mozartian Drumming.' [re timpani] **Music and Musician** 19: 30+, June 1971.

908. BLADES, James 'The Orchestral Instruments of Percussion.'
    In BAINES, Anthony **Musical Instruments through the Ages,** London, Penguin Books, 1961, 383 p. (revised in 1969)
    (For annotation see same entry in Chapter 10/a.)

909. BOWLES, Edmund 'On Using Proper Timpani in the Performance of Baroque Music.' **Journal of the American Musical Instruments Society** 2: 56-68, 1976. (Reprinted in 'Percussionist' 17/2: 55-62, 1980)
    A plea to percussionists and conductors to act on today's knowledge of old instruments and match the timpani to other "old" instruments. Gives detailed descriptions of differences in construction and tone between old and new drums.

910. BROWN, Theodore D. 'The Evolution of early Jazz Drumming.' **Percussionist** 7/2: 39-44, 1969. (Reprinted in 'The Instrumentalist' 27: 47-8, Feb. 1973)
    For a very extensive coverage on this subject see the author's thesis on jazz drumming in this chapter (next entry).

911. BROWN, Theodore D. **A History and Analysis of Jazz Drumming to 1942.** Ph.D. Thesis, University of Michigan, Dept. of Music, 1976, 617 p. (Diss.

Abst. 37: 6128A, April 1977)
This study looks at three areas:
(1) The musical influence of Africa on jazz drumming;
(2) American and European military and dance drumming in the U.S. before 1900;
(3) 20th Century jazz drumming, which includes major changes in styles and their leading drummers (Part 3 takes up most of this extensive study).

912. BROWN, Theodore D. 'Double Drumming.' **Percussive Notes** 20/1: 32-4, 1981.
This term principally refers to the old technique of playing the bass drum with the right hand, and the snare drum with the left hand.

913. BURKETT, E. & TRINKLE, S. 'A Review of the Johann Altenburg Treatise, "Essay on an Introduction to the Heroic and Musical Trumpeters' and Kettledrummers' Art", from the Timpanists' Perspective.' **N.A.C.W.P.I. Journal** 32/2: 19-27, 1984-85.

914. CAHN, William 'The Xylophone in Acoustic Recordings (1877-1929).' **Percussionist** 16/6: 133-52, 1979.
[Includes list of performers and bibliography]

915. DE PONTE, Niel 'Janissary Music and its Influence on the Use of Percussion in the Classical Orchestra.' **Woodwind World, Brass and Percussion** 15/4: 44+, 1976.

916. GANGWARE, E.B. **The History and Use of Percussion Instruments in Orchestration.** Ph.D. Thesis, Northwestern University, 1962, 292 p. (Diss. Abst. 23: 4707, June 1963)
This dissertation traces first of all the use of percussion instruments right back to very early history and finds an interesting continuity to the present day. The paper shows how much of this was lost in Europe during the Roman Empire, how percussion was slowly reinstated again in the orchestra, starting with the timpani, and its rise to importance in the 20th century.

917. GILBERT, D.K. 'Military Drumming in the British Isles 1450-1900.' **Percussionist** 8/1: 4-8, 1970.

918. GILBERT, D.K. 'Military Drumming during the American Revolution, 1775-83.' **Percussionist** 9/1: 1-5, 1971.

919. GILBERT, D.K. 'Rudimental Drumming in the USA, 1860-1900.' **Percussionist** 11/1: 12-4, 1973. [Early method books]

920. HILL, Thomas A. **The Drum.** New York, Franklin Watts (Keynote Books), 1975, 117 p.
The book tries to give a basic historical and musical overview of the evolvement of drumming in ancient times; in Africa and India; the rise of percussion in European (art) music; the strong impact of percussion in the 20th century (with special reference to Stravinsky, Bartok, and others); and the drums in jazz and rock music. The chapters are illustrated with some interesting photos, but are not very authoritative.

921. HOCHRAINER, Richard 'Beethoven's Use of the Timpani.' **Percussionist** 14/3: 66-71, 1977.

This is based on the original article (in German) which appeared in 'Das Orchester' 18, July-Aug. 1970, and praises the composer's bold and musical innovations in tuning and use in the orchestra.

922. HOEFER, G. 'History of the Drum in Jazz.' **Jazz** 4/10: 11-5+, 1965.
Does actually not deal with the instrument ("drum"), but is a listing of the main drummers who contributed to jazz music over the years up to the present.

923. HONG, Sherman 'Percussion in the Orchestra, 1750-1850.' **Percussionist** 8/4: 115-29, 1971.
This informative article follows the various main instruments through this period, giving many examples from the literature.

924. KRENTZER, Bill 'The Beethoven Symphonies: Innovations of an Original Style in Timpani Scoring.' **Percussionist** 7/2: 55-62, 1969.
Discussion by the author of Beethoven's contribution to the timpani gaining more recognition as a musical instrument in the orchestra.

925. LEVINE, Dave 'Percussion Instruments and Performance Practices in Beethoven's Music.' **Percussionist** 15/1: 1-6, 1977.

926. LEVINE, Dave '1957-1982: A Perspective of Drumset Percussion and the Plastic Drumhead.' **Percussive Notes** 20/2: 41-8, 1982.
(For annotation see same entry in Chapter 10/a.)

927. LONGYEAR, R.M. 'Percussion in the 18th Century Orchestra.' **Percussionist** 2/1-2: 1-5, 1965.
Basic article with reference to and description of several compositions of that period, mostly refering to the use of timpani.

928. LONGYEAR, R.M. 'The Domestication of the Snare Drum.' **Percussionist** 3/1: 1-5, 1965.
Delineates the transition of the snare drum from its use in military music to the symphony orchestra in the 18th and 19th century.

929. LONGYEAR, R.M. 'Percussion in Breitkopf's Thematic Catalogue, 1762-1878.' **Percussionist** 7/1: 1-5, 1969.

930. LONGYEAR, R.M. 'Altenburg's Observations (1795) on the Timpani.' **Percussionist** 7/3: 90-3, 1970.

931. LONGYEAR, R.M. 'Ferdinand Kauer's Percussion Enterprises.' **The Galpin Society Journal** 17: 2-7, May 1977.
Longyear presents some rather little-known (or forgotten) facts about F. Kauer's writings and orchestrations for percussion, which show some unusual, if not innovative, use of certain instruments.

932. MICHAELIDES, Solon **The Music of Ancient Greece: An Encyclopedia.** London, Faber, 1978.

933. MODERN DRUMMER (Edi.) 'The Great Jazz Drummers: 1900-1980.' (4 parts) **Modern Drummer** 4/3: 16-20+; 4/4: 16-9,51-5; 4/5: 22-5+, 1980; 4/6: 20-3+, 1980-81.
(For annotation see same entry in Chapter 7/a.)

934. MONTAGU, Jeremy 'Early Percussion Techniques.' **Early Music** 2/1: 20-4, 1974.
This paper demonstrates playing techniques and typical rhythms for tabor, nakers, tambourine, snare drum, timpani, triangle, cymbals and pellet bells.

935. MOORE, James L. 'How Turkish Janizary Band Music started our modern Percussion Section.' **Percussionist** 2/4: 7-13, 1965.
Describes the Janizary bands and their influence on the use of kettledrums, bass drum, cymbals and triangle; including bibliography.

936. NATIONAL SCHOOL OF VIBRACUSSION **Home Study Course in Vibracussion.** Chicago, National School of Vibracussion, 1917. (Twelve Lessons) (Subtitle: 'The Art of Playing Percussion-Vibrated Musical Instruments - For all Mallet Played Instruments.')

937. NISULA, Eric 'The Use of Percussion in Early Music.' **The Choral Journal (USA)** 20/8: 5-8, 1980.
Nisula contests the often held opinion that early music contained mainly regular ostinato rhythms (as advocated by Jeremy Montagu), and gives his reasons why it could (and should today) be performed less rigidly. He then proceeds to analyze the 16th century Spanish carol "Riu, riu", and presents some interesting and detailed possibilities for three percussion instruments accompanying the carol.

938. PETTERS, John 'Jazz Drumming: From New Orleans to Bebop.' (3 parts) **Jazz Journal International** 37/11: 6-8; 38/1: 16-7, 1984; 38/4: 14-5, 1984-1985.
A survey of the development of drumming styles and drummers, including discussions on Baby Dodds, Zutty Singleton, Tony Sbarbaro, Vic Berton, Gene Krupa, Sonny Greer, Chick Webb, Big Sid Catlett, Lionel Hampton, Jo Jones, Kenny Clarke, Buddy Rich, and others.

939. PFUNDT, Ernst **Paukenschule.** Leipzig, Breitkopf & Haertel, 1894.
[School for Timpani; in German]

940. POLLART, Gene 'The Use and Innovations of Percussion in the Works of J.S. Bach and Handel.' **Percussionist** 13/3: 75-81, 1976.
[Refers mainly to the use of kettle-drum]

941. PORTER, Lewis 'A historical Survey of Jazz Drumming Styles.' (2 parts) **Percussive Notes** 20/3: 42-3, 70+; 21/3: 46-7, 78, 1982.

942. POTTER, Samuel **The Art of Beating the Drum.** London, 1815.

943. SABLINSKIS, Paul **The Significance of Percussion in Contemporary Music between 1945 and 1970.** Masters Thesis, Univ. of Melbourne, 1982, 462 p.
(For annotation see same entry in Chapter 3/a.)

944. SACHS, Kurt **The Rise of Music in the Ancient World.** Norton, 1943, 324 p.

945. SANDMAN, Susan G. 'Indication of Snare-drum Technique in Philidor Collection MS 1163.' **The Galpin Society Journal** 30: 70-5, May 1977.
This refers to a manuscript, written in 1686, containing a collection of 91 short pieces (by various composers) for wind band - in combination with snare drum or timpani.

946. SCHULTZ, Thomas 'A History of Jazz Drumming.' **Percussionist** 16/3: 106-32, 1979.

Covers the development of jazz in New Orleans from the year 1900 to the various styles of around 1950. Drummers discussed in more detail include Baby Dodds, George Wettling, David Tough, Gene Krupa, Chick Webb, Cozy Cole, Buddy Rich, Jo Jones, Sidney Catlett, Kenny Clarke, Shelly Manne, and Elvin Jones.

947. SEELE, Otto 'Self Instruction for the Kettle Drums.' **Percussionist** 5/2: 253-9, 1967.

A historic article, written originally in 1895 in Leipzig, here literally translated from the German by Mervin Britton.

948. TANNER, Peter H. **Timpani and Percussion Writing in the Works of Hector Berlioz.** Ph.D. Thesis, The Catholic Univ. of America, 1967, 289 p. (Diss. Abst. 28: 2722A, Jan. 1968)

This paper is dedicated to the great advancements and innovations Hector Berlioz made in orchstration and part-writing for percussion. It discusses in detail the new concepts of tuning and timbral requirements for timpani, and the extensive and new artistic level to which many other percussion instruments were brought in his compositions. For example, the musical use of dynamics, percussion as solo instruments, creating new sounds like the bass drum roll, the use of suspended cymbals, and others.

949. WILSON, C.B. 'Some Remarks about Multiple Timpani and Berlioz.' **The Instrumentalist** 28: 55-6, Nov. 1973.

# CHAPTER 11.

# RESEARCH AND TECHNOLOGY:

## (a) Acoustics and Scientific Research.

950. ANDRUS, Donald **An Analysis of the Acoustics of Tam Tam Sounds.** D.M.A. Thesis, University of Illinois, 1968, 230 p. (Diss. Abst. 30: 352A, July 1969)

951. BALDWIN, John **Some Acoustical Properties of Triangles and their Relation to Performance Practices.** Ph.D. Thesis, Michigan State University, 1970, 164 p. (Diss. Abst. 31: 6091A-92A, May 1971)
The aim of this study was to find a basis from which to predict the sound quality of various triangles and cymbals, knowing the type and size of beaters and instruments. Recommendations are given for various obtainable sound generations.

952. BALDWIN, John 'Some Acoustical Properties of Triangles and Cymbals, and their Relation to Performance Practice.' (2 parts) **The School Musician** 42: 12-4, March; 42: 22+, May 1971.
This is based on the dissertation by the author (Michigan, 1970), listed above.

953. BALDWIN, John 'Some Acoustical Properties of Cymbals.' **Percussionist** 12/1: 15-28, 1974.
This is also taken from the author's dissertation (Michigan, 1970; listed above in this chapter), and contains many charts, graphs and detailed findings.

954. BASSET, I.G. 'Vibration and Sound of the Bass Drum.' **Percussionist** 19/3: 50-58, 1982.
(Not available for annotation)

955. BORK, I. & MEYER, J. 'On the Tonal Evaluation of Xylophones.' **Percussive Notes** 23/6: 48-57, 1985. (Translated by Thomas D. Rossing)
Scientific tests and evaluations were made in reference to the physical parameters which influence the pitch and timbre of the xylophone. The three areas of tests were in reference to tone, pitch impressions, and sound character of the instrument, and conclusions and recommendations are given with regard to tuning of bars.

956. DEARING, Jim 'Are Drums harming your Ears?' **Modern Drummer** 5/8: 25-8, 78-9+, 1981.
An informative article, which deals with this question under the following sub-headings: Physical Properties of Hearing, Will your Ears survive Drumming?, Problems of Hearing & Drumming, Which Drums hurt the Most?, What can you do?.

957. HANSELL, William & PUGH, Greg 'Natural vs. Synthetic - An Evaluation of Xylophone Bars.' **Percussive Notes** 20/1: 60,62-3, 1981.
    This article tries to point out the various differences between these two materials.

958. MOORE, James L. 'Percussion Acoustics; An Introductory Evaluation.' **Percussionist** 5/1: 218-20, 1967.

959. MOORE, James L. 'Percussion Acoustics; Some Basic Considerations.' **Percussionist** 6/3: 86-9, 1969.
    Briefly discusses the acoustic qualities of (1) membrane instruments, (2) wide solid autophone instruments, and (3) bar autophone instruments (including tuning problems of the latter).

960. MOORE, James L. **Acoustics of Bar Percussion Instruments.** Columbus, OH, Permus Publication, 1970, 164 p.
    A large and detailed book on this very specialized subject. Chapter II deals with the individual instruments, their bar characteristics, materials, ranges, mallets, etc. Chapter III is a "Literature Review" of articles and texts available which are related to this subject. Then there is a chapter on "Bar Tuning", one on "Identification of steady state and transient responses", a discussion of the "Results of experimental work", and a final "Summary and Recommendations" (for future work).

961. PAYSON, Al 'A Comparison Test of the Rosewood Bar vs. the Kelon Bar Xylophone.' **Percussive Notes** 14/2: 32-3, 1976.
    A report on a comparison test of five pieces being played (on both types of bars) behind a screen to an audience of percussionists, and the result of their findings.

962. POLLART, Gene 'A Study of Muscle Efficiency Comparing the Matched Grip and the Traditional Grip.' **Percussionist** 4/4: 174-84, 1967.

963. ROSSING, T.D. 'Acoustics of Percussion Instruments. (2 parts) **The Instrumentalist** 30: 55-9, May; 30: 62-5, June 1976.
    Part I at first discusses acoustic principles ("Behaviour of vibrating systems"), and then in more detail the vibrations of bars and the pitch of complex tones. Part II continues with chimes, vibrations of plates and tuned bells. Includes graphs and charts.

964. ROSSING, T.D. 'Acoustics of Tuned Bars.' **The Instrumentalist** 31: 60-2+, Oct. 1976.
    This is a continuation of the author's earlier article (see entry above) on acoustics of percussion instruments. Here he deals specifically with the glockenspiel, marimba, xylophone and vibes.

965. ROSSING, T.D. 'Acoustics of Percussion Instruments.' (7 parts) **Percussionist** 19/3: 6-83, 1982.
    A series of new articles in this special issue on the subject of acoustics of various percussion instruments:
    'Acoustics of Bar Percussion Instruments', pp 6-17.
    'Acoustics of Timpani', pp 18-31.
    'Vibrations of Plates, Gongs & Cymbals', pp 31-41.
    'Chimes and Bells', pp 42-50.
    'Acoustics of Indian Drums' (with W.A. Sykes), pp 58-67.
    'Nonlinear Effects in Percussion Instruments'

(Plates and Gongs), pp 68-72.
'Acoustics of Gamelan Instruments', pp 73-83.

966. ROSSING, T.D. **The Science of Sound.** Reading, MA, Addison-Wesley
Publ. Co., 1983, 637 p.
This is a major and very extensive work on scientific research, facts
and findings on all aspects of sound, and especially with regard to all
musical parameters. Part III, 'The Acoustics of Musical Instruments", is
a 28-page chapter on percussion instruments with detailed findings of
most groups of instruments. Of special interst will also be Part VI 'The
Acoustics of Rooms', Part VII "Electronic Music', and Part VIII
'Environmental Noise'. Each of the 33 chapters also has a list of
references, a glossary of terms, and a list of questions and problems, as
well as detailed graphs and illustrations.

967. ROSSING, T.D. & KVISTAD, G. 'Acoustics of Timpani: Preliminary
Studies.' **Percussionist** 13/3: 90-8, 1976.
Report on measurements of acoustical properties of three timpani
(32", 26" & 20") with plastic heads. Debate of overtones and
fundamentals, vibration frequencies, etc.

968. RYNIKER, Douglas 'Dealing with the Aches and Pains of Drumming.'
**Modern Drummer** 5/5: 29-30+, 1981.
A rare article, offering much experience and advice on prevention and
cure of physical problems arising from drumming. It deals with various
parts of the body, including feet, knees, hands, fingers, wrists, elbows,
shoulders and ears.

969. SIWE, Thomas 'Percussion Growth, Research, and the Future.'
**Percussionist** 2/1-2: 6-9, 1965.
Debates the problems of reliable and practical information on
percussion; what instruments should be included in the percussion family,
the need for a new classification system, which (the author thinks) could
be based on the instruments' sound.

970. STAUFFER, D.W. 'A Motion and Muscle Study of Percussion Technique.'
**Percussionist** 5/3: 290-98, 1968. (Reprinted and abridged from the
U.S.Naval School of Music Clinic Manual, 1959)
With this study the author intends to "present the various principles
underlying the movements required in percussion performance". It
debates motion and muscle efficiency with relevance to the single stroke
and the repetitive stroke.

971. STOUTMEYER, G.L. 'A Detailed Description and Acoustical Study of the
Marimba and Xylophone.' (2 parts) **Percussionist** 9/2: 35-7; 9/3: 59-62,
1972.
The author's objective of this study was to define the difference in
tone quality between the xylophone and marimba, based on scientific
acoustic tests.

972. WHEELER, Douglas 'Bar Materials for Xylophones and Marimbas.'
**Woodwind World, Brass and Percussion** 20/7: 12-3, 1981.
Discussion on the different materials available, especially rosewood
and synthetics, their pros and contras in sound, cost and durability.

973. WHEELER, D.B. **An Analytical Study of Bass Drum Sounds.** D.A. Thesis, Univ. of Northern Colorado, 1982, 173 p. (Diss. Abst. 43: 2826A, March 1983)

Sound experiments were made with a specially designed and built electro-mechanical beating device, which was able to execute sixteen different types of strokes, each with various beaters. The recordings were analyzed with the help of a computer, and findings were then presented regarding the acoustical properties of the bass drum.

# CHAPTER 11.

## RESEARCH AND TECHNOLOGY:

### (b) Sound Recording Techniques and Electronic Developments.

974. BETTINE, Michael 'The Art of Drum Computing.' **Modern Drummer** 8/12: 106-7, 1984.
Short article on basic considerations of this subject.

975. BROOKS, Clyde 'How to prepare a Drum Set for Recording.' **Percussive Notes** 14/3: 20-21, 1976.
Article taken from the author's book: 'The Recording Drummer', dealing briefly with acoustic hints and problems of the individual parts of the drum set.

976. BROOKS, Clyde **The Recording Drummer.** (Edi. by Joel Leach)
New York, Award Music, 1977, 88 p.
A useful book for the drummer wishing to gain knowledge about recording techniques. The first part (28 pages) deals with the preparations of the drum set for recording, mixing techniques, a list of studio terms, and other hints. The remainder of the book consists of examples of 18 drum charts, covering several types of popular rhythms, how they are normally written and how they actually should be played.

977. BROOKS, Clyde 'The Drum Set in the Studio.' **Percussive Notes** 20/1: 42-5, 1981.
An updated article on the same subject as the author's previous article (see 'Percussive Notes' 14/3: 20-21, 1976).

978. BURNS, Roy & FARRIS, Joey **Studio Funk Drumming.** Fullerton, CA, Rhythmic Publications, 1981(?).
(For annotation see same entry in Chapter 6.)

979. CHANDLER, James Jr. 'Electronic Insight: Drum Pickups.' **Modern Drummer** 9/12: 50-52, 1985.
The author explains clearly how to make one's own personalized electronic drums, by using various inexpensive, simple electronic devices and parts; what to use as controllers, how to use them and interface them with other equipment (e.g. keyboards, light controllers, etc.).

980. CHRISTIAN, Bobby & PAYSON, Al **In the Studio - Percussion Recording Techniques.** Park Ridge, IL, Payson Percussion Products, 1980, 74 p.
(For annotation see same entry in Chapter 5/f.)

981. COBHAM, Billy 'Drum Machine Techniques.' (4 parts) **Keyboard Magazine** 11: 74, Apr.; 11: 61, May; 11: 74, June; 11: 31, July, 1985.
Four articles with the following titles: (1) 'Latin-Rock Rhythms', (2) 'Two Contemporary Rhtyhms - Techno-Pop & Break Dance', (3) 'Jazz Rhythms from the Top', (4) 'Basic Rock Beats in 4/4 & 3/4.' (The series is being continued.)

982. COLBERT, P. 'Roland rocks Rhythm (Roland CR 8000 CompuRhythm).' **Melody Maker** 56:35, 12. Sept. 1981.

983. COLBERT, P. '1982's First Star (Roland TR 606 Drum Synthesizer).' **Melody Maker** 56: 57, 19.Dec. 1981.

984. ERNST, David 'Simple Percussion Modifications.' **Modern Drummer** 4/2: 38-9, 1980.
Shows "various methods by which percussion instruments may be modified via electronic devices, including (by) synthesizers", with special application to live performance.

985. ERNST, David 'Percussion Interfaces.' **Modern Drummer** 4/6: 96-7, 1980.
A continuation of the earlier article, in as far as automatically controlled modifications are discussed here.

986. FELDSTEIN, Sandy **Roland Drum Machine Rhythm Dictionary.** Sherman Oaks, CA, Alfred Publ. Co., 1984.
This text explains clearly and to the point how to use one of several Roland machines, lists over 100 rhythmic patterns in many styles, including some ethnic dances and transcriptions of several popular drummers. The rhythms are also notated in drum set notation apart from the graphs relating to the Roland models TR-606, DR-110, and adaptions for TR-707 and TR-909.

987. HENRY, E. 'Build an Electric Drum Pad.' **Polyphony** 10/1: 20-3, 1984.

988. JACOBS, Kenneth 'The "Plugged-In" Percussionist.' **Percussive Notes** 19/2: 40-46, 1981.
Explains the synthezised sound production and possibilities of electronic percussion instruments. Includes a good glossary of terms.

989. LEVINE, Dave 'Electronic Drums - A Head of our Times.' **Downbeat** 52: 53-5, Jan. 1985.
Describes briefly several makes and models of electronic drum systems (incl. Oberheimer, Tama, Simmons SDS 28, Roland MIDI).

990. LISOWSKI, J.A. 'Optical Disc Drum Machine.' **Polyphony** 10/2: 22-4, 1985.

991. LONDIN, L. 'A Positive Bass Drum Sound.' **Modern Drummer** 8/11: 80-1, 1984.
[Studio Recording Techniques]

992. MATTINGLY, Rick 'Equipment Highlights of NAMM 84.' **Modern Drummer** 8/10: 22-9, 1984.
Describes the latest equipment on show at this exhibition in Chicago (June 1984), in the categories of cymbals, electronics, drums and sticks.

993. MURO, D. 'The Musician and the Electronic Medium: Electronic Drums, live Performance Synthesis.' **International Musician** 81: 1+, July 1982.

994. ROGERS DRUM CO. 'Rogers introduces Malletron - Electronic Mallet Instruments.' **The Music Trades** 118: 59, May 1970.

995. RUMBLEY, J.E. 'Techniques and Equipment for the Studio Percussionist.' **Woodwind World, Brass and Percussion** 17/2: 28-9, 1978.

Basic advice regarding attitude, presentations, considerations about equipment, and recording techniques (for popular music).

996. SAMUELS, David 'Miking for Mallet Instruments.' [bar percussion] **Modern Drummer** 8/1: 80, 1984.

997. SAYDLOWSKI, Bob Jr. 'A Look at the Manufacturers of Electronic Percussion Instruments.' **Percussive Notes** 19/2: 46-9, 1981.

Notes the state of development at the manufacturing houses of Syndrum, Synare, Pearl Syncussion, and Simmons.

998. SAYDLOWSKI, Bob Jr. 'Drum Machines: A Comparative Look.' **Modern Drummer** 7/12: 24-7, 1983.

A description and evaluation of the following models: Linn Drum, Oberheim DX, E-Mu Drumulator, MXR 185, Korg KPR-77, Yamaha MR 10, and JTG SR-88.

999. SAYDLOWSKI, Bob Jr. 'Cano Modulus - Electronic Drums.' **Modern Drummer** 8/4: 34, 1984.

1000. SAYDLOWSKI, Bob Jr. 'Electronic Kits.' (4 parts) **Modern Drummer** 9/4: 36-8; 9/4: 66-7; 9/7: 34-6; 9/11: 46-53, 1985.

This report gives a description of the new electronic drums by Pearl, Tama, Gretsch, Ultimate Percussion, Desert Drums, E-Mu Systems, and the Simmons SDS 9.

1001. STEVENS, Mark 'Audio Engineers on Miking & Recording Drums.' (2 parts) **Modern Drummer** 6/9: 10-21, 79+, 1982; 7/1: 18-21, 76+, 1983.

This article is really a series of interviews with seven well-known American recording engineers. They discuss choice, quality and placing of microphones for various types of drums and musical styles.

1002. SWENSON, J. 'Ralph McDonald: The Sound of a Syndrum.' **Rolling Stone** No. 258: 74-6, Feb.9, 1978.

1003. ZARETSKY, S. 'How to get a Great Drum Sound (for Recording).' **Songwriter Magazine** 5: 56-7, Apr. 1980.

# CHAPTER 12.

## AFRICAN MUSIC:

### (a) Instruments.

1004. AKPABOT, S. 'The Talking Drums of Nigeria.' **African Music** 5/4: 36-40, 1975-76.
A short article on the wooden drum, pot drum, calabash drum, hourglass drum, tom-tom, and xylophone drum.

1005. AROZARENA, Pierre 'Notes on some Mossi Drums of Upper Volta.' **The World of Music** 23/1: 26-33, 1981.
Discusses construction, meaning and beliefs relating to the three most important drums: Bendre, Lunga and Gangaogo.

1006. BEIER, U. 'The talking Drums of the Yoruba (Nigeria).' **African Music** 1/1: 29-31, 1954.

1007. BERLINER,Paul **The Soul of the Mbira: Music Traditions of the Shona People of Zimbabwe.** Berkeley, University of California, 1978, 245 p.
This extensive study is about many aspects of musical tradition: the instrument itself (construction, tuning, technique), its role in tradition and society, and the wider historic and social background of musical activities of the Shona people. The original thesis was published in 1974 by Wesleyan University, and it recommends two records as musical illustration (Nonesuch: H-72054, H-72077), which also contain a photographic supplement.

1008. BURT-BECK, C. **Playing the African Mbira.** New York, Ludlow Music, 1983(?), 32 p.
(Not available for annotation)

1009. CARRINGTON, J.F. **Talking Drums of Africa.** New York, Negro University Press, 1969, 96 p. (Orig. London, Carey Kingsgate Press, 1949)
This slender book explains the various types of drums used to send messages with, and how, why and when this is done.

1010. CARRINGTON, J.F. 'The Talking Drums of Africa.' **Scientific American** 90-94, December 1971.

1011. CHAPPELL, Robert J. 'The Amadina Xylophone: the Instrument, its Music and Procedures for its Construction.' **Percussionist** 15/2: 60-85, 1978.
A detailed article on this xylophone, one of the principal instruments of the Buganda tribe in Uganda. Thorough discussion of the music (scales and tuning), performance practice, and various aspects of the music (structure, rhythms, etc.). This is followed by exacting instructions on the construction procedures of the xylophone.

1012. CHENOWETH, Vida 'Marimbas of the Congo.' **Percussionist** 2/3: 15-6, 1965.

1013. DIETZ, B.W. & OLATUNJI, M.B. **Musical Instruments of Africa (Their nature, use and place in the life of a deeply musical people).** New York, Day, 1965, 115 p. (Includes a 7" record)
A good, basic book on the instruments, well illustrated, containing also an interesting chapter on "Body Percussion."

1014. DONALDSON, B. 'Talking Drums of Africa.' **Music Journal** 32: 40-1, May 1974.

1015. ECHEZONA, W. **Ibo Musical Instruments in Ibo Culture.** Ph.D. Thesis, Michigan State University, 1963, 214 p. (Diss. Abst. 25: 1246-7, Aug. 1964)
Specializes on the instruments themselves, with little historic background. The construction, technique, their use and meaning is demonstrated, and the dissertation also contains a plea for the preservation of Ibo musical culture.

1016. ECHEZONA, W. 'Ibo Musical Instruments.' **Music Educator's Journal** 50/5: 23-7+, 1964.
An illustrated article, describing the construction, playing techniques, and relationships to the music of several instruments, in particular the talking drum, gongs and pot drums.

1017. FAGG, Bernard 'The Discovery of Multiple Rock Gongs in Nigeria.' **African Music** 1/3: 6-9, 1956.

1018. GILBERT, Dorothy 'The Lukumbi.' **African Music** 1/2: 21-3, 1955.
[A six-toned slit drum of the Batetela]

1019. HYSLOP, G. **Musical Instruments of East Africa.** Nairobi, Nelson Africa, 1975, 64 p. (Vol.1: Kenya)
The chapter on percussion imstruments (pp 46-61) depicts the drums used in Kenya, describes their playing techniques, the traditional groupings of the drums, and some of the rhythmic patterns.

1020. JOHNSTON, T.F. 'How to make a Tsonga Xylophone.' **Music Educator's Journal** 63: 38-49, Nov. 1976.
Detailed instructions on building the xylophone, and transcriptions of seven Tsonga Mohambi pieces.

1021. JONES, A.M. **Studies in African Music. (2 vols.)** London, O.U.P., 1959, 295 p & 238 p.
A major publication on African music for its time (1959), and original and pioneering in many aspects, but by today's knowledge and level of research perhaps slightly outdated in some areas of approach, analysis and rhythmic transcriptions. Vol.I consists of the text, whilst Vol.II contains the musical scores of dance ensembles. The book is not a fair representation of African music on the whole, but mainly of West Africa, and in particular of the Ewe people.

1022. JONES, A.M. 'Indonesia and Africa: The Xylophone as a Culture-Indicator.' **African Music** 2/3: 36-47, 1961. (Comments by A.T. Tracey: pp 75-7)

1023. JONES, A.M. **Africa and Indonesia: The Evidence of the Xylophone and other Musical and Cultural Factors.** Leiden, Netherlands, E.J. Brill, 1971, 286 p. (First Ed. 1964)

A large part of the book presents detailed studies of the tunings, scales and construction of xylophones, as well as some other instruments. The rest of the book presents other evidence to connect the musical cultures of the two geographical areas.

1024. KIRBY, Percival Robson **The Musical Instruments of the Native Races of South Africa.** Johannesburg, Witwatersrand Univ. Press, 1953, 285 p.

1025. KUBIK, G. 'The Endara Xylophone of Bukonjo (Uganda).' **African Music** 3/1: 43-8, 1962.
    Contains a description of the instrument and the characteristics of the music studied (rhythm and scales).

1026. KUBIK, G. 'Discovery of a Trough Xylophone in Northern Mozambique.' **African Music** 3/2: 11-4, 1963.

1027. KUBIK, G. 'Musical Bowls in South-Western Angola.' **African Music** 5/4: 98-104, 1975-76.

1028. MOYLE, Richard 'Tongan Musical Instruments.' (2 parts) **The Galpin Society Journal** 19: 64-7, 1976; 30: 86-111, 1977.
    Part I discusses and describes some idiophones, whereas Part II deals primarily with idiophones and some membranophones, and includes a useful bibliography.

1029. NKETIA, J.H. **Our Drums and Drummers.** Ghana, Ghana Publishing House, 1968.
    [Not available for annotation; out of print.]

1030. NODAL, Roberto 'The Social Evolution in the Afro-Cuban Drum.' **The Black Perspectives in Music** 11/2: 157-77, 1983.
    The author presents a "brief history of the Afro-Cuban drum from colonial times to the present". Discusses history and construction of various sacred (ritual) and profane drums.

1031. NORBORG, A. **Musical Instruments from Africa South of the Sahara.** Copenhagen, Musikhistorisk Museum og Carl Claudius' Samling, 1982, 91 p.

1032. PRICE, Christine **Talking Drums of Africa.** New York, Charles Scribner's Sons, 1973.
    [Not available for annotation]

1033. SCHLICH, Victor 'The Drums of Africa.' **Modern Drummer** 5/6: 26-7+, 1981.
    Very basic, limited overview of some of the many types of drums in Africa and their uses.

1034. THIEME, D.L. **A Descriptive Catalogue of Yoruba Musical Instruments.** Ph.D. Thesis, The Catholic Univ. of America, 1969, 452 p. (Diss. Abst. 30: 2067A, Nov. 1969)
    Thieme portrays and illustrates 108 instruments, their performance practices, techniques, some historic background and social importance.

1035. THOMPSON, D. 'The Marimbula, an Afro-Caribbean Sanza.' **Yearbook for Inter American Musical Research** 7: 103-16, 1971.

1036. TRACEY, A. 'The Tuning of Mbira Reeds - A Contribution to the Craft of Mbira Making.' **African Music** 4/3: 96-100, 1969.

1037. TRACEY, Hugh **Chopi Musicians: Their Music, Poetry and Instruments.** London, O.U.P., 1970, 193 p. (First publ. in Oxford, 1948)
    Mostly concerns itself with the poetry, songs and dances of the Chopi (Bantu people of South-East Africa), but also includes detailed description of the Timbila xylophones (construction and tuning).

1038. VAN OVEN, C. 'The Kondi of Sierra Leone.' [re Mbira] **African Music** 5/3: 77-85, 1973-74.
    The "kondi" is the Sierra Leone version of the mbira, and the author discusses this instrument, its tuning, sound characteristics, playing techniques and music.

1039. WOODSON, C.D. **The Atumpan Drum in Asante: A Study of their Art and Technology.** Ph.D. Thesis, Los Angeles, University of California, 1983, 792 p. (Diss. Abst. 45: 15A, July 1984)
    A comprehensive study on the construction, social and historic background, playing technique, acoustic properties, and music of the Atumpan drum - "a pair of single-headed, goblet-shaped membranophones with a sound modifier" - talking drums of the Asante in Ghana.

1040. WOODSON, C.D. 'Appropriate Technology in the Construction of Traditional African Musical Instruments in Ghana.' **Selected Reports in Ethnomusicology** 5: 216-48, 1984.
    The first part of this essay presents the current situation of attitudes, needs and abilities in manufacturing traditional instruments in Ghana today. This is then applied to the example of how to construct the Atumpan drum, in a lengthy, detailed, illustrated and technical report. Woodson concludes with comments on implications with regard to performance, education and ethnomusicology.

# CHAPTER 12.

## AFRICAN MUSIC:

### (b) Music Theory and Practice.

1041. AKPABOT, S. 'Standard Drum Patterns in Nigeria.' **African Music** 5/1: 37-9, 1971.
A brief article, discussing some basic rhythmic patterns.

1042. ANDERSON, L.A. 'Multipart Relationships in Xylophone and Tuned-Drum Traditions in Buganda.' **Selected Reports in Ethnomusicology** 5:120-44, 1984.
The author describes and analyzes how the melodic and rhythmic patterns interlock (separately and together) to produce new rhythms and/or melodic patterns (and complete realizations), which are often not present in the individual parts.

1043. AVORGBEDOR, Daniel 'Double Bell Technique among the People of Ghana.' **Percussive Notes** 20/1: 77-80, 1981.
Explains briefly the three different types of instruments found in Ewe, and discusses four techniques used on the double bell (Gankogui) and some general considerations.

1044. BLACKING, John 'Some Notes on the Theory of African Rhythm advanced by Erich von Hornbostel.' **African Music** 1/2: 12-20, 1955.

1045. BLACKING, John 'Patterns of Nsenga Kalimba Music.' **African Music** 2/4: 26-43, 1961.

1046. BROWN, Allen 'African Drumming.' **Percussionist** 12/2: 67-76, 1975.
The subtitle reads:'Three demonstration pieces that help your students get the feel of this unique art'. Without any technical analysis, the author explains some typical characteristics of African drumming rhythms and provides three pieces for drum ensembles, incl. variations for the master drummer.

1047. CHAPPELL, Robert J. 'The Amadina Xylophone: the Instrument, its Music and Procedures for its Construction.' **Percussionist** 15/2: 60-85, 1978.
(For annotation see same entry in Chapter 12/a.)

1048. CHERNOFF, J.M. **African Rhythm and African Sensibility.** Chicago, Chicago Univ. Press, 1979, 261 p.
The subtitle is: 'Aesthetics and Social Action in African Musical Idioms'. Chapter 2 ("Music in Africa") could be of special interest to the percussionist as it includes examples and dicussions of rhythms and forms in drum ensembles, which are expanded in Chapter 3 ("Style in Africa").

1049. COMBS, F. Michael 'An Experience in African Drumming.' **Percussionist** 11/3: 106-115, 1974.

128

The author gives his account of some styles of drumming and xylophone playing which he studied in Ghana (West Africa). The article is very general and basic, the main part consisting of transcriptions of seven dance rhythms (for ensemble), which are badly notated and carry no explanations.

1050. COMBS, F. Michael 'West African Drums and Dance Rhythms.' **Woodwind World, Brass and Percussion** 14/4: 35-8+, 1975.
This is a very similar article to an earlier one by this author (see entry above in this chapter), but has ten transcriptions of West African dance rhythms, most of them different ones from the earlier examples.

1051. COOKE, P. 'Ganda Xylophone Music: Another Approach.' **African Music** 4/4: 62-80, 1970.
A comparison study of the xylophone music and song texts, thereby trying to show how the structure of the music is related to that of the texts.

1052. EKWUEME, L.E. 'Structural Levels of Rhythm and Forms in African Music with particular Reference to the West Coast.' **African Music** 5/4: 27-35, 1975-76.
The author tries to demonstrate a close structural connection between Western and African music (in this case in reference to the West Coast). Many theorists advocate three levels in the structure of Western music (background, middleground and foreground), and so, claims the author, has the rhythm of African music three levels: the background (like the skeleton of the structure), the middleground containing rhythmic motives (patterns), and the foreground (non-structural) provided by decorative motives (e.g. by the master drummer).

1053. EKWUEME, I.E. 'Analysis and Analytic Techniques in African Music: A Theory of Melodic Scales.' **African Music** 6/1: 89-106, 1980.

1054. FAINI, P. 'African Rhythms for American Percussionists.' **The Instrumentalist** 35: 82-7, Oct. 1980.
An over-simplified exposure of some African rhythms to be played on the drum set and/or other percussion, suggestions for substitute instruments to imitate certain African ones, and some available music sources.

1055. FAINI, P. 'East African Percussion.' **Percussive Notes** 19/2: 68-70, 1981.
A short article on this (much less represented than West African) subject, in particular the "Nankasa" dance drum ensemble from Uganda. The four different drums are given a brief description, and the fairly simple dance patterns are notated.

1056. GALEOTA, Joseph 'Kinka.' **Percussive Notes** 23/4: 55-7, 1985.
'Kinka' is a type of dance music of the Ewe people of West Africa; origin, analysis and performance.

1057. GBEHO, Philip 'Beat of the Master Drum.' **West African Revue** 22/290: 1263-4, 1951.
[Brief and vague article]

1058. GBEHO, Philip 'Cross Rhythm in African Music.' **West African Revue** 23/292: 11-3, 1952.

Basic debate of the rhythm in the Agbeko dance, and some other, un-related musical background.

1059. GODSEY, L.D. **The Use of the Xylophone in the Funeral Ceremony of the Birifor of Northwest Ghana.** Thesis, Univ. of Calofornia, 1980, 348 p.
(Not available; see following entry for same subject.)

1060. GODSEY, L.D. 'The Use of Variation in Birifor Funeral Music.' **Selected Reports in Ethnomusicology** 5: 67-80, 1984.
This delineates the musical nature and function of the "Kogyl" xylophone used especially at funerals of the Birifor people of Northwest Ghana. The author also relates his experience of learning the instruments, and concludes with a complete transcription of a performance.

1061. JOHNSTON, T.F. 'Shangana-Tsonga Drum and Bow Rhythms.' **African Music** 5/1: 59-72, 1971.
Explains the drum rhythms of various schools and shows how each belongs to a certain type of vocal music and social event of the Shangana-Tsonga (Central-East Africa).

1062. JOHNSTON, T.F. 'Mohambi Xylophone Music of the Shangana-Tsonga.' **African Music** 5/3: 86-93, 1973-74.
A brief description of the Mohambi xylophone, its style of playing, and analyzed transcriptions of seven traditional tunes.

1063. JONES, A.M. **Studies in African Music. (2 vols.)** London, O.U.P., 1959, 295 p & 238 p.
(For annotation see same entry in Chapter 12/a.)

1064. Jazz Forum (Editorial) 'The African Beat.' **Jazz Forum** No.11: 69-79, 1971.
A broad and sketchy article with a brief description of some instruments; a collection of various unrelated rhythms and melodies, all in relation to the "African Negroid" influence found in jazz music.

1065. KAUFFMAN, Robert 'African Rhythm: A Reassessment.' **Ethnomusicology** 24/3: 393-415, 1980.
The first part of this summarizing article discusses and relates some current theories on African rhythm, e.g. the theory of syncopation (and Hornbostel's); the common fast beat; the "standard pattern" (re A.M. Jones); African hemiola style; and rhythm in West African drum ensembles. Part two then takes a "macro - and micro perspective" of rhtyhm, with some notations of patterns and forms.

1066. KINNEY, S. 'Drummers in Dagbon: The Role of the Drummer in the Damba Festival.' **Ethnomusicology** 14/2: 258-65, 1970.

1067. KNIGHT, Roderic 'Mandinka Drumming.' **African Arts** 7/4: 25-35, 1974.

1068. KOETTING, James 'Analysis and Notation of West African Drum Ensembles.' **Selected Reports in Ethnomusicology** 1/3: 115-46, 1970.
A quote from the author's own introduction: "The article examines, analytically and notationally, various elements in the structure and context of the music of the West African drum ensembles". Koetting discusses the function and structure of the drum ensembles and analyzes

the music "on its own structural terms", that is, he does not compare it with Western ideas of structure and form. He uses a specially developed "Time Unit Box System" to notate the rhythms, which seems quite effective as a graphic overview, and works on the principle of the fastest rhythmic pulse per box unit.

1069. KUBIK, G. 'The Phenomenon of Inherent Rhythms in East and Central African Instrumental Music.' **African Music** 3/1: 33-42, 1962.
Includes a short examination of Wahenga drum rhythms.

1070. KUBIK, G. 'Transcription of Mangwilo Xylophone Music from Film Strips.' **African Music** 3/4: 35-51, 1965.

1071. KUBIK, G. 'Compositional Techniques in Kiganda Xylophone Music; With an Introduction into some Kiganda Musical Concepts.' **African Music** 4/3: 22-72, 1969.
A detailed analysis and description of the Amadinda music and the Akadinda music, and whether and how they are related.

1072. LADZEKPO, A.K. & LADZEKPO, Kobla 'Anlo Ewe Music in Anyako, Volta Region, Ghana.'
In MAY, Elizabeth **Musics of Many Cultures,** Berkeley, University of Calif. Press, Chapter 12, 216-31, 1980.
An article giving a good, basic overview of the cultural background, musical styles, and performance practices of this region. The (percussion) instruments of the dance ensembles are described and illustrated and several dance rhythms are discussed.

1073. LADZEKPO, S.K. & PANTALEONI, H. 'Takada Drumming.' **African Music** 4/4: 6-31, 1970.
This article discusses the drumming in the dance ensembles of the Ewe Takada music (Ghana), and is a follow-up of an earlier article by M. Serwadda & H. Pantaleoni, in which a new notation system was proposed (see entry in this chapter under 'Serwadda'). In the present article K. Ladzekpo provided the musical examples and background, and H. Pantaleoni did the analysis and notation - demonstrating the application of the earlier notation proposal. The instruments of the ensemble are described, their playing techniques, the rhythmic structure is discussed, and the authors conclude with a full-length notation of a dance piece.

1074. LO-BAMIJOKO, J.N. 'Performance Practice in Nigerian Music.' **Black Perspectives in Music** 12/1: 3-20, 1984.
The essay pertains to three instruments in particular: the Oja (flute), the Ubo-aka (thumb piano), and the Ngedegwu (xylophone). It discusses sound quality, musical function, and styles of playing.

1075. LOCKE, David **The Music of Atsiagbeko.** Thesis, Wesleyan Univ., CT, 1979, 681 p.
This large and thorough work deals extensively with this old dance, which used to be danced after battle by the Ewe speaking people of Ghana and Togo. It is divided into three parts: The first one contains a general overview of the Ewe society and in particular the background of the Atsiagbeko dance. In the second section the author discusses the songs of Asiagbeko, as he claims that the analysis of these songs fosters the understanding of the dances (63 songs are analyzed in detail). The final section then deals with the drumming. The southern Ewe rhythmic

principles are debated, the supporting instruments, and finally the leading drum. These analyses are very thorough and detailed, and over one hundred compositions are transcribed.

1076. LOCKE, David 'Principles of Offbeat Timing and Cross-Rhythm in Southern Ewe Dance Drumming.' **Ethnomusicology** 26/2: 217-46, 1982.
    This extensive article is based on Chapter 5 of the author's earlier dissertation 'The Music of Atsiagbeko' (see listing in this chapter) and presents and debates a number of the author's concepts regarding the rhythmic complexities of this music. First, there is a description of instruments in the Southern Ewe drum ensemble, which is followed by an explanation of the basic rhythmic principles (beat, pulse, and meter - including his disregard for polymeters). The larger part of the paper clearly discusses examples of offbeat timing and cross-rhythms, and how they occur in Ewe drumming.

1077. LOCKE, David 'The Rhythm of Takai.' **Percussive Notes** 23/4: 51-4, 1985.
    [Takai is one of the dances of the Dagomba people of Northern Ghana.]

1078. LOCKE, D. & AGBELI, G. 'Drum Language in Adzogbo.' **The Black Perspective in Music** 9/1: 25-50, 1981. (Reprinted from **African Music** 6/1: 32-51, 1980.)
    This article is based on a talk by the author (Locke), which he gave at the Annual Meeting of the Society for Ethnomusicology at the Univ. of Texas (Nov. 1977). In this paper the author puts the origin, instruments, and performance practices of the Adzogbo dance (of the Ewe people) into cultural context. Then six songs are analyzed with regard to their texts and speech-tone patterns, which are compared to the overall rhythmic patterns of the leading drum. The close correspondence of these two patterns is demonstrated in graphs and summarized in the five principles found in the drum language. The songs are also transcribed. [For a further, extensive study of this subject see D. Locke's dissertation 'The Music of Atsiagbeko' (1979), listed in this chapter.]

1079. MERRIAM, A.P. **African Music in Perspective.** New York, Garland, 1982, 506 p. ('Critical Studies on Black Life and Culture', No.21)
    Two chapters of this collection of studies should be of interest. Chapter 9 gives a brief account of the "Musical Instruments and Techniques of Performance among the Bashi" (Republic of Zaire), on pages 169-182, and Chapter 11 is a chronological description of "Drum-Making among the Bala (Basongye)", on pages 191-222. There is also a short discussion on "African musical rhythm and concepts of time-reckoning", and an extensive bibliography.

1080. NKETIA, J.H. 'The Role of the Drummer in the Akan Society.' **African Music Society Journal** 1/1: 34-43, 1954.

1081. NKETIA, J.H. **Drumming in the Akan Communities in Ghana.** London, Nelson (University of Ghana), 1963, 212 p.
    This specialized book could be divided into three groups: The first one (Chapters I to IV) deals specifically with drumming and drums (including descriptions of drums, drumming techniques and rhythmic patterns). Chapter V debates the role of drumming in the community, followed by other chapters on various aspects of ethnomusical considerations, organisations, etc., relating to drumming. Also five appendices with useful tables and glossaries.

1082. NKETIA, J.H. 'Multi-part Organization in the Music of the Gogo of Tanzania.' **Yearbook of the International Folk Music Council** 19: 79-88, 1967.
[With special reference to the Mbira]

1003. NKETIA, J.H. **The Music of Africa.** London, Victor Gollancz, 1975, 278 p. (Originally publ. by Norton, New York, 1974)
A book trying to cover a wide range of areas, with the main sections being : (1) Social and Cultural Background, (2) Musical Instruments, (3) Structures in African Music, and (4) Music and Related Arts.
Percussion Instruments are dealt with on a broad basis (pp 69-97), and there is a chapter analyzing "The rhythmic basis of instrumental music" (pp 125-39).

1084. PANTALEONI, H. 'Three Principles in Anlo Dance Drumming.' **African Music** 5/2: 50-63, 1972.
The author explains these three principles: (1) that Anlo timing is carried by the high sounds (in the ensemble), (2) every timing pattern is asymmetrical, and (3) against the timing pattern every (other) pattern has but one placement.

1085. PANTALEONI, H. **The Rhythm of Atsia Dance Drumming among the Anlo (Ewe) of Anyako.** Ph.D. Thesis, Wesleyan University, CT, 1972. (Diss. Abst. 33: 1189A-9A, Sep. 1972)
The dissertation is divided into two main parts, the first one being a more general one, giving insight into the dance drumming as a means of social expression, and it discusses the songs, dancing, musical structure and rhythmic principles. Part two is more specialized with regard to rhythmic analysis and detailed structure and texture of the instruments in the ensemble and what they play.

1086. PRESSING, Jeff 'Rhythmic Design in the Support Drums of Agbadza.' **African Music** 6/3: 4-15, 1983.
The music in discussion is that of the Ewe people of Ghana, in particular their drum emsemble music 'Agbadza'. The author bases his detailed analysis of the rhythms on his study with master drummer C.K. Ladzekpo, and relates the rhythmic designs, phrasing, and subtle variations within various cycles of the two support drums (Kidi and Kagan) to the rest of the percussion ensemble.

1087. PRESSING, Jeff 'Cognitive Isomorphisms in World Music: West Africa, The Balkans, Thailand and Western Tonality.' **Studies in Music** 17: 38-61, 1983.

1088. SEAVOY, M.H. **The Sisaala Xylophone Tradition.** Ph.D. Thesis, Los Angeles, Univ. of California, 1982, 591 p. (Diss. Abst. 43: 969A+, Oct. 1982)
This dissertation is a comprehensive examination of the "Jengsi" (xylophone), the musical culture it relates to, and the musical tradition of the Sisaala in Northwest Ghana. Part one deals with the overall ethnographic background, and Part two covers the technical-musical details of this tradition.

1089. SELECTED REPORTS IN ETHNOMUSICOLOGY (Edi.) 'Glossary of African Terms.' **Selected Reports in Ethnomusicology** 5: 357-76, 1984.

1090. SERWADDA, M. & PANTALEONI, H. 'A Possible Notation for African Dance Drumming.' **African Music** 4/2: 47-52, 1968.
    The authors offer a graph-tablature notation, where the time moves vertically from the bottom to the top of the page. The notation is meant to indicate the different sounds of sticks, hands, area of drum head, and duration, in the hope to aid the teaching of this ensemble music.

1091. TRACEY, A. & TAPERA, A. 'Mbira Music of the Jege.' **African Music** 2/4: 44-63, 1961.

1092. TRACEY, A. **How to Play the Mbira.** Roodepoort, South Africa, The International Library of African Music, 1970, 25 p.
    This is the first instruction book on the Mbira (for Western use). It covers all the basics and presents five transcriptions of authentic mbira compositions (and their variations) from the Shona people of Zimbabwe/Rhodesia.

1093. TRACEY, Hugh 'The Wood Music of the Chopi.' **Yearbook of the International Folk Music Council** 16: 91, 1964.

1094. UDOW, Michael 'African Percussion Music.' **Percussionist** 9/4: 119-28, 1972.
    A very general, and somewhat muddled, article on various groups of instruments (rattles, xylophones and drums of Ghana) and some of their cultural background and construction, with a little information about the actual music. Much of the article is based on J.H. Nketia's book 'Drumming in the Akan Communities of Ghana' (London, 1963).

## CHAPTER 13.

## INDIAN MUSIC:

## (a) Instruments.

1095. BERGAMO, John 'The Indian Ghatam and Tavil.' **Percussionist** 19/1: 18-23, 1981.
A short description of these two instruments and their playing techniques.

1096. COURTNEY, David **An Introduction to Tabla.** Hyderabad, India, Anaud Power Press, 1982.
The author states in his preface that "it is impossible to learn tabla from a book" and he only tries to supplement and aid students with this book (i.e. one needs a teacher as well). It has a short history of the drums, followed by the listing of drumstrokes (with exercises), examples of compositions and variations, and discussions of various styles.

1097. COURTNEY, David 'Tabla Making in the Deccan.' **Percussive Notes** 23/2: 33-4, 1985.

1098. DAY, C.R. **The Music and Musical Instruments of Southern India and the Deccan.** Dehli, B.R. Publishing, 1974, 181 p. (Reprint of 1891 ed.)

1099. DEVA, B.C. 'Classification of Indian Musical Instruments.' **Journal of the Indian Musicological Society** 4/1: 33-45, 1973.

1100. DEVA, B.C. 'The Santals and their musical Instruments.' **Jahrbuch fuer musikalische Volks - und Voelkerkunde** no.8: 36-46, 1977.
The Santals (approxm. three million people) live in the mid-eastern part of India. The article is a (verbal only) description of their instruments, ordered in the common grouping of idiophones, membranophones (majority of instruments), aerophones and chordophones.

1101. DEVA, B.C. **Musical Instruments of India: Their History and Development.** Calcutta, Firma KLM, 1978, 306 p.
Edward Henry, despite criticism of some of the author's (Deva) musical theories presented, calls this book "the most comprehensive and detailed" so far available on this subject (see his book review in 'Ethnomusicology', May 1980, pp 302-3). The book gives an extensive account of India's instruments and their music, including about 120 photographs. Of special interest to the percussionist should be the technical discussion of the composite drum head, which gives such a unique sound to much of India's music (e.g. the tabla).

1102. FREEBERN, Charles **The Music of India, China, Japan and Oceania: A Source Book for Teachers.** Thesis, University of Arizona, 1969, 176 p. (Dissertation not listed in Diss. Abst.)

1103. KNAVE, Brian 'Introduction to Tabla.' **Modern Drummer** 6/8: 94-5, 1982.

1104. KOTHARI, K.S. **Indian Folk Musical Instruments.** New Dehli, Sangeet Natak Akademi, 1968, 99 p.
     The author describes it as "an expanded catalogue" (of an exhibition in New Dehli, Nov. 1968) with c. 300 instruments listed with annotations and illustrations.

1105. KRISHNASWAMI, S. **Musical Instruments of India.** New Dehli, Ministry of Information and Broadcasting, 1971, 56 p.
     This is meant to serve as a basic introduction (to the Westerner) of Indian instruments. It includes short descriptions and photographs (of a rather poor quality).

1106. LEVITAN, Daniel 'The Tabla as a Contemporary Chamber Instrument.' **Percussive Notes** 16/1: 34-5, 1977.
     (For annotation see same entry in Chapter 5/e.)

1107. RECK, D.B. & RECK, S. 'Drums of India: A Pictorial Selection.' **Asian Music** 13/2: 39-54, 1982.
     A short article with eleven photographs of drums (being played), describing instruments, some history, dances and traditions.

1108. VANDOR, I. 'The Gandi: A Musical Instrument of Buddhist India recently identified in a Tibetan Monastery.' **World of Music** 17/1: 24-7, 1975.

1109. BENNETT, Frank 'The Mrdangam of South India.' **Percussionist** 19/1: 24-40, 1981.
The author deals with the construction of this instrument, the sounds and their notation (list of sounds with their symbols), the "Tala in Karnatic Music", with some common and traditional patterns used in Mrdangam playing.

1110. BERGAMO, John 'Indian Music in America.' **Percussionist** 19/1: 5-8, 1981.

1111. BHOWMICK, K.N. 'On Traditions of Tabla-Riaz in Bnaras School.' **Indian Musician** 12/1-2: 52+, 1981.

1112. BROWN, Robert **The Mrdangam: A Study in Drumming in South India.** Thesis, Los Angeles, University of California, 1965. (2 vols., 361 p & 388 p.)
This is a very extensive study on the playing technique, construction, and rhythmic structures relating to this very specialized drum and its highly skilled techniques. Vol.I contains the text of the study, relating in detail the South Indian rhythmic concepts, drum construction, playing techniques with the various strokes, the tala system, and the explanatory instructions which relate to the 152 mrdangam lessons contained in Vol.II.

1113. DAY, C.R. **The Music and Musical Instruments of Southern India and the Deccan.** Dehli, B.R. Publishing, 1974, 181 p. (Reprint of 1891 ed.)

1114. ELLINGSON, T. 'Ancient Indian Drum Syllables and Bu ston's sham pa ta Ritual.' **Ethnomusicology** 24/3: 431-52, 1980.
The discussion includes some historical background; the Sarvadurgati drum notations, their interpretation and performance; and drum syllables and drum language in India.

1115. GHOSH, N. 'Science and Art of keeping Time in Indian Music.' **Journal of the Indian Musicological Society** 5/2: 27-32, 1974.
The author gives some (historic) background on the evolvement of Tala (time-measure), and tries to show how one can obtain a basic overview of the art of drumming by studying the specific technique of the Tabla, and the use of its 22 different sounds.

1116. GHOSH, N. 'Different Gharanas in the Field of Tabla Art.' **Journal of the Indian Musicological Society** 3/1: 5-10, 1972.

1117. GHOSH, N. **Fundamentals of Raga and Tala, with a New System of Notation.** Bombay, Popular Prakasham, 1978 (1968).

The author proposes in this book a new approach to (Indian) music education, and also presents a combination of occidental and his own graphic (and complex) notation system, which seems of interest, as Raga and Tala are an oral tradition. He also concerns himself with the historical development of Indian music and the book contains a register of instruments, apart from discussing the concept of Raga and Tala.

1118. GOTTLIEB, R.S. **The Major Traditions of North Indian Tabla Drumming.** Munich, Katzbichler, 1977, 205 p. (Includes two audio cassettes)
The aim of the author was to present a "representative survey of main traditions of solo tabla drumming", which he did with the aid of recorded performances by six different soloists from six different musical traditions. The transcriptions are analyzed and discussed, and a summary of theory and terminology is given.

1119. HARTENBERGER, J.R. **Mrdangam Manual.** Thesis, Wesleyan University, Connect., 1974, 626 p. (Subtitle: 'A Guidebook to South Indian Rhythm for the Western Musician')
This large manual is in three volumes: (1) Rhythmic Theory, (2) Analysis of Mrdangam Lessons, (3) Mrdangam Lessons in Mrdangam Notation. Furthermore, there are two volumes (not microfilmed) available for consultation at the Wesleyan Univ. Library: Vol.(4) Mrdangam Lessons in Western Staff Notation, and Vol.(5) Tape Recordings of Mrdangam Lessons. In this study the author shows how to adapt South Indian rhythmic ideas to Western music, based on the lessons, which range from beginner's exercises to very advanced studies.

1120. JEANS, M. 'With Sitar and Tabla.' **Music and Musician** 19: 28-30, Jan. 1971.

1121. KETTLE, Rupert 'Thoughts on Tabla Notation.' **Percussive Notes** 11/1: 21-2, 1972.
The author proposes three different, basic "Westernized" notation systems (using either two staves, one stave, or on two single lines) to help the student understand Indian rhythmic conception.

1122. RAMAMURTY, Dharmala **The Theory and Practice of Mridanga.** Rajahmundry, Saraswathi Press, 1973, 312 p.
A detailed instruction manual for this instrument. It explains the theory of Tala (time-keeping), describes construction and design, covers many styles of the various rhythmic series, contains extensive patterns (in verbal drum notation), and also many tables of Tala, rhythms and patterns. For the serious student.

1123. RICHARDS, Tim 'Banaras Tabla Tradition.' **Percussive Notes** 19/1: 9-17, 1981.
Deals briefly with the history of this tradition, teaching methods, practice and development of technique, composition and improvisation, and the concept of "tal."

1124. RICHARDS, Tim 'The Banaras Gharana Style of Tabla Drumming.' **Modern Percussionist** 1/1: 52-3, 1984-85.

1125. ROBERTSON, Donald **Tabla - A Rhythmic Introduction to Indian Music.** New York, Peer International Corp., 1968, 54 p.
This is a reasonably good tutor which teaches and explains all the

basic rhythms and techniques. Part I is a rudimentary introduction, covering some history, construction details, tuning and playing techniques. Part II explains all the "bols" (the spoken sounds) and the strokes as applied to the drums. Over twenty strokes are described in detail with suitable exercises. Part III contains many rhythmic patterns, explained in the Indian time-keeping tradition and musical phrasing.

1126. RUCKERT, G. 'Theka Supreme (Drum Strokes).' **Percussive Notes** 22/1: 34-5, 1983.

1127. SHEPHERD, F.A. **Tabla and the Benares Gharana.** Ph.D. Thesis, Wesleyan University, Connect., 1976, 349 p. (Diss. Abst. 37: 6134A-5A, April 1977)
    The study examines the "state of the tabla performance today", in particular the school of playing known as Benares Gharana. Special emphasis is on the structure and form of the tabla solo, the construction of the instrument and its playing technique with its many tonal colors.

1128. STEWART, Rebecca Maria **The Tabla in Perspective.** Thesis, Los Angeles, University of California, 1974, 425 p.
    This is a major study on the tabla and its repertoire. There are three main parts to the text, the first one discussing the tabla itself, its playing technique and the various strokes. In part two the large repertoire is presented and debated (types of time-keeping, stroke patterns, and geographical styles), and part three brings the music and the drumming techniques in proper context of functions of the patterns and performance style.

1129. WADE, Bonnie **Music in India: The Classical Traditions.** Englewood Cliffs, NJ, Prentice Hall, 1978, 250 p.
    Discusses background, melody and melody instruments, meter, performance genres, and has a good chapter on "Rhythm instruments and drumming" (23 pages). Furthermore it contains a comprehensive discography, glossary, and an annotated bibliography.

# CHAPTER 14.

## SOUTH-EAST ASIAN MUSIC.

1131. BECKER, J. 'Percussive Patterns in the Music of Mainland Southeast Asia.'
**Ethnomusicology** 12/2: 173-91, 1968.
The author has made an attempt to "classify the great variety of percussive structures" present in the melodies of the music of that area. She explains the terms "colotomic units" and discusses four drum patterns she found: configurative, extented, durational, and metronomic. Several transcriptions illustrate her discussions.

1132. CADAR, Usopay 'The Role of Kulintang in Maranao Society.' **Selected Reports Ethnomusicology** 2/2: 49-61, 1975.
A description of the percussive Kulintang ensemble and its music in northern Borneo.

1133. DYCK, Gerald 'Lung Noi Na Kampam makes a Drumhead for a Northern Thai Long Drum (A photographic Documentary).' **Selected Reports in Ethnomusicolo** 2/2: 183-203, 1975.
35 illustrated steps on the manufacture of this musical instrument.

1134. FAGG, William **Javanese Musical Instruments.** London, British Museum, 1970, 3 p.
(Not available for annotation)

1135. FORREST, W.J. 'Concepts of Melodic Patterns in contemporary Solonese Gamelan Music.' **Asian Music** 11/2: 53-127, 1980.

1136. FRAME, Edward 'The Musical Instruments of Sabah, Malaysia.' **Ethnomusicolog** 26/2: 247-74, 1982.
Includes detailed and illustrated desciptions of several traditional percussion instruments from this area (incl. gongs, Gabbang xylophone, Gendang drum, anc the Tagunggak bamboo tube-drums).

1137. GAETANO, Mario 'Definite pitched Idiophones of the Javanese Gamelan.'
**Percussionist** 15/3: 121-43, 1978.
A listing of instruments, a short theory of Gamelan music, and a description these idiophones, including charts and illustrations.

1138. GILES, Ray 'Ombak in the Style of the Javanese Gongs.' **Selected Reports in Ethnomusicology** 2/1: 159-65, 1974.
An acoustical study relating to the manufacture of large Javanese gongs; "ombak" meaning roughly (in Western terms) an amplitude vibrato, and also a frequency vibrato.

1139. HARRELL, M.C. **The Music of the Gamelan Degung of West Java.** Ph.D. Thesis Los Angeles, University of California, 1974, 290 p. (Diss. Abst. 35: 3036A, Nov 1974)

This small ensemble consisits of gongs, metallophones, drums and flute. Here the Bandung tradition was studied; the scales of the gamelan degung are explained and a modal analysis is given. The patterns of improvisation are examined and some guidelines for performance are given.

1140. HOOD, Mantel **The Evolution of Javanese Gamelan, Book I: Music of the Roaming Sea.** Wilhelmshaven (NY), Heinrichshofen (C.F. Peters), 1980, 229 p.

1141. HYE-GU, Lee **Korean Musical Instruments.** Seoul, National Classical Music Institute of Korea, 1982, 48 p. (Translated by A.C. Heyman)
The booklet is a catalogue of instruments, with colourful illustrations and basic descriptions of construction, playing techniques and their use in Korean music. Contains many photographs of beautifully decorated percussion instruments.

1142. JONES, A.M. 'Indonesia and Africa: The Xylophone as a Culture-Indicator.' **African Music** 2/3: 36-47, 1961. (Comments by A.T. Tracey: pp 75-7)

1143. JONES, A.M. **Africa and Indonesia: The Evidence of the Xylophone and other Musical and Cultural Factors.** Leiden, Netherlands, E.J. Brill, 1971, 286 p. (First Ed. 1964)
(For annotation see same entry in Chapter 12/a.)

1144. KARTOMI, Margaret 'Musical Strata in Sumatra, Java and Bali.'
In MAY, Elizabeth **Musics of Many Cultures,** Berkley, Univ. of Calif. Press, Chapter 7, pp 111-33, 1980.
Discusses various styles of music and instruments found in this area, including the "Talempong" ensemble (Gamelan) of Sumatra, the Gamelan "Slendro-Pelog" in Central Java, and some Gamelan ensembles of Bali. Includes useful glossary, bibliography and discography.

1145. KUNST, Jaap **Music in Java; its History, its Theory and its Technique.** The Hague, Nijoff, 1973, 660 p. (3rd ed.; 2 vols.)
This is a major work on this subject. All the actual text is in Vol.I, which has four major chapters: (1) Tone and Scale Systems (c.100 pages), (2) Historical Survey, (3) Central and East Java, (4) West Java. The last two chapters each discuss vocal and instrumental music separately, with nearly 200 pages of material on percussion instruments. Vol.II contains 165 illustrations, extensive bibliography (407 entries); transcriptions, scores, charts and tables of many kinds.

1146. LINDSAY, Jennifer **Javanese Gamelan.** New York, O.U.P., 1979, 58 p.
A basic, illustrated primer in Gamelan music, with some information on the instruments, tuning and notation, and musical structure.

1147. MATUSKY, P. 'Musical Instruments and Musicians of the Malay Shadow Puppet Theatre.' **Journal of the American Musical Instruments Society** 8: 38-68, 1982.

1148. McDERMOTT, Vincent & SUMARSAM 'Central Javanese Music: The Patet of Laras Slendo and the Gender Barung.' **Ethnomusicology** May: 233-43, 1975.

1149. McPHEE, C. **Music in Bali.** New Haven, London, Yale University Press, 1966, 430 p. (Subtitle:'A Study in Form and Instrumental Organization in Balinese Orchestral Music.')
This large study has been undertaken during the author's visit to Bali in 1931-1939, and deals especially with Gamelan music.

1150. MORTON, David **The Traditional Instrumental Music of Thailand.** Ph.D. Thesis,
Los Angeles, University of California, 1964. (Diss. Abst. 25: 4185-6, Jan. 1965)

1151. MORTON, David 'Instruments and Instrumental Functions in the Ensembles of
Southeast Asia: a Crosscultural Comparison.' **Selected Reports in
Ethnomusicology** 2/2: 6-15, 1975.

1152. MORTON, David **The Traditional Music of Thailand.** Berkeley, Univ. of Californi
Press, 1976, 258 p.
   This well-produced book includes 33 pages of detailed descriptions,
illustrations, and playing techniques of the percussion instruments in Thai
ensembles.

1153. MURPHY, D.A. **The Autochthonous American Gamelan.** Thesis, Wesleyan
University, 1975, 303 p.
   The author addresses this study to the non-specialist, and describes his
experience in studying Javanese Gamelan and the manufacturing of instruments
in the environment of a university department.

1154. ORNSTEIN, R.S. 'The Five-Tone Gamelan Anklung of North Bali.'
**Ethnomusicology** 15/1: 71-80, 1971.

1155. ORNSTEIN, R.S. **'Gamelan Gong Kebjar' - The Development of a Balinese Music**
**Tradition.** Ph.D. Thesis, Univ. of Calif., Los Angeles, 1971, 479 p. (Diss. Abst. 32
4049A, Jan. 1972)
   From the author's summary: "This study examines the ways that music and
other performing arts function in Balinese society and focuses on the Gamelan
Gong Kebjar - a recent Balinese orchestral style". The author obtained her
material in Bali between the years of 1963 and 1966 and deals with the music's
historic and social context in Part I of her study, and discusses the Gamelan Gon
Kebjar in detail in Part II (including tuning, scales, musical forms, instruments,
etc.).

1156. PERRIS, A.B. 'The Rebirth of the Javanese "Anklung".' **Ethnomusicology** 15/3:
403-7, 1971.

1157. RUGOLO, John 'Dong Wook Park and the Music of Korea.' **Percussive Notes** 20/3
64-6, 1982.
   Discusses some of the Korean percussion instruments, like the Changgo, bells,
gongs, and others. Also concerns itself with some rhythmic patterns from the
traditional literature. These are then compared to the modern piece "Contrast"
by Dong Wook Park.

1158. SHEPPARD, Tan Sri 'Traditional Musical Instruments of Malaysia.' **Selected
Reports in Ethnomusicology** 2/2: 171-9, 1975.
   [Brief, illustrated descriptions of the instruments.]

1159. SUMARSAM 'The Musical Practice of the Gamelan Sekaten.' **Asian Music** 12/2:
54-73, 1981.
   Considers problems for and benefits to the musician playing this music (from
melodic and an improvisational point of view).

1160. SURJODININGRAT, R.M. **A First Introduction to Javanese Gamelan Music.**
Oberlin, OH, Oberlin College Board of Trustees, 1978, 40 p.

(Not available for annotation; for book review see 'Ethnomusicology' 25/2: 340-1, 1981.)

1161. SUTTON, R.A. 'Concept and Treatment in Javanese Gamelan Music, with Reference to the Gambang.' **Asian Music** 11/1: 59-79, 1979.

1162. SUTTON, R.A. **Variation in Javanese Gamelan Music: Dynamics of a Steady State.** Ph.D. Thesis, Univ. of Michigan, 1982, 385 p. (Diss. Abst. 43: 3151A, Apr. 1983)
In seven chapters the dissertation looks at variation in many different ways in the music of Gamelan, including the type of composition in question, different versions of one piece, the results of using two melodic parts at the same time, and variation through expansion and contraction. The appendices include descriptions of gamelan instruments and rhythmic structures, and notation of pieces.

1163. TAKACS, Jenoe 'A Dictionary of Philippine Musical Instruments.' **Archiv fuer Voelkerkunde** No.29: 121-218, 1975.
The research for this study was done during the years 1932-1934, with the assistance of Prof. von Hornbostel. The instruments are described, related to their ethnic backgrounds, a short explanation of playing techniques is given, and many instruments are illustrated with line drawings.

1164. TOTH, Andrew 'The Gamelan Luang of Tangkas, Bali.' **Selected Reports in Ethnomusicology** 2/2: 65-79, 1975.

# CHAPTER 15.

# LATIN AMERICAN MUSIC.

1165. ALMEIDA, Laurindo **Latin Percussion Instruments and Rhythms.** New York, Gwyn Publishing Co., 1972, 17 p.

Ten original instruments are illustrated and their playing techniques discussed, with a short musical example of a typical rhythm. However, the cost of the book and the Subtitle ("For jazz and rock") are not justified, and the title should really be "Brazilian Percussion......"

1166. AMIRA, John 'Congas and Caribbean Percussion.' **Modern Drummer** 6/6: 94-5, 1982.

A short article explaining several sounds on the conga, and showing in graph-notation details of the Cuban "Guaguanco" and the Haitian "Yanralon" rhythm.

1167. BARR, W.L. 'The Salsa Rhythm Section.' **The Educator (Assoc. of Jazz Educators)** 12/2: 15-8+, 1980/81.

1168. BARTHOLOMEW, John **The Steel Band.** London, O.U.P., 1980, 49 p.

Covers many aspects of this musical style, including social and historical background of the area (Trinidad). Gives detailed instructions (well-illustrated) on how to manufacture and tune the various sized pans, playing techniques, and how to arrange the music.

1169. BERENDT, J.E. 'Perkussion von Kuba, Salsa und Brasilien ueber Afrika bis Indien.' **Jazz Podium** 30: 6-11, July 1981.
[German; Discussion of styles.]

1170. BROWN, Theodore D. 'More Latin Rhythms: Samba, Baion, Bossa Nova.' **The Instrumentalist** 21: 68-9+, May 1967.

1171. BROWN, Thomas A. 'Let's learn Latin.' **The Instrumentalist** 19: 46-9, Oct. 1964.

A very basic coverage of the main Latin American instruments and rhythmic patterns.

1172. BROWN, Thomas A. **Afro-Latin Rhythm Dictionary.** Sherman Oaks, Alfred Publ. Co., c. 1983, 48 p.

Includes illustrations of instruments, their basic playing techniques and a typical rhythm for each. This is followed by detailed examples of many complementing Latin rhythms.

1173. CHARLES, David **Conga, Bongo, and Timbale Techniques - Live and in the Studio.** New York, Marimba Productions, 1982.

The three sections of this well-presented book (which also includes a record) are: (1) Primary, authentic playing techniques of the instruments, including clave, with rhythms and background information; (2) covers improvisation with given materials, and (3) gives information about studio recording work.

1174. CHENOWETH, Vida **The Marimbas of Guatemala.** Lexington, University of Kentucky Press, 1964, 108 p.
    The book describes in detail and with clear drawings the three main marimbas of Guatemala: the chromatic, the gourd, and the transitional marimbas. Designs, ranges, and typical musical examples are detailed, and chapter 5 gives a history of the development of the marimba. Also included are transcriptions of pieces by some famous marimba players of the 1950's.

1175. CORDY, Ernie 'Combining Conga and Drumset.' **Modern Drummer** 8/4: 78-81, 1984.
    Ideas and hints on using conga together with bass drum and hi-hat: set-up and rhythmic patterns.

1176. DA ANUNCIACAO, L.A. 'Birimbau from Brasil - what is Birimbau and how to play it.' **Percussionist** 8/3: 72-7, 1971.

1177. DARACA, J. **Conga Drumming - Disco, Soul, Raggae, Rock.** Ontario, CA, Congeros, 1980. (Also avail. with cassette)
    (For annotation see same entry in Chapter 6.)

1178. DE LIMA, R.T. 'Folk Music and Musical Instruments of Brasil.' **Student Musicologists at Minnesota** 4: 219-55, 1970-71.
    This is an extensive article, translated by Robert Krueger (from the original "Prima Conferencia Interamericana de Etno-musicologia", Pan-American Union, Washinton, 1965, pp 205-24). It begins with a discussion of the historic influence of African, Eurasian and Amerindian styles of Brasilian Folk Music and its instruments. This is followed by the detailed (verbal) description of 52 instruments, their playing techniques and musical applications. It concludes with a bibliography and discography.

1179. DELP, Ron 'The Conga Drum.' **The Instrumentalist** 29: 58-61, Feb. 1975.
    Explains the construction of the conga (advice on choice) and the basic strokes.

1180. DINELLA, Jim **Conga Come Alive.** Toms River, NJ, Brass Ring Enterprises, 1984, 60 p.
    Covers the technique of mounting and tuning heads, historical information, and general reference. Then it explains roll exercises, hand co-ordination, various types of sounds obtainable, followed by specific rhythms, special effects and other useful hints.

1181. FINK, Siegfried **Percussion Brazil.** Frankfurt, Zimmerman, 1978, 16 p.
    Has tables of ten popular Brazilian rhythms (two versions each), each one nicely set out for ten different percussion instruments.

1182. FORMAN, Steve 'South American Percussion: Cuica speaks.' **Downbeat** 48: 80-81, Dec. 1979.
    Description of the instrument, how to lap the head, and basic playing technique with 11 exercises.

1183. GARFIAS, R. 'The Marimba of Mexico and Central America.' **Latin American Music Review** 4/2: 203-28, 1983.

1184. GIBBS, J.A. **The Unit Steel Band.** Hicksville, NY, Exposition, 1978, 96 p.
    (Not available for annotation; for book review see the 'Music Educator's Journal' 65: 19, Nov. 1978.)

1185. GOLDBERG, Norbert 'Brazilian Percussion: the Cuica.' **Percussionist** 14/1: 29-32, 1976.
Short description of the instrument, its use in Brazilian music, and some exercises and rhythms.

1186. GOLDBERG, Norbert 'Brazilian Drumming: the Samba.' **Modern Drummer** 1/3: 20, 1977.

1187. GOLDBERG, Norbert 'Calypso.' **Modern Drummer** 3/1: 40-1, 1979.

1188. GOLDBERG, Norbert 'Afro Cuban.' **Modern Drummer** 3/2: 40-1, 1979.

1189. GOLDBERG, Norbert 'The Cha Cha.' **Modern Drummer** 3/3: 38-9, 1979.

1190. GOLDBERG, Norbert 'The Mambo.' **Modern Drummer** 3/4: 36-7, 1979.

1191. GOLDBERG, Norbert 'Brazilian Percussion.' **Modern Drummer** 3/5: 46-7, 1979.
A brief summary of the usage of the Surdo, Pandeira, Agogo and the Cuica.

1192. GOLDBERG, Norbert 'New Directions in Latin Drumming.' **Modern Drummer** 4/1: 42-3, 1980.
Some influences of Brazilian, Afro-Cuban, and West Indian rhythms.

1193. GOLDBERG, Norbert 'Brazilian Rhythms.' **Modern Drummer** 4/5: 42-3, 1980.
Basic examples of Samba and Bossa Nova, including the use of brush-and-stick technique.

1194. GOLDBERG, Norbert 'Latin Fills.' **Modern Drummer** 5/4: 56-8, 1981.
Some simple, but authentic, ideas for short Latin fills (for the Drummer).

1195. GOLDBERG, Norbert 'Music of the Andes Countries.' **Percussive Notes** 19/3: 79-80, 1981.

1196. GOLDBERG, Norbert 'The Samba.' **Modern Drummer** 7/12: 106-7, 1983.
This article varies a little from an earlier one by the same author ('Modern Drummer' 1/3: 20, 1977) and includes contemporary mixtures of jazz and funk.

1197. GUERRERO, Frank **Latin Sounds from the Drum Set.** Hollywood, Try Publishing Co., 1974, 312 p.
The aim of this large and thorough book is to help the drummer produce Latin rhythms as close as possible to the original sound ideal, without having the assistance of percussionists. There are two main parts: "Cuban-Rooted Rhythms" and "Brazilian Rhythms". All the various well-known, and not so popular, rhythms are there in great detail, with many variations, exercises, fills and references to all the Latin instruments. To make it really complete, the author gives examples of whole rhythm sections (melody, bass, harmony and drums) to every type of rhythm studied. An enormous amount of information put together with loving care.

1198. HENRIQUE, Jorge **Brazilian Rhythm Instruments - And how to play them.** Santa Cruz, Calif., Brazilian Imports, 1976, 25 p.

Henrique uses a combination of conventional staff and graph notation to show the rhythms and patterns of six diverse instruments. Although with apparent good intentions, the notation is very dense and hard to decipher at first. There is no detailed description or background given of the instruments themselves, but there are several rhythms and effects explained and notated.

1199. HOLEN, Mark 'La Bateria Tropical.' **Percussive Notes** 22/5: 58-60, 1984.

Relates some dance rhythms of Cuba, Colombia, Santa Domingo, Argentina, Venezuela, Chile and Brazil for the drummer and percussionist.

1200. IZIKOWITZ, K.G. **Musical Instruments of the South American Indians.** Wakefield, Yorkshire, England, SR Publishers Ltd., 1970, 433 p. (Reprint of 1935 ed.)

Although an early work (1935), it is a very thorough study of a great number of these instruments, with nearly 200 pages on percussion instruments. The book contains many quality line drawings of drums, xylophones, bells, rattles, shakers, etc., but has no index.

1201. JOE, Montego 'The Conga Drum.' **Modern Percussionist** 1/2: 24-6, 1985.

Brief discussion on choice and characteristics of the congas, how to produce the basic tonal strokes (but no finger technique), and variations on some Latin rhythm.

1202. JOE, Montego 'Timbales.' **Modern Percussionist** 1/4: 28-9, 1985.

Description of the drums, basic playing technique and eleven rhythmic patterns.

1203. JONES, A.M. 'A Kwaiker Indian Xylophone.' **Ethnomusicology** 10/1: 43-7, 1966.

Investigates the specific tuning of this instrument.

1204. KILGORE, B.R 'Conga Technique.' **The Instrumentalist** 38: 90-95, Mar., 1984.

A basic, but clearly presented article on the techniques of conga playing. Playing position and four essential strokes are demonstrated (open, slap, bass, and finger), exercises are given, and a choice of rhythms is given for Cha Cha, Mambo, Samba, Funk, and Bolero.

1205. KURATH, G.P. 'The Kinetic Ecology of Yaqui Dance Instrumentation.' [Amercan Indian] **Ethnomusicology** 10/1: 28-42, 1966.

Discusses meaning, instrumentation, instruments and music of the dance-dramas of the Yaqui (Central Sonora, Mexico).

1206. LASZLO, B. **Latin Drumming.** Kent, England, A. Kalmus. (Includes two recorded discs.)

(Not available for annotation; for book review see 'Jazz Journal International' 37: 17, Apr. 1984.)

1207. LIST, G. 'The Mbira in Cartagena.' [Colombia] **Yearbook of the International Folk Music Council** 20: 54-9, 1968.

1208. McCALLUM, F.K. 'The Marimba's Bass Notes.' **Percussionist** 5/2: 266-9, 1967.

A description of the large marimbas manufactured in Central America, especially Guatemala, of around 6 1/2 octaves.

1209. MENDOZA, Victor 'Vibes in Latin Music.' **Percussive Notes** 22/5: 65-7, 1984.
This article gives some valuable examples and advice for the situation when the vibraphone takes the place of the piano in the rhythm section. The percussionist must familiarize himself with the idiomatic rhythmic patterns of the various Latin dances.

1210. MORALES, Huberto **Latin American Rhythm Instruments.** New York, Henry Adler, 1954, 132 p. (Rights assigned to Belwin Inc. 1966)
Very thorough instruction book of "authentic" Latin American rhythms and playing techniques of all the Latin instruments. They are also combined in many cases to be used on the drum set or in complete percussion sections. Very detailed notation and illustrations; the text is printed in Spanish and English.

1211. NODAL, Roberto 'The Social Evolution in the Afro-Cuban Drum.' **The Black Perspective in Music** 11/2: 157-77, 1983.
(For annotation see same entry in Chapter 12/a.)

1212. O'BRIEN, Linda 'Marimbas of Guatemala: The African Connection.' **The World of Music** 25/2: 99-103, 1982.
Relates some information regarding the Central African origin and similarities of the marimbas and their music.

1213. ORREGO-SALAS, J.A. 'Araucanian Indian Instruments.' **Ethnomusicology** 10/1: 48-57, 1966.
This report includes brief considerations of some percussion instruments used by the Araucanian Indians in Chile.

1214. POLLART, Gene 'Latin Percussion - What and how to select.' **Woodwind World, Brass and Percussion** 18/6: 24, 1979.
Mainly directed at the teacher, advising him about the construction of several Latin instruments, and what to look for when selecting and buying.

1215. RAE, John 'Mambo on the Drum Set.' **Modern Drummer** 5/9: 52-3, 1982.

1216. ROS, Edmundo **The Latin American Way.** London, Morris, 1949.

1217. SANTOS, John 'The Making of a Guiro - The Unsung Thriller of Latin Rhythm.' **Percussive Notes** 23/2: 45-7, 1985.

1218. SARGENT, Wyn 'The Steel Drums of Trinidad.' **Modern Drummer** 6/6: 30-2, 1982.
A short historic background and elementary description of the construction and playing techniques of these drums are given.

1219. SCIARRINO, J. & DE LOS REYES, W. **Salsa Rock.** Sherman Oaks, CA, Alfred Publ. Co., 1978, 24 p. (Subtitle: 'A Complete Guide for Blending the Drum Set with the Latin Rhythm Section.')
(For annotation see same entry in Chapter 6.)

1220. SEEGER, Peter **Steel Drums, and how to play them and make them.** New York, Oak Publications, 1964, 40 p. (Also available with records: Folkways Fi 8367 and Fs 3834)
This book presents detailed instructions on how to make and tune these drums from Trinidad. It depicts the various patterns for each of the drums, the Ping Pong, Second Pan, Cello Pan, Guitar Pan, and Bass Pan. It also shows how to treat and play them. The last 12 pages contain arrangements for the whole band of several typical (and also some more unlikely) melodies, and a suggestion for a new "steelband notation" method, a quasi tablature idea.

1221. SEEGER, Peter 'Tuning the Steel Drums.' **Sing Out** 22/4: 23-5, 1973.
This is one chapter from the author's book 'Steel Drums, and how to play them and make them' (see entry above).

1222. SING OUT (Editorial) 'Teach-in: Bomba Puertorriquena.' **Sing Out** 25/3: 7, 1976.
Explains the "Bomba", a Puerto Rican dance rhythm - with musical notation.

1223. SOEBBING, H.W. 'Latin American Instruments and Rhythms.' **The Instrumentalist** 32: 74-80, 1977.
A basic but clear guide to six of the Latin instruments, with a brief description of the instruments and some of their typical rhythms (claves, guiro, cowbell, timbales, maracas and conga).

1224. SULSBRUCK, Birger **Latin American Percussion.** New Albany, IN, Jamey Abersold, 1983, 183 p. (Includes 3 cassettes)
The book is divided into two parts: the first deals with the instruments, with detailed information regarding origin, illustrations and typical rhythms. Part two contains many examples of Latin American rhythms, amply demonstrated on the three cassettes which come with the book.

1225. TAYLOR, John 'Fundamental L/A Patterns.' (6 parts) **Crescendo International** Aug. 1973 to Mar. 1974.
Six short articles on the following rhythms:
'Mambo' - 12: 38, August 1973.
'Baion' - 12: 38, September 1973.
'Afro Cuban' - 12: 38, February 1974.
'Guaracha' - 12: 38, March 1974.
'Joropo' - 12: 38, July 1974.
'Naningo' - 12: 39-40, August 1974.

1226. TAYLOR, John 'Around the Kit; LA Instruments.' (12 parts) **Crescendo International** from Oct. 1974 to Nov. 1975.
A series of basic articles on the following instruments:
'Maracas' - 13: 37, Oct. 1974.
'Chocollo' - 13: 334, Nov. 1974.
'Tambourine' - 13: 35, Jan. 1975.
'Cabaza' - 13: 34, Feb. 1975.
'Bongos' - 13: 37, March; 13: 37, April 1975.
'Conga Drum' - 13: 37, May 1975.
'Timbales' - 13: 37, June; 14: 37, Aug.; 14: 27, Sep.; 14: 37, Oct.; 14: 35, Nov. 1975.

1227. THIERMANN, D. 'The Mbira in Brazil.' **African Music** 5/1: 90-4, 1971.

1228. THOMPSON, D. 'The Marimbula, an Afro-Caribbean Sanza.' **Yearbook for Inter American Musical Research** 7: 103-16, 1971.

1229. THOMPSON, D. 'A New World Mbira: The Caribbean Marimbula.' **African Music** 5/4: 140-8, 1975-76.
An illustrated description, with historical background information.

1230. TRACEY, A. 'New Development in the Trinidadian Steel Drum.' [re tuning] **African Music** 4/2: 70, 1968.

1231. VELLA, David **Information on the Marimba.** Auckland, N.Z., Institute Press, 1957-58, 77 p. (Editor and translator Vida Chenoweth)
The book discusses the origin and development of the marimba in different parts of the world.

1232. WEINBERGER, Norman 'Aztec Percussion Instruments: Their Description and Use Before Cortes.' **Percussive Notes** 19/2: 76-85, 1982.
Concerns itself with old instruments of the idiophone and membranophone families, and includes a reasonable bibliography.

# CHAPTER 16.

# MUSIC FROM OTHER AREAS.

1233. ABE, Keiko 'The History and Future of the Marimba in Japan.' **Percussive Notes** 22/2: 41-3, 1984.

1234. ABE, Keiko 'Japanese Percussion and Marimba Music.' **Percussive Notes** 22/4: 51-60, 1984.
A compilation of pieces by 450 composers, written before 1983.

1235. ARBATSKY, Yuri **Beating the Tupan in the Central Balkans.** Chicago, Newberry Library, 1953.
Gives details of rhythmic patterns (with their analyoos) and playing techniques of this large bass drum.

1236. BAILY, J. 'A Description of the Naqqarakhana of Herat, Afghanistan.' [Percussion Ensemble] **Asian Music** 11/2: 1-10, 1980.

1237. BOSE, Fritz 'Die Musik der Tukano and Desana.' **Jahrbuch fuer Musikalische Volks- und Voelkerkunde** No.6: 9-20, 1972. [German]
Describes the music and instruments of these American Indian tribes, now living in the Brasilian high-lands (with interesting illustrations).

1238. BRATMAN, C.C. 'A Wealth of Ancient and new Instruments Native to the Orient.' **Percussionist** 6/3: 73-8, 1969.
A brief description (of little value) of many percussion instruments as seen by the author in Japan, Taiwan, Hong Kong, Singapore, Indonesia and India.

1239. CHANDOLA, Anoop **Folk Drumming in the Himalayas (A Linguistic Approach to Music).** New York, A.M.S., 1977, 151 p.
(Not available for annotation; for book review see 'Ethnomusicolgy' 22/3: 519-20, 1978.)

1240. CHENOWETH, Vida 'Defining the Marimba and the Xylophone Inter-culturally.' **Percussionist** 1/1: 4-6, 1963.
A brief discussion on the origins, components and relationships of the xylophone, marimba and vibraphone.

1241. CHENOWETH, Vida (Edi.) **Musical Instruments of Papua New Guinea.** Ukarumpa, P.N.G., Summer Institute of Liguistics, 1976, 80 p.
The book is laid-out in the form of a catalogue, divided into the common grouping of idiophones, aerophones, membranophones, chordophones, plus toys, and borrowed (introduced) instruments. Each entry is specified with province, a brief description, and detail of usage. A great number of percussion instruments are listed, but without illustrations or index.

1242. COURLANDER, H. **The Drum and the Hoe; Life and Love of the Haitian People.** Los Angeles, California University Press, 1960, 371 p.

1243. DELGADO, Mimi Spencer **Zils - The Art of Playing Finger Cymbals.**
Forest Knolls, CA, Jazayer Publications, 1977, 57 p.
(For annotation see same entry in Chapter 8.)

1244. DONALD, Mary Ellen **Doumbec Delight.** San Francisco, Mary Ellen
Books, 110 p. (Also avail. with two cassettes)
A very well-designed and well-written book, explaining all the
techniques of the doumbec in special relation to the music of the Middle
East. The text is clear and progressive.

1245. EL-DABH, Halim **The Derabucca.** New York, Peters, 1965, 8 p.
A very short (and expensive) text on the playing techniques of this
drum. The drum parts, resonance, fingering, hand position and touch are
explained, all with special notation and symbols, and the exercises are
only verbal instructions. The hand-written text and drawings may be
'artistic', but are difficult to read.

1246. FARAOLA, John 'Rediscovering Hawaiian Drums.' **Modern Drummer** 5/1:
28-9, 1981.
In this article a short description of construction and playing
techniques of eleven percussion instruments are given.

1247. FICHTER, George **American Indian Music and Musical Instruments.** New
York, David McKay Co., 1978, 115 p.
The first part gives a very basic overview and examples of Indian
music and songs, but the more unusual part is the second half of the
book, which gives illustrated instructions on how to make a number of
simple Indian percussion instruments.

1248. FREEBERN, Charles **The Music of India, China, Japan and Oceania: A
Source Book for Teachers.** Thesis, University of Arizona, 1969, 176 p.
(Dissertation not listed in Diss. Abst.)

1249. GARFIAS, R. **Music of a Thousand Autumns; The Togaku Style of
Japanese Court Music.** Los Angeles, California Univ. Press, 1975, 322 p.

1250. GREGOIRE, C. **Aegyptische Rhythmik; Rhythmen und
Rhythmusinstrumente im heutigen Aegypten.** Strassburg, Heitz, 1960, 70
p. (German; Translation: 'Egyptian Rhythmic; Rhythms and Rhythm-
Instruments in Egypt of today.')

1251. HARICH-SCHNEIDER, Eta **The Rhythmical Patterns in Gagaku and
Bugaku.** Leiden, E.J. Brill, 1954.
A detailed study of the rhythmic structures in this old Japanese court
music, that is the instrumental music only. It analyzes musical forms,
patterns, notation (Japanese and Western), and instrumental techniques
(with a large percentage being percussion instruments).

1252. HERNDON, M. **Native American Music.** Norwood, PA, Norwood, 1980,
233 p.

1253. HOFSINDE, R. **Indian Music Makers.** Clifton, NJ, Morrow, 1966.
Describes the construction of a variety of percussion instruments used
by American Indians; also debates the significance of music in the daily
life of the Indians, and of ceremonial occasions.

1254. HOWARD, Joseph **Drums in the Americas.** New York, Oak, 1964.
Mainly about the instruments and their history; a very small part on rhythm and drumming; extensive glossary and bibliography.

1255. KAEPPLER, Adrienne **Pahu and Piniu - An Exhibition of Hawaiian Drums.** Honolulu, Bernice Panahi Bishop Museum, 1980, 39 p.
An interesting collection of 74 Pahu and Piniu drums, some with fascinating wood carvings, including historic background.

1256. KARAMATOV, F. 'Uzbek Instrumental Music.' **Asian Music** 15/1: 11-53, 1983.
This article is the main part of Chapter I. of the author's book by the same title (Tashkent, 1972). It includes detailed discussion of the "usuls" (rhythmic structures, usually for percussion instruments) of the Uzbecks (Soviet Union); description and playing technique of the Doira drums, and 18 pages of transcriptions of drum patterns and dances.

1257. KAUFMANN, W. **Musical Notations of the Orient.** Bloomington, Indiana Univ. Press, 1967, 498 p. (Subtitle: 'Notational Systems of Continental East, South and Central Asia')
A fascinating collection of notational systems and techniques from China, India, Tibet and Korea, with a specially interesting chapter on "The Drum Words and Drum Phrases of North Indian Music" (pp 218-63). This includes the description of basic strokes for the Tabla and Mrdanga, and an extensive listing of the various combined strokes of Tabla and Bayan drums (notated in drum syllables and Western notation).

1258. KENNEDY, K. 'Australian Aboriginal Corroboree Sticks.' **The Townsville Naturalist** 5: 8-10, Oct., 1967.
The author decribes three sets of Corroboree sticks, used for keeping time in Aboriginal ceremonial music. [Sticks in collection of the Anthropological Museum, Townsville]

1259. KUNDRAT, Steve **Fun with the Doumbek.** Mid-East Manufacturing Co. (USA), 1977, 16 p.
The subtitle promises: 'Instructions and 50 rhythm variations from one amateur to another'. After an introduction and explanation of a basic playing tecnique, there are 50 two-bar patterns, notated in 4/4 and 9/8, with special (unexplained) names, to be used at the drummer's own discretion.

1260. LIANG, David Mingyue 'The Symbolic and Compositional Language of Chinese Percussion Music.' **Percussive Notes** 23/3: 17-33, 1985.
This debates the meaning of percussion music in society, historic and symbolic background, examples of several "Luogu" styles, with rhythmic charts, musical examples and illustrations.

1261. MALM, W.P. **Japanese Music and Musical Instruments.** Ruttland, VT, Charles E. Tuttle, 1959, 299 p.
This beautifully presented book divides the music into nine styles and discusses the various aspects within each group. The music, instruments and their basic playing techniques are defined, and there is an abundance of detailed illustrations, a combined glossary-index, and an annotated bibliography.

1262. MASON, B.S. **Drums, Tom Toms and Rattles.** New York, Barnes & Co., 1938, 205 p. (now assigned to Dover)
[Gives descriptions of (American) Indian percussion instruments.]

1263. MOYLE, Alice **Aboriginal Sound Instruments.** Canberra, Australian Institute of Aboriginal Studies, 1978, 75 p.
This is actually the 'Companion Booklet for a 12" L.P. Disc, Cat. No. AIAS/14'. It describes and illustrates all the instruments recorded, has complete transcriptions of all the pieces, and includes the main percussion instruments of the Australian Aboriginal people.

1264. PENG XIUWEN 'Chuida Music of Sunan.' [Percussion Ensembles] **Asian Music** 13/2: 31-8, 1982. (Reprinted from radio lectures published by Beijing Music Publ. Co. 1957; includes glossary.)

1265. PICKEN, Laurence **Folk Musical Instruments of Turkey.** London, O.U.P., 1975, 685 p.
The reviewer in the 1976 'Yearbook of the International Folk Music Council' (Kurt Reinhard, pp 139-41) claims that this is not only by far the best book on Turkish instruments, but the best book of this kind on any selection of instruments. It is extensive, detailed, authoritative and covers all direct or indirect aspects of the instruments.

1266. PIGGOTT, Francis **The Music and Musical Instruments of Japan.** New York, Da Capo Press, 1971, 196 p. (Reprint of the 1909 ed.)
This reprint of an old, but interesting, book contains about twenty pages of information on Japanese percussion instruments.

1267. PRESSING, Jeff 'Cognitive Isomorphisms in World Music: West Africa, The Balkans, Thailand, and Western Tonality.' **Studies in Music** 17: 38-61, 1983.

1268. RECK, David **Music of the Whole Earth.** New York, Charles Scribner's Sons, 1977, 545 p.
(For annotation see same entry in Chapter 8.)

1269. RUSSELL, L. 'Percussion in Hawaii.' **Percussionist** 5/2: 272-3, 1967.

1270. SCHOENFELDER, G. 'Zum Gebrauch der Schlaginstrumente im traditionellen chinesischen Musiktheater.' **Studio Musicologica** 13/1-4: 137-76, 1971.
[Article on the use of percussion in Chinese Music Theatre; German]

1271. SHINER, Kristen 'Ensemble Nipponia: A continuing Tradition in Today's World.' **Percussive Notes** 21/4: 33-5, 1983.
A description of this ensemble, which plays contemporary music on traditional Japanese instruments.

1272. SYMONETTE, Neil 'Junkanoo.' **Modern Drummer** 7/10: 64-8, 1983.
[Several examples of percussion ensemble music from the Bahamas.]

1273. TOHSHA, Naritoshi 'Japanese Traditional Percussion Instruments and their Music.' **Percussive Notes** 22/2: 44-59, 1984.
An illustrated report, with many musical examples, describing the instruments, solo and ensemble music.

1274. TONG, K.W. **Shang Musical Instruments.** Ph.D. Thesis, Wesleyan Univ., 1983, 400 p. (Diss. Abst. 44: 1240A, Nov. 1983)
This concerns the historic culture of Shang (China), c. 16th - 11th century B.C., and is a study of their music and instruments. There is also a lengthy article (based on this thesis) published in 'Asian Music' (15/1: 103-51, 1983).

1275. VANDOR, I. 'Cymbals and Trumpets from the "Roof of the World".' [Tibet] **Music Educator's Journal** 61: 106-9+, Sep. 1974.
A description of some instruments and music found in Tibetan monasteries.

1276. VENNUM, Thomas Jr. **The Ojibwa Dance Drum: Its History and Construction.** Washington, Smithsonian Institution Press, 1982, 320 p.
This is a specialized, illustrated study on this particular drum, which is used by the North American Indians, the Ojibwa. It covers a broad history of the instrument and its music, and contains details on its construction, decoration and accessories.

1277. WOODSON, C.D. 'The Effect of a Snare on the Tone of a Single-headed Frame Drum, the Moroccan Bendir.' **Selected Reports in Ethnomusicology** 2/1: 107-17, 1974.

# APPENDIX I.

## A SELECTED LIST OF PERCUSSION MUSIC, TRANSCRIPTIONS AND ANALYSES.

1278. ABEL, Alan **20th Century Orchestra Studies for Percussion.** New York, Schirmer, 1970, 77 p.

A helpful and varied collection of 39 percussion excerpts, ranging from snare drum to all keyboard and multi percussion, as well as for 2 and 4 percussionists.

1279. ABEL, Alan **20th Century Orchestra Studies for Timpani.** New York, Schirmer, 1970, 69 p.

The author has compiled and annotated a useful collection of 36 lengthy excerpts from the contemporary repertoire.

1280. ALFORD, E.E. **Identification of Percussion Performance Techniques in the Standard Orchestral Percussion Repertoire.** D.M.A. Thesis, The Univ. of Oklahoma, 1983, 637 p. (Diss. Abst. 45: 676A, Sep. 1984)

(For annotation see same entry in chapter 5/f)

1281. BAKER, Donald 'Percussion Solos and Studies.' (Annual reviews) **The Instrumentalist** 34: 73-4, Dec. 1979.

1282. BEDFORD, F. 'A Survey of 20th Century Music for Percussion and Harpsichord.' **Woodwind World, Brass and Percussion** 17/6: 40-3, 1978.

1283. BETTINE, Michael 'Style and Analysis: Bill Bruford.' **Modern Drummer** 8/10: 72-4, 1984.

Discusses six transcribed examples of his recordings.

1284. BOULDER, J.E. **Brazilian Percussion Compositions since 1953: An Annotated Catalogue.** D.M.A. Thesis, American Conservatorium of Music, 1983, 114 p. (Diss. Abst. 44: 3534A, June 1984)

1285. BROOKS, William 'A Drummer Boy looks back: Percussion in Ives's Fourth Symphony.' **Percussive Notes** 22/6: 4-45, 1984.

An in-depth analysis of the role of percussion in this composition, suggested aims and innovative techniques of the composer, together with performance problems and comparative charts of instrumentation.

1286. BROWN, Merrill 'Repertoire for Percussionists.' **The Instrumentalist** 31: 67-70, Feb. 1977.

This is a summary of the results of a survey among 700 (US) university music departments and music colleges, based on frequency of performances of percussion music (ensemble and solo).

1287. BYRON, Kent 'Transcription: "High Heel Sneekers", Drum Solo by Steve Gadd.' **Modern Drummer** 9/2: 88-9, 1985.

1288. CHEADLE, R.D. **A Bibliography of Multimedia Solo Percussion Works with an Analysis of Performance Problems.** D.A. Thesis, Univ. of Northern Colorado, 1983, 185 p. (Diss. Abst. 44: 2919A+, Apr. 1984) (For annotation see same entry in Chapter 5/g.)

1289. CHILDS, Barney 'A Catalogue and some Comments', **Percussive Notes** 22/6: 59-77, 1984.
     A discussion by the composer of some of his works featuring percussion.

1290. DE PONTE, Niel 'No.9 Zyklus: How and Why?' **Percussionist** 12/4: 136-49, 1975.
     An in-depth discussion and analysis of this piece. The author also relates some background regarding the composer's intentions and plans for this work. Despite the seemingly great amount of freedom and choice the percussionist has in playing "Zyklus" (e.g. the new "constructive principle of relative variability"), the author demonstrates how Stockhausen has "serially mediated all the parameters of the piece". It also includes the complete review by F.B. Zimmermann of the recording and live performance ('Notes' 21/1-2: 241-3, 1963-64).

1291. DODGE, Stephen 'The "Concerto pour batterie et petit orchestre" by Darius Milhaud with a Look at Percussion in his Musical Life.' **Percussive Notes** 17/3: 58-9, 1979.

1292. EYLER, David 'The Top Ten Ensemble Works.' **The Instrumentalist** 34/10: 20-4, 1980.
     A discussion on instrumentation and performance difficulties of the ten percussion ensemble compositions most frequently performed during the years of 1976-1979 (as listed in the section "Programs" of the 'Percussive Notes' magazine). The first three were "Toccata" (C. Chavez), "Gainsborough" (T.Ganger), and "October Mountain" (A. Hovhaness).

1293. EYLER. David 'The Top 50 Percussion Solo and Ensemble Compositions of Today.' **Percussive Notes** 18/1: 38-9, 1980.
     Order of listing is according to repeated number of performances.

1294. FINK, Ron 'Timpani Repertoire (Index to Orchestral Studies).' **Percussionist** 2/4: 19-23, 1965.
     Lists the repertoire as found in six popular timpani tutors.

1295. GANN, Kyle 'The Percussion Music of John J. Becker.' **Percussive Notes** 22/3: 26-41, 1984.
     Discussion and analysis of his music, especially his two pieces for percussion ensemble "The Abongo" (1933) and "Vigilante 1938."

1296. GOLDENBERG, Morris (Comp.) **Classic Overtures for Timpani. [1961] Classic Symphonies for Timpani. [1963] Romantic Symphonies for Timpani. [1964] Standard Concertos for Timpani. [1969]** New York, Chappell & Co.

1297. HAUN, E.E. **Modal and Symmetrical Pitch Constructions in Bela Bartok's "Sonata for Two Pianos and Percussion."** D.M.A. Thesis, Austin, Univ. of Texas, 1982, 106 p. (Diss. Abst. 43: 3748A, June 1983)

1298. HELLER, G.N. **Ensemble Music for Wind and Percussion Instruments; A Catalogue.** Washington, National Education Association, 1970, 160 p.

1299. HINGER, Fred **The Timpani Player's Orchestral Repertoire.** Hackensack, NJ, Jerona Music Corp., 1981, 72 p. (Vol.1: Beethoven Symphonies) (For annotation see the same entry in Chapter 5/b.)

1300. HONG, Sherman **Percussion in the Aggregate Textures of Selected Orchestral, Band and Chamber Compositions written between 1920 and 1970.** Thesis, Univ. of Southern Mississippi, 1974, 242 p.
Seven compositions were studied in this paper, ranging from orchestral context to free design and chance pieces. They include Bartok's "Sonata for two pianos and percussion", E. Varese's "Arcana", Hovhaness' "Symphony No.4", Haubenstock-Ramati's "Mobile for Shakespeare", and E. Brown's "Available Forms."

1301. HOWE, Warren 'The Percussionist's Guide to Darius Milhaud's "La Creation Du Monde".' **Percussionist** 17/1: 37-48, 1979.

1302. HURLEY, Mark 'Transcription: "Green Dolphin Street", Drum Solo by Shelly Manne.' **Modern Drummer** 9/6: 48-9, 1985.

1303. HUSA, Karel 'Three Dance Sketches.' [by the author] **Percussive Notes** 21/3: 36-46, 1983.

1304. JACOB, I.G. 'The Use of Percussion in Symphony No.6 by Vincent Persichetti: A Functional Analysis.' **Percussionist** 15/1: 17-20, 1977.

1305. JOHNSTON, Ben 'The Genesis of "Knocking Piece".' **Percussive Notes** 21/3: 25-31, 1983.
[Composition by the author]

1306. KAUFFMAN, Robert 'Transcription: Elvin Jones Solo "Effendi".' **Modern Drummer** 4/3: 64, 1980.

1307. KEEZER, R. 'A Study of Selected Percussion Ensemble Music of the 20th Century.' (5 parts) **Percussionist** 8/1: 11-23; 8/2: 38-44, 1970; /3: 94-9; 8/4: 134-6+; 16-23. 1971.
This is a very worthwhile series of articles in five parts, giving a brief biography of seven contemporary composers, and discussing one major work of each composer. All the discussions are more descriptive than analytic and cover the performer's interests.
Part (1) deals with Henry Cowell's "Ostinato Pianissimo" and John Cage/L. Harrison's "Double Music", the latter analysis being more detailed. Part (2) covers Alan Hovhaness' "October Mountain". Part (3) debates Armand Russell's "Percussion Suite" reasonably well. Part (4) is extremely brief and talks about Barney Child's "Take Five". Part (5), Edgar Varese's "Ionisation", is the most comprehensive and also contains a bibliography.

1308. KERRIGAN, Chuck 'Transcription and Analysis: "One Word", Drum Solo by Billy Cobham.' **Percussive Notes** 14/3: 27-9, 1976.

1309. KERRIGAN, Chuck 'Spotlight on Joe (A transcription of the drum solo from "Take Five" by Joe Morello).' **Modern Drummer** 1/2: 23-5, 1977.

1310. KETTLE, Rupert 'Transcription: Max Roach Solo "Big Sidd".' **Modern Drummer** 4/1: 60-1, 1980.

1311. LARRICK, G.H. 'Eight Pieces for Four Timpani by Elliott Carter (Analysis).' **Percussionist** 12/1: 12-5, 1974.
This is the second one of two articles on Carter's pieces appearing together in the same journal (see: R. McCormick, entry in this chapter). This author concentrates on the pieces "Recitative", "Improvisation", "Adagio", and "March", and discusses aspects of rhythm, type of sounds (timbre), form, and performance problems. Again, it lacks depth and real insight, and is mainly a description (rather than an analysis). For example, neither author could see past the obvious rhythm in "March" to the clever sonata structure built on sustaining accents.

1312. LARRICK, G.H. 'Gary Burton: "The Sunset Bell" - Analysis.' **Percussionist** 13/2: 48-54, 1976.

1313. LARRICK, G.H. 'Paul Creston: "Concertina for Marimba and Orchestra", Opus 21.' [Analysis] **N.A.C.W.P.I. Journal** 32/3: 4-18, 1984.

1314. LATHAM, Rick 'Steve Gadd: Up close.' **Modern Drummer** 4/5: 50-1, 1980.
A brief article, showing seven examples taken from recordings by Steve Gadd.

1315. LATHAM, Rick **Advanced Funk Studies.** Dallas, TX, The Author, 1981. (Also avail. with two cassettes)
This text aims to give insight into today's funk and fusion music; with relevant exercises, transcriptions of rhythms by well-known drummers (e.g. Steve Gadd, James Mason, and others), and ten well written solos.

1316. LAWRENCE, V.C. '"Ionisation" - Edgar Varese.' **Percussionist** 7/4: 122-5, 1970.
A general, but rather skimpy analysis, lacking the necessary and clarifying depth.

1317. MAHADY, T.J. **A Comparative Study of the Technical and Interpretative Problems of the "Concerto for Five Kettledrums and Orchestra" by Robert Paris and the "Concerto for Timpani and Orchestra" by Werner Thaerichen.** D.A. Thesis, Ball State University, 1977, 163 p. (Diss. Abst. 38: 5791A, Apr. 1978)

1318. McCORMICK, R. 'Eight Pieces for Four Timpani by Elliott Carter (Analysis).' **Percussionist** 12/1: 7-11, 1974.
This is one of two articles on Carter's pieces appearing together (see also G.H. Larrick's entry in this chapter). The analysis discusses some performance techniques used in the compositions, and describes tunings, rhythms and metric modulations of "Canaries", "Moto Perpetuo", and "March". However, most of the discussion is taken straight off the score and the introduction, and has not much insight into the composer's less obvious intentions.

1319. MINTZ, Billy **Different Drummers.** New York, Amsco Music, 96 p. (Includes record)
The book contains transcriptions of drummers like Billy Cobham, Buddy Miles, Ray Hanes, Tony Williams, Elvin Jones, Bernard Purdie and Max Roach, as well as some simple exercises and solos written in the style of these drummers. Interesting material - not for beginners.

160

1320. MIZELLE, D.J. 'Sound and Idea in "Soundscape".' ["Soundscape for Percussion Ensemble" by the author] **Percussive Notes** 21/3: 47-74, 1983.
Detailed discussion with many musical examples from the score, plus a list of notational symbols used.

1321. MORGAN, Graham 'Graham Morgan (edi. by Ken Laing).' **The Professional Musicians' Journal (Melbourne)** Feb.: 29-32, 1983.
Contains three pages of transcriptions of rhythms and patterns from recordings, including Steve Gadd and Billy Cobham, and some exercises.

1322. MORTON, James 'John Bonham: In Retrospect.' **Modern Drummer** 5/1: 20-3, Jan./Feb. 1981.
The article gives 44 transcriptions of short rhythms and patterns from popular recordings of this heavy-metal rock drummer.

1323. MORTON, James 'Transcription: "Get Closer", Drum Part by Russ Kunkel.' **Modern Drummer** 8/11: 104-5, 1984.

1324. MORTON, James 'Transcription: "Rock Steady", Drum Chart played by Bernard Purdie (1972).' **Modern Drummer** 9/11: 70-1, 1985.

1325. MURRAY, G. & J. 'Ensemble Insight: Basic Repertoire (of percussion music).' **Modern Percussionist** 1/2: 36-7, 1985.
This discusses the criteria and some typical characteristics of music for percussion (after 1930), and recommends some pieces for various ensembles.

1326. OWEN, Charles 'Paul Creston's Concerto for Marimba' (A Master Lesson).
**Percussive Notes** 21/2: 62-4, 1983.

1327. PETERS, Gordon 'Motivation for Saint-Saens' Use of the Xylophone in his "Dance Macabre".' **Percussionist** 5/3: 305-7, 1968.

1328. SABLINSKIS, Paul **The Significance of Percussion in Contemporary Music between 1945 and 1970.** Masters Thesis, Univ. of Melbourne, 1982, 462 p.
(For annotation see same entry in Chapters 3/a and 10/b.)

1329. SANDERSON, Gillian **The Dramatic Role of Percussion in Selected Operas of Benjamin Britten.** Thesis, University of Alberta, 1980.

1330. SENN, Dan 'Standard Performance Practice, Soundsculpture and Scrapercussion.' **Percussive Notes** 21/6: 23-45, 1983.
(For annotation see same entry in Chapter 5/g.)

1331. SIMPSON, J. 'Milt Jackson's Solo on "Milano" - A Vibes Transcription.' **Downbeat** 52: 50-51, Feb., 1985.

1332. SMITH, Stuart 'The early Percussion Music of John Cage.' **Percussionist** 16/1: 16-27, 1978.
An essay on some of Cage's philosophy and the pieces "Imaginary Landscape No.3" (1942) and "Quartet: 12 Tom Toms" (1943).

1333. SMITH, Stuart 'Lou Harrison's Fugue for Percussion.' [Analysis] **Percussionist** 16/2: 47-56, 1978.

1334. SMITH, Terry **The Mallet Master Series.** Shell Lake, Wisconsin, Etoile Music Inc.
This consists of three vibraphone solos (with piano accompaniment), well transcribed by the author:
(1) "Moonchild/In a Quiet Place" (Gary Burton and Keith Jarret);
(2) "Green Mountain", by Steve Swallow, played by Gary Burton;
(3) "John Brown's Body", as played by Milt Jackson.

1335. SNIDER, Robert 'A Guide to Percussion Excerpts.' **Percussionist** 16/3: 153-76, 1979.
A handy guide which takes thirteen better-known tutors and albums, and then catalogues all the excerpts according to composers and instrumental groupings: where to find the excerpts and whether they are complete or not.

1336. SOAMES, Cynthia 'Harold Faberman: Concerto for Timpani and Orchestra.' [Analysis] **Percussionist** 14/1: 32-5, 1976.

1337. SOAMES, Cynthia 'Feldman - "The King of Denmark".' [Analysis] **Percussionist** 15/2: 86-7, 1978.

1338. SPAGNARDI, Ron 'Krupa in Solo.' [Transcription and analysis] **Modern Drummer** 3/5: 26-7, 1979.

1339. STOCKHAUSEN, Karlheinz 'Bartok's Sonata for two Pianos and Percussion.' **New Hungarian Quarterly** 11/40: 49-53, 1970.
Stockhausen analyzes this composition with special regard to the treatment and relationship of rhythm vs. melody.

1340. TOMLINSON, Dan 'Transcription: "Lazy Bird", Drum Solo by Philly Joe Jones.' **Modern Drummer** 8/8: 96-7, 1984.

1341. UDOW, Michael 'An Interview with Karlheinz Stockhausen.' **Percussive Notes** 23/6: 4-47, 1985.
(For annotation see same entry in Chapter 5/f.)

1342. VANLANDINGHAM, Larry **The Percussion Ensemble: 1930-1945.** Ph.D. Thesis, Florida State University, 1971, 114 p. (Diss. Abst. 32: 2125A, Oct. 1971)
The author's intent was to trace the percussion ensemble's evolution through these years, and he shows on hand of six selected pieces how the "treatment of instrumentation, timbre, and rhythm" has appeared and changed. The pieces are: A. Roldan's "Ritmica No.5", E. Varese's "Ionisation", L. Harrison's "Canticle No.3", J. Cage's "Imaginary Landscape No.3", C. Chavez's "Toccata", and Hovhaness' "October Mountain". Basically, his conclusive opinion on instrumentation is: (1) use of standard orchestral percussion (in Roldan and Varese); (2) a trend away from standard percussion (in Harrison and Cage); (3) return to standard percussion (in Chavez and Hovhaness).

1343. VANLANDINGHAM, Larry 'The Percussion Ensemble 1930-1945.' (6 parts) **Percussionist** vol.9, no.3, 1971 to vol.10, no.4, 1973.
A series of articles taken from the author's dissertation by the same title (see previous entry above):
9/3: 71-81; 9/4: 106-118; 10/1: 11-25, 1971.
10/2: 55-62, 1972. 10/3: 87-95; 10/4: 118-125, 1973.

1344. VINCENT, David W. 'Commercially available Excerpts for Kettledrums.' **Percussionist** 14/3: 98-105, 1977.

1345. VINCENT, David W. 'Commercially available Excerpts for Percussion.' **Percussionist** 15/1: 40-4, 1977.

1346. VINCENT, David W. **A Percussionist's Guide to Orchestral Excerpts.** Columbia, SC, Broad River, 1980, 71 p.
   The contents is grouped by individual and miscellaneous instruments, and each composition is referred to by code to one of the 33 albums and manuals listed at the rear of the book.

1347. WHITWELL, D. & JOHNSON, R. 'Three Multi-Timpani Works before Berlioz.' (Works by Druschetzky) **The Instrumentalist** 27: 36-7, Dec. 1972.

1348. WILLIAMS, J. Kent 'A Survey of Writings on Bartok's Sonata for Two Pianos and Percussion.' **Percussionist** 17/1: 3-22, 1979.
   The author gives a summary of this piece with examples of other reviews and critiques of performances and analyses. The sections of the article are: "History: The Commission and Composition" (including first performances), "General Outline and Analysis", "Analysis by Erno Lendvai" (discussing the Axis System, the Golden Section, and chord and interval usage), and a bibliography.

1349. WILSON, Patrick 'Elliott Carter: Eight Pieces for four Timpani.' [Interview with the Composer] **Percussive Notes** 23/1: 63-5, 1985.

1350. WOOD, David 'Transcription: "Slow Trane", Drum Solo by Art Taylor (1957).' **Modern Drummer** 8/3: 64-5, 1985.

1351. YORK, Wesley 'A Draft of Shadows.' **Percussive Notes** 22/3: 42-67, 1984.
   Detailed discussion of the achievement, structure, musical relation to the text, and overal concept of this composition.

# APPENDIX II.

## RELEVANT BIBLIOGRAPHIES, INDEXES AND REVIEWS.

1352. BAKER, Donald 'Percussion (annual review of solos and studies).' **The Instrumentalist** 35: 37-40, Dec. 1980.

1353. BAKER, Donald 'New Music, Sounds and Approaches in Percussion Literature.' **The Instrumentalist** 36: 38+, May; 36: 52-5, June 1982.

1354. BAKER, Donald 'New Percussion Solos and Methods.' (Annual reviews) **The Instrumentalist** 37: 78+, Feb., 1983.

1355. BALDWIN, James 'Multipercussion: Techniques and Materials.' **The School Musician** 41: 10+, May 1970.

1356. BERKLEY, Dick 'An Index of Articles appearing in Percussionist, arranged according to Subject (May 1963 - March 1970).' **Percussionist** 7/4: 127-31, 1970.

1357. BRUECHE, B. **Music Bibliographies for all Instruments.** Munich, The Author, 1976, 96 p.

1358. COMBS, F. Michael 'Reviews of Percussion Materials.' **The Instrumentalist** 26: 48-9, Dec. 1971.

1359. COMBS, F. Michael 'Percussion Ensemble Literature.' **The Instrumentalist** 28: 56-9, Oct. 1973.

1360. COMBS, F. Michael 'Snare Drum Method Books.' **The Instrumentalist** 29: 53-5, Sep. 1974. (Eleven texts are annotated.)

1361. COOVER, J. **Musical Instrument Collections: Catalogues and Cognate Literature.** Detroit, Information Coordinators, 1981.

1362. DRUMS UNLIMITED **The Drums Unlimited Percussion Publications Catalogue.** Bethesda, ML, Drums Unlimited, yearly, c.50 p.
    This is a large yearly listing of publications which has been available for several years now. It normally includes (1) methods and studies, (2) solos, and (3) ensembles. Each section is further divided into detailed groupings. The methods are not actually annotated, but contain the odd explanatory comment, and the music literature is graded in levels of difficulty of performance. However, the entries provide only information about author, title, cost and order number (i.e. no publisher, pages, year, etc.).

1363. DUTTON, J. **Solo and Ensemble Literature for Keyboard Percussion Instruments.** Brookfield, IL, Musser, 1963, 25 p.

1364. FINK, Ron 'Percussion Articles which have appeared in the "International Musician," 1950-64.' **Percussionist** 3/1: 19-22, 1965.

1365. FRY, J.H. **New Musical Notation: a Bibliography.** Ph.D. Thesis, The University of Rochester, Eastman School of Music, 1977, 107 p. (Diss. Abst. 38: 17A, July 1977)
From the author's summary: "This bibliography deals with the writings on new symbols as they are used by composers today and the allied subjects of interpretation, inadequacies in traditional notation, reform and new systems". The paper does not include ethnomusicological, computer or analytical notations.

1366. GALM, John 'The Percussionist's Bookshelf.' **Percussionist** 7/2: 45-54, 1969.
An annotated bibliography of texts and articles grouped into areas of interest (of Western music).

1367. GALM, John 'A Survey of Latin American Percussion instructional Materials.' **N.A.C.W.P.I. Journal** 24/2: 42-4, 1975-76.
[Ten texts are reviewed]

1368. GASKIN, L.J.P. (Compiler) **A Selected Bibliography of Music in Africa.** London, International African Institute, 1965, 83 p.
An extensive - if somewhat dated - work, containing over 3000 entries, but not annotated, ordered in cross-reference by musical subjects within geographical groupings.

1369. HOWLAND, Harold 'The Vibraphone: A summary of historical observation with a catalogue of selected solo and small ensemble literature.' **Percussionist** 15/1: 20-40, 1977.
(For annotation see same entry in Chapter 10/a.)

1370. HUBER, G.K. 'Recent Books (on instruments).' **Journal of the American Musical Instruments Society** 2: 104-17, 1976.

1371. HUBER, G.K. 'Recent Books (on instruments).' **Journal of the American Musical Instruments Society** 5-6: 218-27, 1980-81.

1372. HUBER, G.K. 'Recent Books (on Instruments).' **Journal of the American Musical Instruments Society** 9: 144-8, 1983.

1373. JASTROW, William 'The Solo Percussion Ensemble: Literature.' **Percussive Notes** 22/5: 70-2, 1984.

1374. JAZZ JOURNAL INTERNATIONAL (Edi.) 'Record Reviews: The Vibraphone in Jazz.' **Jazz Journal International** 37: 37-8, Feb., 1984.

1375. JENKINS, Jean (Edi.) **International Directory of Musical Instrument Collections.** Buren, Knuf, 1978, 166 p.

1376. KIMMEL, D. 'Book Reviews (List of books on the dulcimer).' **Bluegrass Unlimited** 14: 27, Nov. 1979.

1377. KOCH, K. 'A Review of Selected, Successful Drumset Books.' **The School Musician** 56: 16-8, Nov., 1984.
This is, in my opinion, a very poor selection, and the reviews are very basic.

1378. KUZMICH, John 'Texts on Theory, Compositions and Arranging.' **The Instrumentalist** 34: 42-7, Dec. 1979.

1379. LAMBERT, James 'Annual Review of Solos and Studies: Percussion.' (2 parts) **The Instrumentalist** 39: 46+, Apr.; 39: 62-3, May, 1985.

1380. MASONER, B. 'A Continuing Index of Percussion Articles in other Periodicals.' (2 parts) **Percussionist** 5/1: 238-40, 1967; 6/1: 29-31, 1968.

1381. McKINNEY, James 'A Band Director's Guide to Percussion Texts.' **The Instrumentalist** 29: 75-8. June 1975.

1382. MEAD, Rita H. **Doctoral Dissertations in American Music; A Classified Bibliography.** Brooklyn, Institute for Studies in American Music, 1974, 155 p.

1383. MECKLENBURG, C.G. **1970 Supplement to the International Jazz Bibliography (IJB) and International Drum and Percussion Bibliography.** Vienna, Universal, 1971, 102 p.

1384. MOORE, James L. 'A selective Bibliography of Material Pertaining to the Acoustics of Percussion Instruments.' **Percussionist** 7/1: 23-6, 1969. [Contains brief annotations.]

1385. MOSES, Lennard 'An Annotated Bibliography of the History and Music of Trinidad.' **Percussive Notes** 22/3: 77-83, 1984.

1386. MUELLER, Kenneth 'Percussion Articles and Biographies printed in "The Ludwig Drummer" (1961-1967).' **Percussionist** 4/3: 164-9, 1967.

1387. NAVARA, B. 'Bibliography of Articles appearing in the "National Association of College Wind and Percussion Instruments Journal" (Vol.41).' **N.A.C.W.P.I. Journal** 32/1: 36-8, 1983.

1388. NELSON, Robert 'An Index of Percussion Articles: "Instrumentalist" (1960-1972), "School Musician" (1960-1972), "NACWPI Bulletin" (1958-1972).' (2 parts) **Percussionist** 10/2: 69-73; 10/3: 100-4, 1973.

1389. PERCUSSIONIST (Editorial) 'Percussion Literature from "The Instrumentalist" (May 1946 to May 1965).' **Percussionist** 2/3: 18-21, 1965.

1390. PERCUSSIVE ARTS SOCIETY **Solo and Ensemble Literature for Percussion.** Terre Haute, Percussive Arts Society, 1978, 93 p. (Chairman of P.A.S.: F. Michael Combs)
    The listing is grouped by instruments (solo) and various ensemble groupings, stating composer, publisher, and grading (e.g. E; M; D;). It includes extensive list of publishers.

1391. READ, Danny 'An Annotated Survey of Jazz History Material.' **The Educator** 13/1: 38, 1980.

1392. READ, Danny 'Drumset Study Materials Guide.' **Modern Drummer** 6/7: 28-40, 1982.
    [Includes publishers' costs and brief annotations]

1393. ROSEN, Michael 'A Survey of Compositions Written for the Percussion Ensemble.' (3 parts) **Percussionist** 4/2: 106-12; 4/3: 137-43; 4/4: 190-5, 1967.
    An informative series of articles which traces the development of the

percussion ensemble (in Western art music) in the 20th century up to the present time (1967). Composers and their main works under discussion include: L. Russolo, G. Antheil, E. Varese, W. Russell, L. Harrison, J. Cage, C. Chavez, A. Hovhaness, M. Colgrass, W. Benson, and B. Childs. The article concludes with a discography and bibliography.

1394. SCHIETROMA, Robert 'Materials for Drum Set.' [Methods and tutors] **Percussive Notes** 20/2: 49-51, 1982.

1395. SEWREY, James 'An Index of Articles on Percussion in "The School Musician".' **Percussionist** 3/1: 17-8, 1965.

1396. SHAPIRO, Harry **A - Z of Rock Drummers.** New York, Proteus Publishing Co., 1984.
    Informative, well illustrated, with biographies and references to past work.

1397. SKEI, Allen **Woodwind, Brass, and Percussion Instruments of the Orchestra - A Bibliographic Guide.** New York, Garland Publishing, 1985, 271 p.
    The only serious attempt of a percussion bibliography I have seen so far. But out of 271 pages only 16 (^) deal with percussion alone, and in the general chapters it is sadly under-represented.
    The organisation of the book is not always clear and logical. Sixteen main chapters are divided into further 39 minor sections, often without a seemingly good reason. However, most of the major traditional books and articles on orchestral percussion are listed, but no instructional methods, not much on notation and contemporary performance, nothing on rock or jazz music, and nothing on Non-Western percussion at all.

1398. SMALL, E.P. 'An Index of Percussion Articles appearing in "Downbeat".' **Percussionist** 7/2: 77-81, 1969.

1399. STANDIFER, J.A. & REEDER, B. **Source Book of African and Afro-American Materials for Music Educators.** Washington, Music Educators National Conference, 1972, 148 p.

1400. SZWED, J.F. (and others) **Afro-American Folk Culture: An Annotated Bibliography of Materials from North, Central and South America and the West Indies.** Philadelphia, Institute for the Study of Human Issues, 1978, 466 p & 405 p. (2 vols.)
    Contains over 1000 entries on the subject of music and instruments.

1401. THE INSTRUMENTALIST (Ed.) 'Buyer's Guide: A Comprehensive Listing of Companies Supplying the Needs of Instrumental Music.' **The Instrumentalist** 37: 22-31, July, 1983.
    The listing refers only to companies operating (or represented) in the U.S.A., with the main sections being (1) Instruments & Accessories, and (3) Printed Music and Publications.

1402. THIEME, D.L. **African Music; A briefly Annotated Bibliography.** Westport, CT, Greenwood Press, 1978, 55 p. (First publ. by Library of Congress, Washington, 1964)

1403. WARFIELD, Gerald **Writings on Contemporary Music Notation: An Annotated Bibliography.** Ann Arbor, MI, Music Library Association, 1976, 93 p.

A comprehensive bibliography, covering material from the years 1950 - 1975, and selected listings back to 1900. Percussion entries (15 in number) can be located in the subject index.

1404. WILLIAMS, J. Kent 'A Survey of Writings on Bartok's Sonata for Two Pianos and Percussion.' **Percussionist** 17/1: 3-22, 1979.
(For annotation see same entry in Appendix 1.)

1405. WINESANKER, M. (Compiler) **Books on Music: A Classified List.** Tarleton, TX, Texas Association of Music Schools, 1979, 165 p.

1406. WINICK, S.D. **Rhythm: An Annotated Bibliography.** Metuchen, NJ, Scarecrow, 1974, 150 p.
A comprehensive text, covering the years 1900-1972, divided into three main sections : Background, Psychology, and Pedagogy (of rhythm).

# APPENDIX III.

## LISTING OF PERCUSSION MAGAZINES AND OTHER MUSICAL JOURNALS WITH REGULAR FEATURES ON PERCUSSION.

1407. **African Music** (African Music Society, Rodenpoort; irregular.)
Contains, very frequently, often extensive research articles on African percussion music and instruments.

1408. **Asian Music** (The Society for Asian Music, New York; semiannually.)
Many of its research articles relate to percussion, in particular with regard to music of South-East Asia.

1409. **The Black Perspective in Music** (Foundation for Research in Afro-American Creative Arts, New York; twice a year.)
This journal from time to time publishes essays relating to percussion music and/or instruments in the area of African and jazz music.

1410. **Brass and Percussion**
This journal was published from 1973-1975 and then incorporated into **Woodwind World - Brass and Percussion** (see entry in this appendix under 'Woodwind').

1411. **Down Beat** (Maher Publications, Chicago; monthly.)
Brings several feature articles and interviews per year on well-known jazz and fusion drummers. Occasionally it also has a technical article on drumming techniques under the regular heading of 'Pro Sessions.'

1412. **Ethnomusicolgy** (Society for Ethnomusicology, Ann Arbor; three issues annually.)
Among the many articles in this journal about traditional musics from most parts of the world, a great deal are concerned with percussion. One of the regular features is the usually very comprehensive "Current bibliography and discography", and the extensive and knowledgable book reviews are another important feature of this publication.

1413. **The Instrumentalist** (The Instrumentalist Co., Northfield; monthly.)
This journal covers a wide range of musical activities and styles: however, the regular "New Music Reviews" deals mainly with marching band and concert band music, jazz band, and some string and ensemble music. It has very frequent percussion articles, mostly of a technical nature, and an annual review of percussion texts and literature.

1414. **Modern Drummer** (Modern Drummer Publications, Cedar Grove, NJ; monthly.)
The articles in this publication are divided into basically two types of contributions: "Features" (biographical news and interviews) and "Columns". The latter group contains the subject areas of Education, Equipment, Reviews, Profiles, News, and Departments. The current (1985) regular series of articles includes these titles, with some of the

regular authors mentioned in brackets:
"Jazz Drummer's Workshop" (Mark Hurley, Chuck Kerrigan).
"Driver's Seat" [re big band].
"The Musical Drummer" (Bill Molenhof).
"Club Scene" (Rick van Horn).
"In the Studio."
"Strictly Technique."
"Electronic Insight" (R. Havok).
"Drum Soloist" [transcriptions and some analyses].
"Rock Charts" [transcriptions].
"Product Close-Up" (Bob Saydlowski).
"Shop Talk" [re equipment].
"Reviews" [of books, recordings, and video tapes - by various authors].

1415. **Modern Percussionist** (Modern Drummer Publications, Cedar Grove, NJ; quarterly.)
A very welcome new music journal on the thinly represented subject of percussion (first issue: Jan. 1985). This is an "off-spring" publication of the **Modern Drummer** (see previous entry) and is designed in much the same way, that is that there are main "Features" (mostly reports on personalities) and "Columns" - a series of regular articles, some of which are listed below, again with their regular authors stated in brackets:
"Timp Talk" (Vic Firth).
"Orchestral Percussionist" (Arthur Press, Morris Lang).
"Marimba Perspectives" (L.H. Stevens).
"Vibraphone Viewpoint" (Dave Samuels).
"Marching Percussion" (J.W. Nebistinsky).
"Corps Scene" (D. De Lucia).
"Latin Symposium" (Montego Joe).
"Ensemble Insight" (G. & J. Murray).
"Critique" [Reviews of percussion music literature, instruction books, and recordings - by various authors].
"Tracking" [studio work] (Gordon Gottlieb).

1416. **Percussionist** (Percussive Arts Society, Terra Haute, U.S.A.; quarterly.)
This journal was published from 1963 to 1980 under this title, from 1980 till March 1982 it appeared under the combined titles of **Percussionist** and **Percussive Notes**, when it was totally incorporated into **Percussive Notes** (see following entry for details).

1417. **Percussive Notes** (Percussive Arts Society, Terra Haute, U.S.A.; six issues annually.)
Prior to the incorporation of the **Percussionist** in March 1982 this journal was published only three times a year. The current arrangement is that out of the six issues Nos. 3 and 6 are classified as "Research Editions", each of up to 100 pages, containing a small number of extensive research-type articles, usually of a very high standard. The remaining issues of **Percussive Notes** (which are slightly larger in format, with similar page numbers) as a rule have a particular subject theme per issue. They also contain regular feature articles, which include the following titles (with the regular editors - as of 1985 - in brackets):
"Marimba Clinic" (L.H. Stevens, G. Stout).
"Marimba Exchange" (Linda Pimentel).
"Drum Set Forum" (Ed Soph).
"Symphonic Percussion" (R. Weiner, C. Owen).
"Ethnic Percussion" (Norbert Goldberg).

"Vibe Workshop" (Ed Saindon).
"Focus on Timpani" (K. Cherry).
"Percussion on the March" (G. Whaley).
"Terms used in Percussion" (Michael Rosen).
"Selected Reviews" - of percussion music (solos and ensembles), percussion tutors and texts; also regular reviews of recordings and video tapes.

1418. **Woodwind World - Brass and Percussion** (Swift-Dorr Publications, Oneonta, NY; five issues annually.)
  This journal has a leaning towards band music, but features regular articles on a wide range of percussion subjects. Some are of a very basic nature (often aimed at the general music teacher), but others are more detailed and analytic. The regular feature "Reviews" usually has some evaluations of percussion music.

# AUTHORS INDEX

ABE, Keiko 1233, 1234
ABEL, Alan 1278, 1279
ADAIR, Yvonne 775
ADATO, J. & JUDY, G. 1
ADLER, Samuel 136
AGOSTINI, Dante 180
AKINS, T.N. 262
AKPABOT, S. 1004, 1041
ALBIN, W. 137, 776
ALBRIGHT, Fred 181
ALFORD, E.E. 1280, 415
AI MEIDA, Laurindo 1165
ALTENBURG, J.E. 903, 904
AMEELE, David 182, 374, 394
AMIRA, John 1166
ANDERSON, Dean 316
ANDERSON, L.A. 1042
ANDERSON, W.A. 1130
ANDRUS, Donald 950
APPICE, Carmine 497, 498
ARBATSKY, Yuri 1235
ARBEAU, (?) 905
AROZARENA, Pierre 1005
ASHWORTH, Charles 906
AVGERINOS, Gerassimos 2, 263
AVORGBEDOR, Daniel 1043

BAILEY, Colin 638, 639
BAILY, J. 1236
BAKER, Donald 37, 438, 1281, 1352, 1353, 1354
BALDWIN, James 439, 499, 951, 952, 953, 1355
BARR, W.L. 1167
BARTHOLOMEW, John 1168
BARTLETT, Harry R. 3
BASSET, I.G. 954
BECK, J.H. 500
BECKER, J. 1131
BEDFORD, F. 1282
BEGUN, Fred 264
BEIER, U. 1006
BELLSON, Louie (Louis) 501, 502, 503, 504, 640, 641, 642
BELLSON, L. & BREINES, G. 777, 778
BENJAMIN, R.E. 38
BENN, Billy 505
BENNETT, Dick 506
BENNETT, Frank 1109
BENNETT, R. 24
BENSON, Allen 183, 184, 463, 464, 465

171

HANSELL, William & PUGH, Greg 957
HARDING, J.R. 879
HARICH-SCHNEIDER, Eta 1251
HARRELL, M.C. 1139
HART, W.S. 397
HARTENBERGER, J.R. 1119
HAUN, E.E. 1297
HEADINGTON, C. 28
HELLER, G.N. 1298
HENRIQUE, Jorge 1198
HENRY, E. 987
HERNDON, M. 1252
HERRICK, Joey 669
HIEBERT, C.W. 803
HILL, Thomas A. 920
HINDEMITH, Paul 804
HINGER, Fred 281, 282, 1299
HOCHRAINER, Richard 212, 283, 377, 378, 670, 805, 806, 807, 921
HOEFER, G. 922
HOFSINDE, R. 1253
HOLDSWORTH, C. 880
HOLEN, Mark 1199
HOLLAND, James 10, 150
HOLLY, R. 808
HONG, Sherman 94, 213, 214, 809, 810, 923, 1300
HONG, Sherman & HAMILTON, Jim 477
HOOD, Mantel 1140
HOPKIN, Bart 52
HORST, Thomas 53, 54
HOULLIF, Murray 216, 550, 551, 552, 671, 672, 811
HOULLIF, M. & PETERCSAK, J. 215
HOUNCHELL, R. 812
HOUSTON, Robert 151, 284, 478
HOWARD, Joseph 1254
HOWE, Warren 1301
HOWELL, S. 881
HOWLAND, Harold 882, 1369
HUBER, G.K. 1370, 1371, 1372
HUGHES, Harry 553
HUMPHREY, Paul 554, 673
HURLEY, Mark 555, 813, 1302
HUSA, Karel 1303
HYE-GU, Lee 1141
HYSLOP, G. 1019

IDA, T.T. & JOZSEF 398, 762
IZIKOWITZ, K.G. 1200

JACKSON, H.J. 217
JACOB, Gordon 152
JACOB, I.G. 883, 1304
JACOBS, Kenneth 988
JAKOB, Friedrich 11
JAMISON, R. 95
JASTROW, William 1373
JAZZ FORUM 1064